AF608298

RECALLING RECITATION IN THE AMERICAS

Borderless Curriculum, Performance Poetry, and Reading

JANET NEIGH

Recalling Recitation in the Americas

Borderless Curriculum, Performance Poetry, and Reading

UNIVERSITY OF TORONTO PRESS
Toronto Buffalo London

Toronto Buffalo London
www.utorontopress.com

ISBN 978-1-4875-0183-9

Library and Archives Canada Cataloguing in Publication

Neigh, Janet, 1977–, author
Recalling recitation in the Americas : borderless curriculum, performance poetry, and reading / Janet Neigh.

Includes bibliographical references and index.
ISBN 978-1-4875-0183-9 (hardcover)

1. Oral interpretation of poetry. 2. Performance poetry – Social aspects. 3. Poetry – Social aspects. 4. Poetry – Study and teaching. 5. Recitation (Education) – Social aspects. 6. Johnson, E. Pauline (Emily Pauline), 1861–1913 – Criticism and interpretation. 7. Hughes, Langston, 1902–1967 – Criticism and interpretation. 8. Bennett, Louise, 1919–2006 – Criticism and interpretation. I. Title.

PN4151.N45 2017 808.5'45 C2017-903572-X

This book has been published with the assistance of Penn State Erie, The Behrend College.

University of Toronto Press acknowledges the financial assistance to its publishing program of the Canada Council for the Arts and the Ontario Arts Council, an agency of the Government of Ontario.

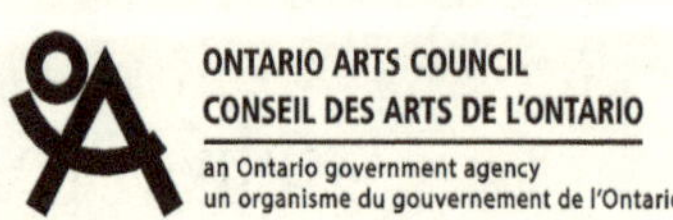

Funded by the Government of Canada | Financé par le gouvernement du Canada

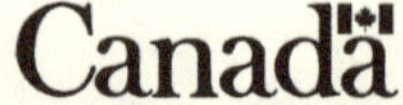

Contents

Acknowledgments

For generous financial support thanks to the Department of English, the Center for the Humanities, and the College of Liberal Arts at Temple University, the School of Humanities and Social Sciences and the Chancellor's Office at Penn State Behrend, and the Social Sciences and Humanities Research Council of Canada.

I was incredibly fortunate to work with outstanding professors throughout my degrees. Suzanne Gauch, Jena Osman, and Harvey Neptune deserve a special thank you here because they provided me with crucial encouragement and advice in the very early days of this project. I'm especially grateful to Rachel Blau DuPlessis for her lightning speed and her unwavering support every step of the way. Thank you to Jahan Ramazani for his mentorship and for his incredible generosity. While studying at Temple, I had the opportunity to engage in interdisciplinary research that helped me to expand my thinking beyond my literary training. My colleagues in the Women's Studies Program and in the Center for the Humanities research seminars helped me to figure out ways to pursue some of the research questions that I ask in this book.

I also need to thank Michael Bucknor who took a moment at the Association for Commonwealth Literature and Language Studies (ACLALS) conference in Vancouver in 2007 to give me the call for papers for the Noh Lickle Twang: Louise Bennett-Coverley: The Legend and the Legacy conference. This was a small thing, but so much of this book initially took shape during my trip to the Noh Lickle Twang conference at the University of the West Indies in 2008. I have also received excellent advice and feedback from scholars and friends whom I have met at conferences in Canada, the United States, the Caribbean, and South Africa.

I owe a great debt to Siobhan McMenemy and Mark Thompson at the University of Toronto Press for invaluable guidance and encouragement throughout this long process. I'm also grateful to the anonymous reviewers for their generous and detailed feedback.

Thank you to the librarians and support staff at Penn State Behrend, the William Ready Division of Archives and Research Collections at McMaster University, the Special Collections and the Library of the Spoken Word at the University of the West Indies, Mona campus, and the Archives of Ontario. For editing assistance, thank you to Kate Epstein and Katie McDonough.

At my intellectual home at Penn State Behrend, I am fortunate to have many wonderful and supportive colleagues who have sustained me as I wrote this book. John Champagne, Eric Corty, Sara Luttfring, and Craig Warren have been especially warm and helpful.

So many of my friends made writing this book easier by giving me advice, by reading drafts and providing insightful feedback, by encouraging me to take a break from working and then return to my desk refreshed, by listening to me, by talking shop, and by talking about everything but shop. Thank you to Hilary Baker, Gabriel Cutrufello, James De Lorenzi, Christa DiMarco, Daniel Ellis, Phil Maciak, Jennifer Maloy, Melanie Micir, Kathy Lou Schultz, Andrea Strudensky, Mara Taylor, Sarah Turner, and Aileen Wang.

A few friends deserve special thanks for going above and beyond the call of duty. Thanks to Julia Bloch for her willingness to listen and for being the best conference roommate. Thanks to Megan Walsh for being such a supportive neighbour across state lines. Thanks to Sarah Dowling for endless feedback and encouragement. To remind myself how lucky I am, I often think about what a happy accident it was that our Canadian selves both ended up at Temple in 2004.

I could not have completed this project without the support of my family. I am so grateful to have been born into the crazy exuberance of the Neigh family. Thanks to Scott, Stacey Ritz, Kathryn, Dave, David Scott, Eve, Yiggy, and Liam. A special thanks to my parents, Ed and Margaret Neigh, who taught me to question the world, to love multiple Englishes, and to work incredibly hard. Although my dad is not here to see this book in print, his brilliance inspired me in so many ways. I dedicate this book to his memory, his bagpipes, and his unique life of performance.

This book could not have been written without the loving support of Dan Schank. For everything and more, thank you. I could not ask for a better reader and life partner.

RECALLING RECITATION IN THE AMERICAS

Borderless Curriculum, Performance Poetry, and Reading

Introduction

As fast as the squirrel-eye one finish smoke one cigarette, he light another one. He aint saying nothing, only listening. At last he put out his cigarette, he say, "Recite the alphabet."
"Say what?"
"The alphabet. Recite it."
And just so I know I get catch. The question too easy. Too easy like a calm blue sea.

Earl Lovelace, "Joebell and America"

Reciting the alphabet likely conjures up memories of childhood, an innocuous melody, or perhaps a classroom setting. However, the epigraph from the Trinidadian author Earl Lovelace's short story "Joebell and America" depicts something more unexpected – a combative scene of recitation in an immigration interrogation room in a Puerto Rican airport. Set in the 1980s, Lovelace's story laments the failure of Independence to empower the lives of working-class individuals in Trinidad. The main character, Joebell, attempts to enter the United States with a fake passport, hoping to make it big in the America that he has learned to idolize through popular culture. Joebell takes a flight to Puerto Rico, believing that it will be easier to enter the United States from there. The airport setting evokes the tension between legacies of colonization and contemporary politics of globalization at play in borderland spaces in the Americas, where luxury vacations and the surveillance state go hand in hand. From the beginning of his interview, the border guards immediately suspect Joebell's bluff; however, they must prove this through verbal interrogation, demonstrating the power of speech acts in border spaces. Joebell manages to answer almost all of the immigration officials' questions by relying on his extensive knowledge of American music, television, and film, until the border guards order him to recite the alphabet. He suspects immediately that the question is "too easy," comparing the easiness of the question with the deceptively "calm blue sea," which has never been calm for black people attempting to cross it.

When he pronounces the last letter according to British standards, as "zed" rather than "zee," he reveals his Trinidadian citizenship.[1] The pronunciation of this single letter marks him as a subject of British colonization and mars his performance in the eyes of his US interlocutors. Lovelace's border performance illustrates how psychological decolonization often involves a public battle with one's memory. Recitation, defined broadly in this study as the performance of internalized verbal art and texts, becomes a crucial site of action where this struggle often takes place.

The border guards' enforced homogeneity of speech evokes the practices of the "old" British imperial regime. However, unlike students in a colonial school, Joebell fails his recitation test because of his mastery of British pronunciation. His education undermines his agility as a diasporic subject in the Americas. Saying "zed" suggests that his schooling, shaped by the legacy of British colonization, trumps his US assimilation. Throughout the story, Joebell speaks in different vernacular forms and rejects standard British English, but in this moment his education controls him. Like many post-colonial writers, Lovelace points to how children learning the English alphabet play a pivotal role in the colonial project. Moreover, he exposes the power of schoolroom memorization and the difficulty of deflecting this psychological control later in life. The authoritarian setting of the interrogation room demonstrates how this form of colonization depends on forcing a subject to make public what he has internalized.

Through Joebell, we witness how disenfranchised subjects in the Americas are often coerced into performing their identities in public spaces. More crucially, we see how dominant scripts, like the alphabet, orchestrate everyday scenarios. While his recitation evokes the experiences and desires of a poor Trinidadian in the 1980s, his disciplinary performance resembles the experience of many people throughout the history of the Americas. As the Cuban-American artist Coco Fusco highlights in her essay "The Other History of Intercultural Performance in the Americas," objectifying performances of the racial other are at the heart of the invention of New World imaginaries. Such performances extend as far back as Columbus's first voyage in 1492 when he brought

Arawaks back with him and put them on display in the Spanish court. These performances reached the height of their unfortunate popularity during nineteenth-century circuses and freak shows.[2] Similarly, Diana Taylor draws attention to the disciplinary uses of performance in the colonization of the Americas and cautions against the simplistic alignment of performance with "anti-hegemonic challenge."[3] By returning us to the colonial classroom and making us aware of its lasting effects, Joebell's recitation of the alphabet exposes a more complicated relationship between performance, memory, and decolonization than we often acknowledge.

Borderless Curriculum

Recitation practices are common in many cultures, and people use them for a wide range of purposes, including sharing knowledge, entertainment, passing on culture, and spiritual devotion; however, when the border guards command Joebell to "recite" the English alphabet, the word means something much more specific. Here *recite* evokes the history of Western elocution and the pedagogy of rote learning, which began in Britain in the late eighteenth century and eventually spread throughout the Americas as well as the British Empire. In the nineteenth century, rhetoric handbooks and elocution manuals containing poetry, speeches, and other texts for recitation proliferated in the Americas. The popularity of elocution ensued from the elevation of English as a scholarly language and from the invention of the printing press. The expansion of the print industry in eighteenth-century Britain encouraged the standardizing of the English language.[4] As spelling and punctuation rules arose, ideas about proper pronunciation and demeanour also advanced to standardize speech practices. Elocution played a central role in teaching the proper alliance between voice, body, and language. In England, anxiety about the purity of upper-class English speech coincided with the spread of public education to the working class, especially after the Elementary Education Act in 1870, which set the foundations for elementary education to become compulsory in Britain.[5] The export of the British education system (and along with it the English language) to the Americas exacerbated these fears over the purity of English. Poetry memorization and rote learning also became widespread in North America because they were easy devices to implement in understaffed rural schoolrooms.[6]

Schools used recitation in the classroom for multifaceted reasons that shifted depending on location, historical moment, and the particular teacher. Studying the pages of recitation manuals published in the last 150 years reveals consistent themes, such as improving memory and cognitive capacity, broadening a sense of language patterns, building vocabulary, cultivating literary taste and character, aligning body and mind, instilling public-speaking skills, promoting democracy, and inspiring passion for the material studied. While poetry memorization is no longer a core part of school curricula, national recitation contests for students, such as Poetry in Voice in Canada, Poetry Out Loud in the United States, and the Jamaica Festival's annual Speech Competition, attest to its continued popularity. Today many educators and poets still promote the value of poetry recitation and challenge the idea that it fosters "a culture of servility."[7] For example, in a podcast for the Poetry Foundation, the poet Dan Beachy-Quick proposes that memorizing a poem increases his levels of engagement and "creates a new channel of intelligence" in him.[8] Defences of poetry memorization like his reject the idea that the practice is old-fashioned and conservative. My study complicates definitions of poetry recitation, which rely too much on progressive/conservative dichotomies and fail to acknowledge the more nuanced ways disenfranchised populations in the Americas have internalized these practices and put them to subversive use.

To explore these nuances, we need to move beyond educators' stated learning objectives for poetry recitation and make the hidden curriculum – critical pedagogy's term for "the tacit ways in which knowledge and behavior get constructed" – visible.[9] For disenfranchised populations, the ideological goal was often cultural and linguistic assimilation. The "new channels of intelligence" that Beachy-Quick discusses were often the behaviours and norms the dominant culture expected. Teachers employed this "civilizing pedagogy" in institutional settings as diverse as First Nations residential schools in Canada, black schools in the American South, citizenship classes at settlement houses for new immigrants in New York City, and British colonial schools in the West Indies.[10] In fact, rote learning was the predominant pedagogy in most classrooms in the United States, Canada, and the anglophone Caribbean in the early twentieth century. Didactic poems, often designed specifically for memorization, played a pivotal role in these practices. Across these diverse settings, students recited many of the same texts, selected from recitation manuals and anthologies such as the popular *Palgrave's Golden Treasury*.[11] The internalization of texts from the recitation canon provided an efficient way to simultaneously indoctrinate pupils by introducing them to anglophone culture and by improving their proficiency in "Standard English."[12] Yet these coercive performances also presented opportunities for readers, introducing them to poetry and public expression. In certain cases, they became occasions for readers to engage in a public battle with the distortion of personal memory often imposed by this form of indoctrination.

What were the effects of this borderless curriculum that sprawled across the British Empire and throughout the Americas? How did students' experiences with poetry recitation shape their sense of performance practices and their ideas about poetry? Since recitation was so ubiquitous, what effect did it have on performance poetry in the twentieth century?

Recalling Recitation in the Americas argues that schoolroom recitation had a significant influence on the development of twentieth-century performance poetry aimed at decolonization. This study illustrates how poetry recitation, an assimilationist pedagogy, transforms from its roots in the elocutionary tradition invested in "proper" speech and behaviour into a performative reading strategy aimed at the decolonization of cultural forms and knowledge practices. Through a comparative analysis of poets' engagements with recitation in the late nineteenth century and early twentieth century, *Recalling Recitation in the Americas* reassesses the motivations for widespread oral performance in multiethnic poetries of the Americas, establishing how it refashions the institutional uses of poetry to decolonize language and builds new literacy practices. By examining how Western oral modes were imposed on disenfranchised people like Joebell, this book illustrates how poets challenge dominant scripts of identity by manipulating the imperative to perform for the imperial gaze and by crafting their own racial meanings in the Americas.

The three main figures in this study – Mohawk author E. Pauline Johnson (Tekahionwake) (1861–1913), African American author Langston Hughes (1902–1967), and Jamaican author Louise Bennett (1919–2006) – recall recitation traditions and remake them.[13] Despite their different geographic origins and ethnicities, these poets share some striking commonalities, namely their use of performance to become prominent national figures at a time when their racial identities made this exceedingly difficult. They also share a commitment to promoting their respective oral traditions and a belief in the value of children's education, which led to their own poetry becoming part of recitation curricula. This study traces their performance innovations back to their early experiences with poetry as children, revealing that they all experienced recitation as an early poetic model. As an enactment and metaphor for the dynamics of colonial control, recitation taught these poets how to harness the power of embodied performance and to use this form of mimicry to reclaim language from within dominant forces. By bringing their multi-genre artistic projects into dialogue with one another, as well as the subsequent generations of performance poets whom they have influenced, *Recalling Recitation in the Americas* examines how their complicated legacies as national icons obscure their engagements with broader questions about New World identities and their similar approaches to resisting anglicization through performance.

The hemispheric dialogue among these popular national poets crystallized for me several years ago at the Norman Manley International Airport in Kingston, Jamaica, when I was returning to the United States. After officials in the final corridor checked my Canadian passport, visa, and boarding pass, I walked by a gigantic portrait of Louise Bennett in the hallway that led to my boarding area. Although I had just attended a conference in her honour at the University of the West Indies, and spent five days researching her Creole poetry at the National Library of Jamaica, her portrait as a Jamaican national hero in this borderland setting seemed more evocative of the dichotomies in her performance poetry than anything that I found in the archives.[14] The photograph recalls the image on the cover of the paperback edition of *Jamaica Labrish*, and shows her whole body with her face and hands animated, as if she is in the midst of reciting one of her Creole poems. She is dressed in her peasant costume, designed by her mother in the 1930s, replete with a head-tie and red plaid skirts hemmed up at the side to appear as if she has hitched up her skirts to wade across a shallow river. The action shot depicts her lively performance style, yet the picture freezes her in time and space in this departure corridor. Despite her outfit's implied rural setting, in Bennett's own life she was more likely to walk down an airport hallway such as this one than cross a stream. Her portrait loomed larger than life, yet in just a couple of short hours, once my plane touched down in Miami, where few people know of her, she shrank from public view. In the United States, Langston Hughes, whose poems are taught in elementary schools, invoked by presidential candidates, and cited on public monuments, takes Bennett's place as the unofficial poet laureate for a black cultural nationalism.[15]

Much farther north, my own experience of the popular national poet growing up was E. Pauline Johnson, whom I remember first learning about in a grade three unit about famous Canadians. Like Bennett and

Hughes, Johnson became a national symbol, and she was featured on a 1967 postage stamp to commemorate one hundred years since Confederation. Yet her poetry performances in the late nineteenth century, in which she appeared in a Native costume based on an illustration of Minnehaha from Henry Wadsworth Longfellow's *The Song of Hiawatha*, have also elicited criticism and discomfort throughout the years. Although even children study these poets, they all have minimal recognition beyond their own countries' borders. Even Bennett, clearly a hemispheric poet who lived for periods in Miami and New York, where she befriended Langston Hughes, and then spent the last twenty years of her life in Toronto, where she played an active role in the Caribbean community, receives little critical attention in North America. By exploring the dialogue among their performance projects, this book expands their community of readers across borders of race, gender, ethnicity, and nationality.[16]

Borders animate the heart of this book's conceptual framework. Rather than study recitation practices within a specific national literary tradition, I track the borderless curriculum of schoolroom recitation as it shifts and re-forms in various contexts, paying attention to border containment and restrictions, as well as to moments when borders collapse or come undone. To capture the ways English speakers in North America understand poetry recitation, we need to reconceptualize their practices through the shared political geography of the British Empire that established poetry recitation practices in the first place.

Using this border-crossing approach, *Recalling Recitation in the Americas* builds on recent book-length studies that examine the history of poetry recitation in the United States and Great Britain, namely Angela Sorby's *Schoolroom Poets: Childhood, Performance and the Place of American Poetry 1865–1917* (2005), Joan Rubin's *Songs of Ourselves: The Uses of Poetry in America* (2007), and Catherine Robson's *Heart Beats: Everyday Life and the Memorized Poem* (2012).[17] These scholars explore the disjunction between the institutional histories of poetry memorization and the varied embodied experiences of everyday readers subjected to these practices. They demonstrate how an attention to readers as performers of poems reshapes our understanding of poetry's impact on social life. As Rubin puts it, "the meanings of texts are inseparable from the ideological and cultural tensions in play at sites for reading."[18] All three scholars establish that poetry recitation became a widespread practice because of its ability to foster national and imperial patriotism. They also stress that an attention to poetry recitation provides an alternative version of literary history. For example, Rubin argues that "the 1920s were as much an era of Henry Wadsworth Longfellow as of [T.S.] Eliot" when one views poetry history from the perspective of everyday readers, rather than from the perspective of an elite group of modernist writers and scholars.[19] Similarly, Sorby contrasts the public prominence of US poets such as Longfellow and Felicia Hemans in the United States in the nineteenth and twentieth centuries with their marginal treatment in literary studies. She traces a transatlantic genealogy connecting British schoolroom poets, including William Shakespeare, Hemans, Robert Louis Stevenson, and Alfred Lord Tennyson, with the New England schoolroom poets, such as Longfellow, John Greenleaf Whittier, James Russell Lowell, and Oliver Wendell Holmes. She defines the tradition loosely, to include any poets whose work frequently appears in schoolroom readers from this period; however, she focuses on Longfellow and Whittier, who actively promoted and developed memorization and recitation as a central part of the schoolroom poetry tradition. Although Rubin, Sorby, and Robson recognize the transatlantic scope of the recitation canon and its widespread implementation throughout the British Empire, they limit their investigation to the United States and Great Britain.[20]

They also suggest that the recitation canon (although a force in public life and readers' interior worlds) plays an inconsequential role in the development of twentieth-century poetry and poetics. While scholarship on the social history of reading establishes the myriad ways in which readers act as producers rather than just consumers of literature, very little scholarship explores the crossover between these two roles. *Recalling Recitation in the Americas* questions what happens when readers subjected to these practices go on to become poets themselves. Sorby proposes that schoolroom poetry had "a negligible influence on modern and postmodern poetry" because the purpose of classroom recitation was "not to engage with literary history but rather to make social history by forming communities."[21] However, this performative sociality is precisely what appealed to Johnson, Hughes, and Bennett, who were drawn to poetry as a form that could be used to imagine community and to build new reading publics.

Although recitation was relevant to many immigrant and working-class communities in early twentieth-century North America, scholars have yet to thoroughly investigate its role in Indigenous, African American, and Caribbean communities. By bringing together Indigenous- and African-descended cultures in the Americas, *Recalling Recitation in the*

Americas deepens our understanding of how recitation provides power to dispossessed peoples who come from predominantly oral cultures and shows how oral performance dynamics transform reading from a solitary act into a social one.

Colonial Mimicry in the Classroom

My theoretical framework also differs from previous work on recitation in that I draw on post-colonial theories of mimicry, cultural hybridity, and critical pedagogy to understand the politics of recitation and its complicated relationship to assimilation and cultural intermixture in the New World. Reciting a British poem in a colonial school quite literally transforms people into what V.S. Naipaul describes as "mimic men."[22] Naipaul uses this term pejoratively to criticize the colonized subject's internalized sense of inferiority and his desire to emulate the imperial culture. However, many post-colonial thinkers have questioned this limited perspective. In his essay "The Caribbean: Culture or Mimicry?" Derek Walcott rejects Naipaul's interpretation of mimicry as uncreative. Walcott situates the Caribbean in an inter-American framework and posits mimicry as a key part of New World aesthetics. Using calypso as his example, he argues that new cultural forms in the Americas emerge through a process of mimicking, remaking, and negotiating "the sanctions imposed on [them]."[23] Walcott draws on the biological meaning of mimicry as a form of survival, creative adaptation, and redesign.[24] His perspective suggests that while a Caribbean reader reciting a British poem might be mimicking the colonial culture, she may also be remaking that culture in the process. As chapter 1 will explore, Johnson's recitations of Longfellow's *The Song of Hiawatha* move our understanding of poetic influence beyond a binary of originality and imitation. Moreover, it is insufficient to interpret her mimicry as de facto proof of her assimilation.

In addition to Walcott's focus on mimicry as part of New World aesthetics, Homi K. Bhabha addresses its broader relationship to psychological colonization. Although he never mentions poetry recitation directly, he identifies the colonial classroom as a primary site for mimicry performances. He characterizes mimicry "as one of the most elusive and effective strategies of colonial power and knowledge."[25] Yet it also draws attention to the ambivalence of colonial power. As he puts it, "colonial mimicry is the desire for a reformed, recognizable Other, *as a subject of a difference that is almost the same, but not quite.*"[26] The slippage of "*almost the same, but not quite*" becomes enacted when the subject fails to perfectly mimic the dominant culture. Mimicry also becomes a form of camouflage, yet a student in a colonial classroom can never completely blend in to the colonial environment. Mimicry functions as a test with a built-in expectation of failure (or at least of average performance), rather than complete mastery. To consolidate imperial power, the mimic's difference must remain visible. Yet this creates what Bhabha calls "its *double* vision which in disclosing the ambivalence of colonial discourse also disrupts its authority."[27] The necessary incompleteness of assimilation takes on a more subversive agenda within this framework.

While Bhabha suggests that the ambivalence of mimicry has the potential to destabilize colonial authority, he refrains from explaining in great detail whether or not there are certain approaches to mimicry in which this disruption becomes more effective than others. Anne McClintock cautions that we "need to elaborate how colonial mimicry differs from anti-colonial mimicry" and asks, "if colonial and anti-colonial mimicry are formally identical in their founding ambivalence, why did colonial mimicry succeed for so long?"[28] Poetry recitation proves especially useful when addressing these questions because the dynamic between performance and reception implies a spectator – mimicry almost always happens in front of a real or imagined audience. More specifically, the performer's body plays a key role in the production of meaning and potential subversion. Studying poets' experiences with poetry recitation and their refashioning of it becomes a laboratory for understanding the disruptive contours of mimicry as a force of creative production. On a more intimate level, it reveals how a young student negotiates (and sometimes even deflects) the force of assimilation.

Édouard Glissant insists that to study the conquest of the Americas we must "return to the point of entanglement, from which we were forcefully turned away."[29] He challenges scholars to counter colonial histories that often direct attention away from this entanglement and miscategorize cultural intermixture as assimilation, because they ignore the contribution of the subordinated culture. Studying mimicry helps us to unravel the messiness of the colonial encounter. While the classroom often gets interpreted as a primary site of assimilation, I interpret it as "a point of entanglement" in which the young student – although in an uneven power relationship – contributes aspects of her culture.

My analysis of the classroom space draws on the work of critical pedagogy scholars who interpret it as a site of struggle and negotiation. While rote memorization seems to epitomize what the renowned education activist Paulo Freire defines as the banking concept of education, when students have to recite they may gain a limited sense of agency to reformulate what they have internalized.[30] Recitation exams, where students demonstrate their reading skills through the number of lines they can successfully memorize, can be aptly characterized as what Peter McLaren calls "a classroom ritual" in his foundational study *Schooling as Ritual Performance*. Such regulatory rituals encourage students to embody ideology and make the hidden curriculum visible as a form of "corporeal shaping."[31] He reveals how rituals reproduce the dominant social order by uniting "gestural display and symbolic meaning," at times becoming even more important than the curriculum and the lessons themselves. However, because these acts participate in "reality *construction* rather than simply reality *reflection*," he proposes that openings exist for students to claim power.[32]

In her novel *Lucy*, Jamaica Kincaid demonstrates how recitation functioned as a classroom ritual and as a form of mimicry in Caribbean schools in the mid-twentieth century. Her protagonist, Lucy, becomes haunted by William Wordsworth's daffodil poem, "I Wandered Lonely as a Cloud," because of her experience reciting this poem when she was ten years old in Antigua. When she immigrates to the United States to work as a nanny, her employer, Mariah, shows her a field of daffodils. Rather than see their beauty, she sees only "sorrow and bitterness," because they trigger her memory of Wordsworth's poem:[33]

> I had been made to memorize it, verse after verse, and then had recited the whole poem to an auditorium full of parents, teachers, and my fellow pupils. After I was done, everybody stood up and applauded with an enthusiasm that surprised me, and later they told me how nicely I had pronounced every word, how I had placed just the right amount of emphasis in places where that was needed, and how proud the poet, now long dead, would have been to hear his words ringing out of my mouth. I was then at the height of my two-facedness: that is, outside I seemed one way, inside I was another; outside false, inside true. And so I made pleasant little noises that showed both modesty and appreciation, but inside I was making a vow to erase from my mind, line by line, every word of that poem. (18)

Despite the fact that Lucy "vow[s] to erase" the poem from her mind, she still recalls the ritual itself – having to memorize the poem through repeated drills and then having to perform it in front of a large audience.

Many scholars interpret this scene as an example of the damages inflicted by a colonial education that contains no Caribbean material. Yet what causes harm here is not just the content of the curriculum, but also the pedagogical devices used to enforce it.[34] Like Joebell's, Lucy's memory of her colonial education can only be "temporarily submerged," rather than completely forgotten.[35] Her "two-facedness," which Alison Donnell aptly renames her "double consciousness," reveals the ambivalence of mimicry as a form of colonial control.[36] Her parents, teachers, classmates, and even the imagined gaze of Wordsworth reveal how surveillance plays a key role in securing mimicry's power, yet Lucy merely pretends to be fully assimilated through her performance of "modesty and appreciation." Lucy never identifies Wordsworth by name to challenge his cultural authority, yet this act of defiance is undermined because the canonical prestige of the text means that most readers can infer the identity of the author.

Despite her efforts to resist his authority, which to her represents the tyranny of British aesthetics and Romantic ideals, she cannot escape it: "The night after I had recited the poem, I dreamt, continuously it seemed, that I was being chased down a narrow cobbled street by bunches and bunches of those same daffodils that I had vowed to forget, and when finally I fell down from exhaustion they all piled on top of me, until I was buried deep underneath them and was never seen again" (18). Her nightmare vividly underscores how this experience overtakes her sense of self, revealing the sinister power of poetry recitation's hidden curriculum. Throughout the novel, daffodils become a metonym for whiteness and imperial violence, representing her employer Mariah's "pale-yellow skin and yellow hair" (27).[37] She even describes Mariah's family as "six yellow-haired heads," as if they are decapitated daffodil blossoms, disrupting the beauty of the symbol with an undertone of violence (12). She evokes the sickliness of yellow, rather than the purity of white, to challenge skin-colour hierarchies that are bound up in colonial aesthetics. By having Mariah, Lucy's US employer, insist that Lucy recall Wordsworth, Kincaid underscores the United States as a direct descendant of British imperial legacies and aesthetics. Rather than a precious flower to be cherished, the daffodil becomes something Lucy needs to uproot from her unconscious. But like an aggressive weed, its roots have become entangled in her psyche and she cannot isolate them from the other parts of herself and pull them out. Accordingly, they threaten to destroy her own sense of beauty and wonder and ultimately her identity. Kincaid reveals how the naivety of the Romantic subject, represented by Mariah, who does not understand why Lucy does not see beauty in the flowers, can be better understood as a wilful ignorance. Mariah's idealization of the daffodil as a symbol of English beauty becomes part of her refusal to see the violence of English colonialism in Lucy's country and elsewhere. Moreover, this scene reveals the distinction between rejection and resistance in the ambivalent space of mimicry. Lucy *rejects* Wordsworth's poem by refusing to privilege daffodils and the colonial aesthetic system they represent, yet she cannot *resist* the damaging power of the ritual over her sense of self.

One might interpret this fictionalization of recitation as a confirmation that mimicry has limited effectiveness as a form of subversion, but to do so overlooks Kincaid's role as author. The entire novel can be interpreted as Kincaid's sardonic rewriting of Wordsworth's "I Wandered Lonely as a Cloud," where her protagonist, Lucy, wanders lonely in New York City. Through her subversive reinterpretation, Lucy's experience of alienation as a West Indian immigrant starkly contrasts with Wordsworth's portrayal of joyful solitary contemplation. In this way, Kincaid revisits her own experience of poetry recitation in schools. Using a first-person narrator, she constructs a very different persona from the one that students are forced to mimic when they recite a Romantic lyric. Although Kincaid's British education was damaging, it also fuelled her creativity and provided her with resources to disrupt its power. According to Romantic principles, which influenced the development of recitation curricula, performing a memorized poem is an innocent act that helps a young student experience the pleasures of poetry; however, Kincaid reveals how it works as a subtle form of psychological control that persists well into adulthood.

In his influential lecture *History of the Voice: Development of Nation Language in Anglophone Caribbean Poetry*, delivered at Harvard in 1979, Kamau Brathwaite also briefly alludes to poetry recitation as a form of colonial control in Caribbean schools that contributes to the colonization of the voice:

> But the point is that for the needs of the kind of emerging society that I am defending – for the people who have to recite "The boy / stood on / the burn / ing deck" for so long, who are unable to express the power of the hurricane in the way that they write their words – at last, our poets, today, are recognizing that it is essential that they use the resources which have always been there, but which have been denied to them – and which they have sometimes themselves denied.[38]

Brathwaite argues that the process of internalization and performance involved in learning a poem by heart prevents a person from expressing her own cultural identity. In assessments of Brathwaite's canonical essay, his mention of recitation often gets overlooked. However, for Kincaid's Lucy, having to embody and perform the daffodil joy of Wordsworth's poem is far more damaging than just having to silently read about it. To make his point, Brathwaite cites the opening lines of Hemans's "Casabianca" (1826), one of the most memorized and recited poems in the British Empire.[39] Hemans's poem describes a young Corsican sailor who remains at his post while his ship becomes engulfed in flames in the Battle of the Nile in 1798. Brathwaite's selection of this poem, which glorifies a young island boy's extreme loyalty to the French imperial ruler who causes him to lose his life, seems particularly apt. He questions the effects of young children in the Caribbean being forced to internalize and then repeatedly perform this message of self-sacrifice for the Empire. He relates the "the burning deck" image in the poem to the precarious stages on which children at British colonial schools in the Caribbean had to recite. Kincaid's character Lucy illustrates that children were often critical of the sentiment they had to perform. Brathwaite proposes that the memorization and recitation of poems like Hemans's play a role in the colonization of the voice; however, he minimizes the impact and the opportunities for subversion such acts of mimicry provide. When he proposes that poets like Bennett "use the resources ... which have been denied to them," he refers to African-descended oral language and music traditions. Yet these oral forms both come into conflict with Western literary print forms and become rearticulated through the disciplinary use of oral performance in colonial society.

Refashioning Recitation

Bennett, Johnson, and Hughes refashion recitation practices to abandon the burning deck of the classroom ritual. In doing so, they carve out more than a means of escape; they also cultivate new national voices. These poets' careers suggest that poetry on the page is not enough to make one a popular national poet in the Americas – a poet must take to the stage and also encourage her readers to do the same, to weave one's words into national collective memory. Their iconic lines, such as Johnson's "By right, by birth we Indians own these lands"; Hughes's "I, too, sing America. / I am the darker brother"; and Bennett's "Yuh gwine kill all English dialec / Or jus Jamaica one?" echo in their respective nations as appeals for a more inclusive citizenship.[40]

Recalling Recitation in the Americas complicates nationalist accounts of Bennett's, Hughes's, and Johnson's careers, which uphold them as anomalies within their socio-historical moments. In late nineteenth-century Canada, few women writers before Johnson had composed their own verse to perform on the stage. As a mixed-race woman in Native dress, she created a completely new performance voice. In mid-twentieth-century Jamaica, Louise Bennett, who wore a traditional peasant woman's dress to enact her vernacular ballads on stage, was championed as one of the first writers to use the Jamaican vernacular. In the United States, Langston Hughes became famous for his groundbreaking poetic innovation with blues and jazz forms and African American oral traditions in the early twentieth century. While these insights about their work reflect aspects of their contributions to literary history, the hemispheric approach used here avoids making an argument of singularity that "works against broader emancipatory politics because it detaches events from the context that might help explain them."[41] A comparison of their performance strategies reveals how each manipulates recitation pedagogy to contend with the intrusion of Anglo-dominant cultures in the Americas, to create empowering reading practices, which incorporate oral knowledge systems, and to represent their racial identities.

Bennett, Johnson, and Hughes were all intensely critical of their countries, yet they were all deeply committed to the idea of nation as a potentially liberating social formation, and they each used their poetry to build more inclusive and empowering scripts of citizenship than their dominant societies offered them. To become popular national poets, Johnson, Hughes, and Bennett paradoxically depended on transnational travel and exchange. Bennett, for example, travelled extensively and spent a significant portion of her life outside of Jamaica.[42] Similarly, Johnson lived a life of performance in motion, functioning without a permanent address from 1892 to 1909 as she performed her poetry throughout North America and the United Kingdom. Hughes aligned himself with Pan-Africanism and worked to build international community through his poetry, travels, and cultural work. Scholars associate all three with the nations of which they were citizens; however, to build their careers as performance poets they had to travel internationally, both to support themselves and to build an audience.

Living through turbulent times when social empowerment appeared on the horizon but was rarely realized, Johnson, Hughes, and Bennett began to focus more on reaching audiences of children as their careers progressed. Bennett lived through the Jamaican Independence movement and saw how working-class Jamaican women lost rights after Independence.[43] During Johnson's lifetime, she witnessed an increase in discrimination towards First Nations peoples, which she initially had hoped would decrease after Confederation. Hughes personally dealt with the disappointments caused by white patronage in the Harlem Renaissance, and then later the repressive effects of McCarthyism. All three poets increasingly recognized that social change must be tied to the education of young children. If they wanted their poetry to facilitate the decolonization of language practices, they would have to reach children who were in the process of learning their ABCs.[44] They shared a sense of the poet's role as an inclusive educator, and their work anticipates critical pedagogy's emphasis on literacy education as a central part of decolonization. In recent decades, promoting diversity in the classroom has been a prominent issue, and I share rhetoric scholar Susan Kates's concern that "educational history does not surface as a crucial consideration, as a way to shape our responses to new pedagogical problems."[45] The following chapters examine how Johnson's, Hughes's, and Bennett's poetry and cultural work respond to pedagogical problems they encountered in their education, and show how their work can become a valuable resource for language and literature educators.

Poetry recitation was popular in anglophone schools in North America for over half a century, beginning in the 1890s and ending roughly in the 1960s.[46] Clearly, countless poets were exposed to recitation during their education, and this book lays the groundwork for more scholarship on the connections between poetry history and education history. Bennett's, Hughes's and Johnson's recitation legacies reveal how the institutional uses of poetry have had far-reaching effects on the development of modern and contemporary poetics. Twentieth-century poetics is much more tied to education history than has been previously acknowledged, and critics have frequently overlooked the significance of poets' engagements with poetry as a pedagogical form. For literary scholars, the classroom remains "the most unloved and understudied aspect of our discipline's history," write Rachel Sagner Buurma and Laura Heffernan.[47] Yet studying recitation reveals the classroom as one of the main sites where literature happens in the world – where it gets read and performed, and where it influences societal values.

Focusing on the classroom also forces us to revise our understanding of literary genealogies. The surprising attention I devote to Longfellow within this book underscores how the borderless curriculum of recitation creates unforeseen shared inheritances. When looking for precursors to twentieth-century performance poetry, scholars, particularly from the United States, often point to Walt Whitman.[48] His democratizing voice and emphasis on poetry as song make him a likely candidate, yet when we look to the classroom and consider poetry as a pedagogical device different types of literary ancestors come into view. Johnson, Hughes, and Bennett all encountered Longfellow in their education, a testament to his ubiquitousness in recitation readers; his "work appears with more frequency in the hundreds of anthologies for recitation that appeared throughout the English-speaking world than any other poet but Shakespeare."[49] However, they all continued to engage with his recitation poetics past childhood. Access in part drives this, especially in the cases of Johnson and Bennett. While they both incorporate Mohawk and Jamaican oral traditions, respectively, their colonial worlds offered them few models of non-white poets or poetic speakers whom the dominant society would have seen as legitimate. Even for Hughes, *The Song of Hiawatha* was likely the only poem he read as a child with a man of colour as the hero. Yet Longfellow's Anglo-American influence is more constructive than one might expect given the circumstances. Studying these poets' relationships to his work reveals the complexity of uneven cultural intermixture in the Americas and the agency readers possess to radically reinvent poetic traditions for their own purposes.

Critics such as Kirsten Silva Gruesz propose that Longfellow's sentimental poetry might be more conducive to cultural difference than his reputation suggests. She attributes his fame in Latin America in the nineteenth century to his extensive work in translation. He built his career by translating many foreign works into English and by appropriating poetic forms and material from other cultures for his own poetry. For example, for his infamous *Song of Hiawatha*, he copied the trochaic tetrameter from the Finnish epic *Kalevala* and took material from the Indian agent Henry Rowe Schoolcraft's inaccurate Anishinaabe ethnography. Gruesz establishes how Longfellow's promotion of a "translative" approach to poetic production challenged the "aesthetic value that seeks to conceal the seam or the difference of translation."[50] Although he participated in blatant cultural theft, he never sought to hide it. For nineteenth-century poets such as Juan de Dios Peza (who was actually nicknamed the Mexican Longfellow), his "fundamental faith in the need for writers to look outside the Anglo-American tradition to prevent a dangerous myopia" was particularly appealing.[51] Johnson,

Hughes, and Bennett also found in Longfellow a fraught example of how to become a popular national poet in the New World by combining European languages and literature with North American culture and folk traditions. Unlike many nineteenth-century white men, he regarded oral culture as a suitable poetic material.

Literacy and Performance Poetry

In the colonial takeover of the Americas, the authority of the written word discredited oral forms of knowing and non-European performance practices. One only has to think of the Canadian government legislation that outlawed potlatch ceremonies and Indigenous dancing in the nineteenth century, or British colonial policies in the nineteenth century that limited carnival celebrations in Trinidad, to recognize that the suppression of oral performance traditions was widespread.[52]

Although dominant cultures have continually suppressed oral cultures in the Americas, those denied subjectivity in the Americas use performance to transmit cultural memory and identity.[53] Scholars typically understand the popularity of oral performance in multi-ethnic poetries of the Americas as a celebration of musical and oral language traditions and as a resistance to this suppression.[54] In these assessments, spoken language becomes aligned with a vernacular tradition and written language with Western print culture. Oral and musical traditions have greatly shaped black diaspora and Indigenous poetics, yet the emphasis on orality as non-Western overlooks the presence of oral traditions within imperial centres and also the ways in which such poetries transform reading practices and create new hybridized oral forms. In the case of Johnson, who managed to access traces of her oral tradition through Longfellow's appropriation of it, we need to question what is at stake in this cultural detour. I share Paul Gilroy's perspective that to view black Atlantic oral performance "as the simple power of a latent but omnipotent Africanity … is to trivialize the urgent question of cross-cultural trafficking and to obscure its potential and actual political effects."[55] Too often in poetry scholarship the term *performance* gets used as a synonym for a social group's orality, and a poet's use of performance to take agency in cultural intermixture gets lost.

Because of the emphasis on oral traditions in Caribbean, African American, and Indigenous studies, the contribution of reading practices to the development of decolonized literary genres has drawn little scholarly attention. This is especially the case with performance poetry, which is more connected to poetry's oral roots than other literary genres. However, modern performance poetry's links to nineteenth-century verse recitation culture reveal an intimate relationship with reading. Tracing poets' refashioning of recitation provides an opportunity to explore how subjects who have historically been denied a right to literacy, or who have been forced to adopt English literacy as a form of social control, use performance strategies to adapt literacy practices for their own purposes and to challenge hierarchies of cultural ownership in the Americas. It also provides insight into how Western, Indigenous, and African practices converge to form new approaches to reading and textuality. John Miles Foley has established how our accounts of what it means to read have mostly been explained from a "Western alphabetic" perspective.[56] When scholars study performance poetry only in oral terms, they overlook how the genre challenges ethnocentric assumptions about literacy and radically redefines what it means to read.

The literacy scholar Brian Street distinguishes between an "autonomous" model – the most popular in mainstream society – where literacy gets studied as an individual skill-based pursuit, and an "ideological" model, where literacy becomes a plural concept tied to the social environment.[57] The latter allows us to understand how "one culture's or group's literacy may not look much like another's."[58] Using this ideological lens, I examine the cultural and political dimension of literacy practices in specific settings. It is especially crucial to address the diversity of literacy practices when studying post-colonial literature. As Walter D. Mignolo points out, many post-colonial texts, especially when experimenting with vernacular forms, establish new orally infused approaches to reading.[59] Since poetry has a life off the page, it is particularly well suited for this.

The spoken-word artist forms one of our main images of what it means to be a poet in popular culture. Television productions, such as the hit HBO series *Russell Simmons Presents Def Poetry* (2002–7), have improved the visibility of performance poetry in mainstream society (a visibility that it once held through the ubiquity of recitation). Yet scholars have paid little attention to performance-based poetries, often dismissing spoken word as a contemporary trend, disconnected from broader literary histories. Performance poetry differs from the conventional poetry reading, which typically involves a poet reading her poetry aloud from the page without adding much dramatic emphasis, often in an academic setting.[60] As Kenneth Sherwood points out, "The very phrase 'poetry reading' shows how criticism marginalizes performance, tending to see it as subsidiary, a secondary mode of presentation."[61] In contrast, performance poets favour recordings to disseminate their work, and explicitly engage the theatricality of language in their compositions, both on the page and in performance. As a multimedia art, performance poetry complicates conventional approaches to literary study that focus primarily on the text. Most performance poets utilize live performance and recordings as well as publications to gain the widest possible audience for their work.[62]

While performance-based poetries go by many different names – spoken word, verbal arts, oral poetry, and even just poetry – I favour the inclusive term *performance poetry* because it acknowledges the work's relationship to poetry history and explicitly links it to the field of performance studies.[63] As a category, performance poetry does have limitations, particularly its association with upper-class (and often white) society. Certain practitioners, such as T.L. Cowan, prefer the term *spoken word* because it challenges "the perceived elitism of 'academic' poetics."[64] As Carolyn Cooper notes, "when 'dub' poetry is dubbed 'performance' poetry it goes genteelly up-market." Yet she also suggests that "the all-encompassing term does have the decided advantage of confirming the breadth and complexity of the performance/print, oral/scribal literary continuum along which both 'performance' and 'non-performance' poets operate."[65]

As a critic, I also take my lead from the poets themselves. While Johnson, Bennett, and Hughes might be characterized as spoken-word artists if they were alive today, during their lifetimes they firmly asserted that their performance-based work should be viewed as poetry, even when their literary establishments refused to acknowledge it as such. In the late nineteenth century, the leading sites of performance poetry in North America were literary societies and school recitals. In the late twentieth century, spoken-word events and slam competitions became some of the most prominent venues for the form. In turn, today's elementary school student is far more likely to encounter a unit on spoken-word poetry than a lesson on Longfellow.[66]

In the past few years, scholars have begun to pay more attention to performance poetry in African American and American studies; however, they have been silent about the form's relationship to literacy practices and to classroom histories. These scholars have also focused on the United States despite the prevalence of performance poetries throughout the Americas.[67] In a similar vein, although recitation curricula cross many borders, recitation scholarship has yet to pursue a transnational approach, revealing the pervasiveness of national frameworks in literary studies. By making the reception of a widespread institutional use of poetry in North America its focal point, *Recalling Recitation in the Americas* reveals how national frameworks limit our understanding of the pervasiveness of legacies of indoctrination, and how such legacies break down and become disrupted by linguistic hybridity.

New Maps for Literature of the Americas

The cross-border scope of this book takes inspiration from hemispheric studies. Also known as New World studies, literature of the Americas, or inter-American studies, this field examines points of connection and dialogue between interlinked histories and cultural formations in the Americas. Originating in Latin American studies, it has become a prominent field of research in the past two decades.[68] Yet as texts such as Michael J. Dash's *The Other America: Caribbean Literature in New World Context* (1998), and more recently Winfried Siemerling and Sarah Phillips Casteel's edited collection *Canada and Its Americas: Transnational Navigations* (2011), have addressed, US/Latin American relationships have tended to dominate this field. My study reorients this North/South axis by examining other circuits of exchange between the Caribbean, Canada, and the United States to understand the intimacies created between and among the cultures of North America by such forces as geographical adjacency and common imperial histories.[69] While Canadian critics such as Herb Wylie caution that a hemispheric approach will further marginalize non-US literatures by incorporating them into one category, I maintain that such an approach offers one of the only opportunities to culturally distinguish these literatures from capital "A" American literature and to challenge the dominance of US definitions of New World identity.[70]

The Tobagonian Canadian poet M. NourbeSe Philip rejects the dominant Euro-American construction of the New World as a place of discovery and conquest by drawing attention to how white settlers irrevocably interrupted the lives of First Nations people and Africans as well as countless others. She suggests that "to understand the Caribbean one needs to understand it and the entire New World as a site of massive interruptions."[71] In the anglophone Americas, the enforcement of the English language has been one of the primary agents of psychological colonization, interrupting memories, identities, thoughts, and intimate relationships. As the Anishinaabe poet Annharte addresses, "The death and mutilation of our peoples' spirits and bodies accompanied the teaching of English."[72] Like Kincaid, Philip recalls Wordsworth's "bloody" daffodils to illustrate the violence of linguistic control: "If there is one central image that sums up english literature studies in the Caribbean for me it would be the daffodil. Every school child had to engage with Wordsworth's daffodils at some time, although we had never seen them, and most of us would probably never see them. And yet our very futures depended on being able to write about these bloody flowers." For Philip, this disruptive experience (although negative) infuses artistic experimentation, which Kincaid's *Lucy* also substantiates. Philip proposes that writers must play "with the structure of language to destabilize the image of the daffodil."[73] Although it takes quite different forms, Afro-diasporic and Aboriginal groups both share this devastating linguistic interruption – churches and schools forced English on them and took away their native tongues, often through rote learning and recitation. How to express (and perform) these experiences of "rupture" and "break" has become a prominent theme in both literatures.[74]

Hemispheric conversations that focus on African-descended and Indigenous groups are both vital and risky. Their intertwined histories of "rupture" and "break" are undeniable, yet scholars and activists have been unsure how to build alliances between them. Indigenous scholars such as Craig Womack, Jace Weaver, Robert Warrior, and Janice Acoose's emphasis on Aboriginal literary nationalism as an extension of the political struggle for self-governance and land claims seems incompatible with Paul Gilroy's rejection of rootedness as a basis for identity in his groundbreaking study *The Black Atlantic*.[75] In addition to a rift between their conceptual frameworks, one reason scholars have been reluctant to pursue conversations between them is because such dialogues can potentially mute significant cultural differences and distinct experiences of oppression. However, when undertaken with care, they offer the opportunity to explore how blackness and indigeneity intertwine in racial discourses (often in complex and problematic ways).

In their edited collection *Cultural Grammars of Nation, Diaspora and Indigeneity in Canada*, Christine Kim and Sophie McCall suggest that scholars need "to examine tensions within and between concepts of indigeneity and diaspora, and to analyze the ways those tensions transform concepts of nation."[76] McCall also stresses that we must build "a hinge between diasporic and Indigenous-sovereigntist viewpoints."[77] While their book focuses on Canadian literature, its main claims are illuminated by recent work in Caribbean studies, which reveals how post-Independence Caribbean societies invoked the vanishing Native ideology as part of nation building.[78] To prevent the reinscription of imperial myths, we must track across borders how notions of blackness and indigeneity get constructed in relation not only to hegemonic whiteness but also to each other in the Americas. The comparative approach used here deepens our understanding of how racial identities in the Americas are constructed not in isolation but rather through cross-border exchange, intermixture, and appropriation. Each chapter examines how poets use performance to craft their own racial meanings in the Americas by refashioning dominant frameworks and by crossing borders between different identity categories. For example, in chapter 2, I discuss Hughes's childhood fascination with Longfellow's *The Song of Hiawatha* and how his Indigenous heritage informed his understanding of his African American identity.

Many Native activists and scholars are sceptical about using postcolonial theory to address Indigenous issues. These concerns are certainly justified because, unlike an island like Jamaica, in Canada the white colonizers never left.[79] However, McCall argues that "theories of diaspora may offer some insights into the history of displacement of Aboriginal peoples," particularly when racial hybridity is also present.[80] The Canadian government's implementation of the reserve system and residential schooling in the late nineteenth century removed countless Indigenous people from their tribal homes and forced many of them to relocate to urban settings. Drawing on the Caribbean writer George Lamming's writings about exile, the Cree poet and scholar Neal McLeod characterizes "this condition of alienation" as both "ideological" and "physical diaspora."[81] Although E. Pauline Johnson never attended residential school, the fact that she was a mixed-race poet who spent the majority of her adult life on tour and living far from her Mohawk nation makes a diasporic lens particularly appropriate. In chapter 4, I will discuss two contemporary First Nations women poets who claim her as a literary predecessor – the Mohawk-Tuscarora Janet Marie Rogers and the Anishinaabe (Marie) Annharte. Both women live in urban environments away from their reserve communities and both identify with Johnson's mobile approach to her Indigenous identity. Certainly the displacement felt by an Afro-Jamaican immigrant such as Louise Bennett, when she lived in Toronto, differs from the displacement felt by a Mohawk woman such as Johnson, who eventually settled on Coast Salish territory in Vancouver; however, exploring the dialogue between these two distinct experiences of displacement can help us "to build coalitions between disparate minority histories."[82]

Although the following chapters have a chronological arrangement, they reveal multiple trajectories in North American performance poetry, rather than a unified history. Their sequence – from late nineteenth-century Canada to the early twentieth-century United States, to mid-twentieth-century Jamaica, and finally to late twentieth- and early twenty-first-century First Nations and Afro-Jamaican poetry in the diaspora – draws attention to the unevenness of performance in different sites. I examine commonalities as well as discontinuities between the various practices of memory, recitation, poetry, and reading to more fully understand their roles in decolonizing language.

Chapter 1 examines Johnson's relationships with the work of Longfellow and Whittier. While she professes to love these authors, a close reading of archival evidence and her performance strategies reveal a submerged critique of their Native-themed poetry. Because scholars have wanted to emphasize Johnson's feminism and her Mohawk and Canadian identities, they have overlooked the complicated influence of American schoolroom poets and verse recitation on her innovation of poetic performance. Performance played a key role in her efforts to represent racial hybridity during a period when racial mixing was either invisible or viewed as a sign of degeneracy. Johnson's experimental use of performance to represent her hybrid subjectivity anticipates Louise Bennett's and Langston Hughes's more radical remaking of memorization and recitation practices in the twentieth century.

While modernist poets like Ezra Pound often rejected the Victorian idea of poetry as a form directed primarily at children, Hughes and Bennett did not view using poetry to instruct children as a fundamental problem. However, they also sought to prevent poetry from being used to enforce "Standard English" grammar and British culture. The chapters devoted to Hughes and Bennett examine how they developed their literacy politics through their engagements with recitation practices. To help readers resist the hegemony of white culture, both poets provided them with representations of black culture, and both taught readers how to manipulate the Western texts they encountered. Rather than view Hughes's work with children and his avant-garde poetics as separate aspects of his career, I interpret his children's literature and teaching as pedagogical enactments of his modernist blues and jazz poetics. By encouraging recitation among his readers, rather than controlling their speech, he gave his readers agency by making the embodied process of reading explicit. Similarly, Bennett's reputation as an oral poet overshadows her promotion of Creole literacy practices in her poetry. In chapter 3, I examine Bennett's gendered critique of Western literacy and how she drew on feminine vernacular knowledge to transform colonial recitation into a strategy of subversive mimicry.

For contemporary authors, having the opportunity to learn a poem by Johnson, Hughes, or Bennett in school, rather than (or in addition to) the Euro-centric recitation canon, opened up a world of possibility. Chapter 4 considers how this broadened recitation canon contributed to the development of performance poetry in the late twentieth century. Studying dub poets' writings about Bennett and Hughes as well as First Nations women poets' writings about Johnson, I reveal how these authors built on the work of their predecessors to create a resistant memory politics. The Joebell example illustrates 1) the difficulty of overcoming what one has been forced to internalize, and 2) how performing one's voice in the era of globalization becomes complicated by competing social scripts. The poets discussed in the final chapter – dub poets Lillian Allen, Mutabaruka, Linton Kwesi Johnson, and Jean "Binta" Breeze as well as the First Nations poets Rogers and Annharte – develop performance strategies to decolonize personal and collective memories put under duress by repeated displacements and forced internalizations.

Performance Traces

To conclude this introduction, let me briefly address methodology. Since Johnson, Hughes, and Bennett pushed their audiences to interact with their poems in new ways, I, too, have had to widen my critical approach. When studying Native literatures, Susan Berry Brill de Ramírez suggests that scholars abandon print-based methods and use the literature itself that is infused by oral traditions to "directly inform the scholarly process."[83] Taking my lead from the poets themselves, I view all forms of reading and interpretation as performative acts. In addition to examining a poem's production, distribution, circulation, and, if possible, reader/listener reception, I focus on the kind of interaction a poem implicitly (or, in the case of some of the texts examined here, explicitly) invites from its audience.[84]

I seek out what various academic fields that focus on marginalized histories refer to as "the trace" (such as subaltern studies, book history, reception studies, and feminist literary criticism). As Roger Chartier points out, "reading is always a practice embodied in acts, spaces, and habits," which makes it difficult to excavate histories of reading.[85] In turn, the ephemerality of performance also evades conventional scholarly methods of literary analysis. I look for traces of reading acts and performance events in a variety of sources that include printed versions of performance poems; audio and video recordings of performances (when available); poets' letters and unpublished manuscripts; newspaper reviews of performances; interviews; and promotional material for performance tours, such as posters and programs. Being attentive to the traces of oral dynamics in this evidence is crucial. As Foley emphasizes, this entails "a sensitivity to the role of context, a commitment to understanding and portraying verbal art on its own terms, and an awareness of expressive signals beyond the usual repertoire of textual cues."[86] Because poets rarely address their views on recitation directly, I look at how recitation is staged in their fiction and autobiographies to study what they reveal about its politics and its influence on the development of modern performance poetry.

To build cultural alliances between different subordinated social groups, *Recalling Recitation in the Americas* illustrates that we must move across national divides and conventional identity politics frameworks. As Audre Lorde establishes, we must build coalitions across racial groups to transform elitist literary canons and dismantle intersecting systems of oppression.[87] As a researcher undertaking this project, I have had to come to terms with my position as a white middle-class feminist who has benefited from the colonialism of the Americas. Like other Canadian feminist critics who have negotiated the politics of writing about Native literature as "cultural outsiders" – such as Jennifer Andrews and Helen Hoy, as well as Gerson and Strong-Boag – I adopt Trinh T. Minh-ha's concept of "speaking nearby." Her term is particularly resonant for my project's focus on the politics of voices. As Minh-ha explains, "speaking nearby or together with certainly differs from speaking for and about."[88] For me, "speaking nearby" involves listening to these poets within their own social locations and to how their own communities have engaged with their work. *Recalling Recitation in the Americas* puts these poets' performance projects in dialogue with each other, but avoids creating a false sense of equivalency between them.

The verb *recalling* in my title evokes memory as an active force in the present. To recall is to summon something from the past back to awareness, often through performance. This book explores how the act of remembering and the act of performing overlap and how the intersection between them shapes language practices. To explore the contradictory legacies of recitation, I emphasize the multiple meanings of recalling, such as to fondly remember that which seems familiar and to revoke, cancel, or send back. Johnson, Hughes, and Bennett express affection for poetry recitation as a positive aspect of their childhoods, which paradoxically helped them to sustain a vital connection to their oral traditions, even as education practices sought linguistic control through it.

How do subjects in the Americas contend with this intimate form of invasion? To refer back to Lovelace's short story, how does a person like Joebell take authority over the English alphabet that he internalized as a child? What happens when we study performance both as a verbal art and as an act that is often tied to some form of textual practice? What types of mimicry disrupt colonial authority and which ones reinforce it? More broadly, how do colonized people become authors of their own histories, rather than passive recipients of dominant cultural discourses? By focusing on the political and poetic dimensions of recitation, the following chapters take up such questions to unravel the interruptions and the entanglements of New World identities.

Chapter One

E. Pauline Johnson (Tekahionwake) and Her "Dear Dead Longfellow"

She was a poet – whose poem "The Song My Paddle Sings" was standard fare in Canadian school readers until the 1950s. She was also what would now be known as a performance artist, but was called at the time an elocutionist – that is, she gave public performances in drawing-rooms and theatres, at which she recited her own poetry to great dramatic effect.

Margaret Atwood, *Strange Things*

"The Song My Paddle Sings" has been memorized and recited by more Canadian children in the last one hundred years than perhaps any other poem in the nation's history.[1] Shortly after its initial publication in *Saturday Night* magazine in 1892, participants began to recite it at canoe meets in Canada and the northern United States.[2] Its rhyme scheme mimics the rhythmic stroke of the paddle, making the poem a perfect anthem for amateur canoeists. Johnson created a text that refuses to stay still on the page and even to stay indoors. At summer camps, children would chant the poem around campfires: "West wind, blow from your prairie nest."[3] For much of the twentieth century, it appeared as a staple in school readers and children's literature anthologies. For many students, it was the only work of literature by an Indigenous author that they would get to study. In the epigraph, Margaret Atwood suggests that its popularity in the classroom declined in the 1950s, which coincides with the general decline of memorization and recitation pedagogy in North America; however, personal accounts suggest that the poem continued to be studied and performed in the second half of the twentieth century. Even though recitation has fallen out of fashion in schools, children still study the poem today.

I remember reading (but not memorizing) the poem in the 1980s at age eight in an Ontario classroom, less than sixty miles from the Six Nations Reserve and Johnson's childhood home, Chiefswood. To me, it evoked the excitement of my own family canoe trips in Algonquin Park; she became another Canadian woman writer whom I adored, along with L.M. Montgomery. My teacher told the class that Johnson was part Mohawk and that "Native people" were a proud part of Canadian heritage, but she failed to mention that the school was built on traditional Attawandaron territory or that Johnson had been a defender of Native rights.

In *Inheriting a Canoe Paddle: The Canoe in Discourses of English-Canadian Nationalism* (2013), Misao Dean establishes how nationalist ideology promotes "the belief that by paddling a canoe we make ourselves Canadian," which explains why Johnson's lyric poem provides an ideal script for school children to perform national identity.[4] Fostering patriotism in the classroom through recitation was as much a priority in anglophone Canada as it was in the United States and Great Britain. Like Louise Bennett in 1940s Jamaica, Johnson began writing when her Commonwealth country sought a distinct national literary culture, and "The Song My Paddle Sings," with its celebration of the Canadian wilderness, fit the bill perfectly. But what made it even more popular for recitation was its usefulness in the (not so) hidden curriculum of indigenization. Terry Goldie developed this term to characterize how settler Canadians appropriate Indigenous identities to feel a sense of rooted belonging. While "The Song My Paddle Sings" is not an overtly "Native poem," the subject of canoeing evokes an Indigenous practice without naming it as such. To put it in the terms of Philip Deloria, one could "play Indian" without explicitly taking on an Indigenous identity because of the unraced persona in the poem.[5]

But is the popularity of Johnson and her classic recitation poem merely a product of indigenization? Carole Gerson suggests that Johnson's books are "the major medium of [her] enduring celebrity" because many of them have never been out of print since their initial publication.[6] However, we should not discount the force of recitation traditions, education history, and oral memory in creating the popular national poet. Moreover, Johnson herself deserves more credit for creating a poetics that lives primarily through performance.

Johnson's complicated reception history reveals how her legacy depends on who remembers her and when. Many things have been named after her, including chocolates, schools, and a First World War machine gun. Her poetry and her politics have been praised as radical by some and dismissed as derivative and assimilationist by others. As is often the case with poets in the recitation canon, Johnson's popularity in the schoolroom has done more to jeopardize her literary reputation than it has to validate it, which might explain why her relationship with recitation has yet to be explored in depth.[7] In this chapter, I recall her as a recitation poet, an often-forgotten but vital lens for understanding how she formulated her poetic voice.

"The Indian Poet-Reciter"

From the very start of her performance career, Johnson aligned herself with recitation traditions. Promotional posters and advertisements characterized her as "an Iroquois Elocutionist," "the Mohawk Indian Poetess and Reciter," and "the Indian Poet-Reciter" (see figure 1). Nineteenth-century verse recitation evoked the idea that the work of renowned writers could impart wisdom, knowledge, and cultural competence to its performing readers. Yet, as many contemporary reviewers of her work noted, Johnson made a decisive break from this tradition in the 1890s by performing poetry that she wrote rather than reciting the canonical verse of others. While certain well-known male authors, such as Charles Dickens and Mark Twain, began to perform their own work in the 1850s, it was far more common for trained elocutionists to read the work of others. Nineteenth-century audiences generally believed a trained elocutionist would read better than a poet, but Johnson anticipated twentieth-century audiences' preference for performance by poets and the flourishing of poetry readings in the Americas.[8] Many of her contemporaries even recognized that her poems depended on performance. As one 1892 reviewer put it, "Her poems are literary gems but one cannot thoroughly appreciate them without hearing them read by the authoress."[9]

Of course, poets have been performing their own work since the earliest days of the art form; however, print-centric frameworks dominated nineteenth-century views of poetry in North America, and the term *poetry reading* held no implicit meaning that the author would perform his or her own work. It was not until the 1920s that audiences began to view public poetry performances as "manifestations of authentic authorial presence," rather than as an activity for trained readers and elocutionists.[10] Johnson anticipated this change three decades before it occurred.

In the epigraph, Atwood proposes that if Johnson were performing today she would be "known as a performance artist," rather than as an elocutionist.[11] Marvin Carlson's definition of performance art supports Atwood's interpretation of Johnson. He explains that performance

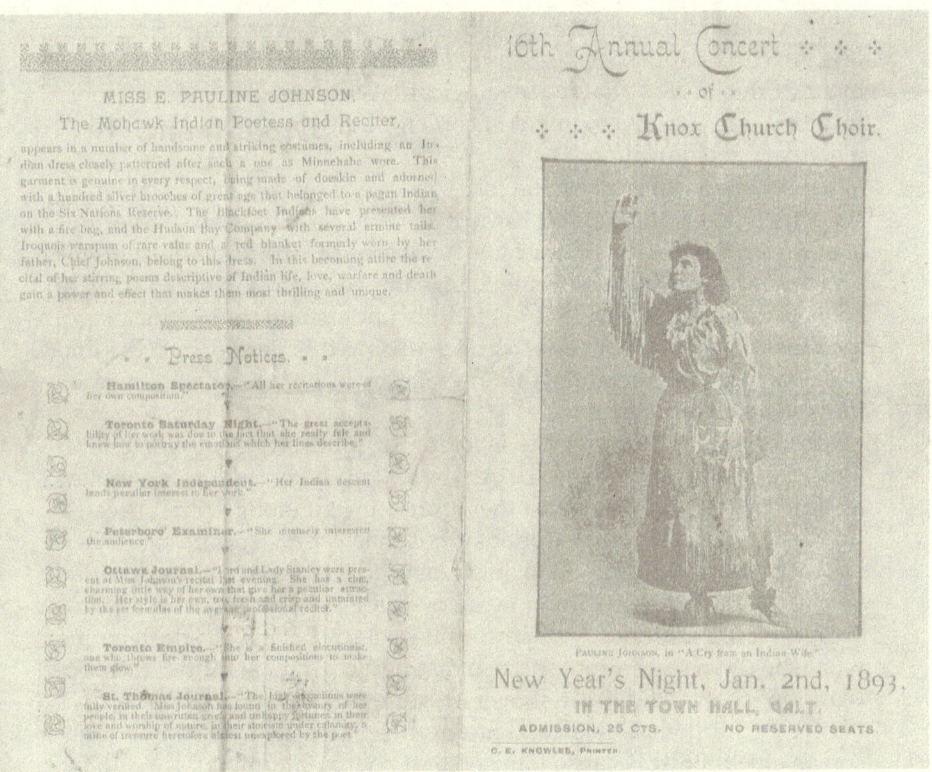

MISS E. PAULINE JOHNSON,

The Mohawk Indian Poetess and Reciter,

appears in a number of handsome and striking costumes, including an Indian dress closely patterned after such a one as Minnehaha wore. This garment is genuine in every respect, being made of doeskin and adorned with a hundred silver brooches of great age that belonged to a pagan Indian on the Six Nations Reserve. The Blackfoot Indians have presented her with a fire bag, and the Hudson Bay Company with several ermine tails. Iroquois wampum of rare value and a red blanket formerly worn by her father, Chief Johnson, belong to this dress. In this becoming attire the recital of her stirring poems descriptive of Indian life, love, warfare and death gain a power and effect that makes them most thrilling and unique.

Press Notices.

Hamilton Spectator.—"All her recitations were of her own composition."

Toronto Saturday Night.—"The great acceptability of her work was due to the fact that she really felt and knew how to portray the emotions which her lines describe."

New York Independent.—"Her Indian descent lends peculiar interest to her work."

Peterboro' Examiner.—"She intensely interested the audience."

Ottawa Journal.—"Lord and Lady Stanley were present at Miss Johnson's recital last evening. She has a chic, charming little way of her own that give her a peculiar attraction. Her style is her own, too, fresh and crisp and untainted by the set formulas of the average professional reciter."

Toronto Empire.—"She is a finished elocutionist, one who throws fire enough into her compositions to make them glow."

St. Thomas Journal.—"The high expectations were fully verified. Miss Johnson has found in the history of her people, in their unwritten griefs and unhappy fortunes, in their love and worship of nature, in their stoicism under calamity, a mine of treasure heretofore almost unexplored by the poet."

16th Annual Concert
of
Knox Church Choir.

Pauline Johnson, in "A Cry from an Indian Wife."

New Year's Night, Jan. 2nd, 1893.

IN THE TOWN HALL, GALT.

ADMISSION, 25 CTS. NO RESERVED SEATS.

C. E. KNOWLES, PRINTER

1. A performance brochure for one of Johnson's performances (The William Ready Division of Archives and Research Collections, McMaster University Library.)

artists, unlike theatre actors, "do not base their work upon characters previously created by other artists but upon their own bodies, their own autobiographies, their own specific experiences in a culture or in a world, made performative by their consciousness of them and the process of displaying them for audiences."[12] Johnson's combining of writing, costume, and performance to explore her lived experience as a mixed-race individual anticipated contemporary art practices. Atwood implies that she was only called an elocutionist because the performance-art genre, which now covers her innovative art practice, had not yet been invented. Since her experiences on stage were explicitly word-based, *performance poetry* seems like the more apt term. In fact, the Mohawk/Tuscarora poet Janet Rogers (who will be discussed in chapter 4) identifies Johnson as an early spoken-word poet.[13] Regardless, Atwood's and Rogers's comments both corroborate a central argument of this book – that a genealogical link connects the elocutionary tradition and the development of contemporary performance practices aimed at decolonization.

In the century of criticism on Johnson, one of the few things on which scholars agree is that her art thwarts generic classification. Part of this stems from the fact that in the nineteenth century, the terms elocutionist and reciter were often used interchangeably to describe a broad array of solo performances.[14] We have yet to fully understand the significance of the elocutionist and reciter categories during this period, and the liminal space between reading, oral performance, and creative innovation that the terms evoke.

Most scholars interpret the labelling of Johnson as an elocutionist and a reciter as strategic. Like Atwood, they imagine that promoters assigned the terms to her and that Johnson went along with it because they had more respectable connotations than *actress*. According to Gerson and Veronica Strong-Boag, Johnson used the respectability afforded by the elocutionary tradition as a cover for her incorporation of less "respectable" material and performance techniques. By designating what she did as recitation, she also distinguished herself from the popular, low-brow Wild West shows of Buffalo Bill, which also featured Native performers. Gerson and Strong-Boag also do not consider Johnson an elocutionist because Johnson had no formal training.[15] Yet in the late nineteenth century the elocution movement changed considerably and began to encourage a DIY approach. It became "more democratic and entertainment-oriented and less instructive."[16] Popular recitation manuals, such as *The Canadian Elocutionist*, were designed for both the self-taught learner and the classroom pupil. It is likely that Johnson learned how to perform by studying one of these books, which were ubiquitous in middle-class homes of the period.[17]

The assertion that Johnson was not a real elocutionist because she lacked formal training minimizes the formative role memorization and recitation practices played in the development of Johnson's performance poetics. During a cultural moment of extreme assimilation, nineteenth-century verse culture made a stage career a possibility for an aspiring poet such as Johnson. Recitation provided her with a model for how to blend reading, writing, and performance, and helped her to achieve a degree of public authority for her voice. Through the guise of Western recitation modes, she was able to incorporate elements from the Mohawk oratory tradition into her poetry. She used embodied performance to gain agency in the process of cultural intermixture and the representation of racial hybridity – a power typically afforded only to those in positions of power.

As was common for children during this period, Johnson's exposure to verse culture began at an early age. By age nine she had memorized lengthy passages from Henry Wadsworth Longfellow's *The Song of Hiawatha* (1855) as well as many other British and American poems.[18] Reciting this poem to guests in her parents' home on the Six Nations Reserve, Johnson likely appeared as a model of Anglo-assimilation. The poem's inaccurate account of a peaceful exchange of power between Native Americans and whites, especially when performed by a young mixed-race child, perhaps eased some of the tensions and contradictions settlers felt in the newly confederated Canada in the 1870s.

Johnson was the daughter of a Mohawk chief and an English-born mother. Her parents raised her to uphold Victorian British values and behaviour, partly because they were anxious about her acceptance in white Canadian society.[19] Yet they also taught her to value her Native heritage. She adored her grandfather John "Smoke" Johnson (Sakayengwaraton), nicknamed the "Mohawk Warbler," who was a legendary storyteller, and she learned some Iroquois from her father, who spoke several Iroquois languages.[20] For most of her education, she was homeschooled by her mother, who taught her British refinement and manners so she could enact Anglo-Canadian identity as protection from discrimination. Through these lessons, Johnson learned to understand identity as performance. Her memorization and recitation of great English and American poems played a central role in her education. Since Johnson's childhood experiences with recitation happened outside of the formal classroom (unlike most of the other poets in this study), perhaps she felt more of a personal connection to the work she memorized and felt less constrained by institutional expectation. The poems that Johnson loved the most as a child were the Native-themed texts by the American poets Henry Wadsworth Longfellow and John Greenleaf Whittier. By age twelve, she claimed that she had read everything that Longfellow had ever published.[21] These men became primary influences in the development of her self-proclaimed "Canadian born" poetic project.[22]

National frameworks can obscure an understanding of the strange and often forced intimacies between the cultures of the Americas. This becomes abundantly clear when one considers Johnson's performance of *The Song of Hiawatha* – a white US poet's appropriation of Anishinaabe and Haudenosaunee culture – in a Mohawk territory in Canada in the late nineteenth century. While Johnson's childhood parlour performances seem firmly entrenched in verse recitation culture and seem to hold no traces of the disruptive forces of modernism, through these early experiences she began to formulate her racialized poetics and adopt embodied performance as a strategy to take agency in cultural intermixture. In an 1890 letter to her friend Archie Kains, Johnson declares that she wants "in all my work and all my strivings … to upset the Indian Extermination and noneducation theory – in fact to stand by my blood and my race."[23] However, in her efforts to champion Native rights in her work, she drew on appropriated white US representations of her own Mohawk culture. Poetry memorization and recitation produced a transatlantic "archive of popular memory" that Johnson could access more readily than the collective memory of her Mohawk tribe because English was her mother tongue.[24] In her childhood recitations, she parroted back the dominant scripts of her Native identity for a white audience. As an adult, she began writing her own poetic scripts, which she brought to life on the stage to disrupt this hegemonic form of mimicry.

Johnson aligned herself with Whittier and Longfellow, two of the most prominent poets in verse recitation culture in North America, to claim literary authority for her voice in the public sphere. Whittier wrote to her early in her career, in 1891, and praised her poems: "They have strength as well as beauty, and study and patient brooding over thy work will enable thee to write better still. It is fitting that one of their own race should sing the songs of the Mohawk and the Iroquois in the English tongue. There is a splendid opportunity before thee."[25] Johnson's promotional material often cited this quotation as a critical endorsement of her work.[26] Relating her excitement about Whittier's compliments to Kains in a letter, she wrote, "Ah Archie you do not know how I love the dear old man now who has penned with his trembling aged hand those dear encouraging words to me. His is such a beautifully simple pure mind and he so loves all races in America that my heart goes out to him, as it did in my childhood to dear dead Longfellow."[27] Johnson expresses her admiration for Whittier's championing of "all races in America," connecting his abolitionist politics to the struggle for Aboriginal rights. His words of encouragement came at a pivotal moment in Johnson's development as a writer, when she felt as though her poetry would never achieve the literary recognition that she desired. Later in her career, she shared with an interviewer, "I owe to Whittier all I have ever accomplished for he first gave me faith in myself."[28]

These idealizing comments about Whittier and "dear dead Longfellow" suggest Johnson had no objections to the Native stereotypes represented in their poetry. However, a closer examination of her engagement with their reader-centred verse reveals how she manipulated Longfellow's and Whittier's versions of nineteenth-century verse recitation culture to perform a racial hybridity and to challenge the fantasy of the vanishing Native. Many of her contemporaries, as well as her twentieth-century critics, believed that she would have been more successful as a poet if she had avoided a stage career.[29] Here we have another example of "our familiar book-idiom" depreciating the value of oral aesthetics.[30] However, becoming a reciter of her own verse allowed her to use both language and her own body to make her critique.

Johnson established herself as a writer before she began to pursue performance. Her first poems appeared in newspapers and magazines in North America in the early 1880s. She became a recitalist as a calculated move. Issues of gender and race prevented her poetry from achieving recognition in her colonial environment. While her poems about the Canadian landscape had much in common with the work of the Confederation Poets (as critics would later term them), the literary elite of Canadian society at the time would never have counted a mixed-race woman who never graduated from high school as part of this tight-knit group of well-educated white men. Due to a lack of recognition for her written work, Johnson turned to performance to earn a living and build an audience. Her successful debut at a literary event in Toronto in 1892 began her performance career. Frank Yeigh, who would become her first manager, organized the event, "Evening with Canadian Authors." The literary evening reflected the national desire during this post-Confederation moment to develop an autonomous Canadian identity. According to most accounts, Johnson's dramatic performance of "A Cry from an Indian Wife" stole the show. Descriptions of her delivery indicate that she was thoroughly versed in the elocutionary principles of the period.[31] While the other writers at the event read their work from the page, Johnson recited her work from memory, as she had learned to do as a child. With her hands and her eyes unconstrained by the page, she won over the audience through the power of expression and gesture.[32] Johnson's successful use of elocution techniques in her first poetry performance points to the importance of her early training.

Performing Racial Hybridity

Soon after her debut, Johnson began wearing a Native outfit to perform her dramatic monologues written in the voices of Indigenous women (see figure 2). Many twentieth-century critics disparaged her for basing her costume on an image of Hiawatha's love interest, Minnehaha, from her childhood copy of Longfellow's poem, rather than on the traditional clothing of her Mohawk tribe.[33] Yet, in her cultural moment, aligning herself with Longfellow was a calculated move to give her voice credibility. Her promotional material highlighted the origins of her costume to make her connection to Longfellow clear to her audiences (see figure 1). In her asymmetrical buckskin dress adorned with fringes, fur pelts, Iroquois silver medallions, wampum belts, and her father's hunting knife, Johnson embodied a fictional Native heroine on stage.

Does Johnson's Minnehaha-inspired dress represent her conforming to white stereotypes of the Indian maiden or her taking on the stereotype to subvert it?[34] In other words, to what extent did her mimicry reinforce colonial power and to what extent did her mimicry disrupt it? These questions are at the heart of contemporary debates about Johnson, and our inability to easily answer them reflects the ambivalence of mimicry itself. For example, Ruth Phillips argues that Johnson "exploited popular stereotypes of Indianness through dress and stage props as a strategy for affirming a positive Native identity"; however, Emma LaRocque maintains that Johnson falls into the trap of colonial mimicry because she relies on "words and tropes" in nineteenth-century literature by white men like Longfellow.[35] Yet we need to take a deeper look at the intertextual conversation between Johnson and Longfellow, in both her performances and her texts, before we assume that her relationship with his work discounts the disruptive potential of her mimicry. These debates often overlook the murky terrain between Johnson's self-fashioning and audience reception, as well as her dual mimicry. She mimics the stereotype of the fine Anglo-Canadian lady as well as the stereotype of the Native heroine.

From 1892 to 1909, Johnson performed her poetry in small communities and cities across North America – in drawing rooms, churches, schoolrooms, town halls, mechanics institutes, mining camps, and sometimes in actual theatres.[36] She wore her buckskin dress to recite her Native-themed poetry in the first half of each performance. During the intermission she would change into an evening gown and reappear on stage to recite nature poetry about the Canadian landscape. One

2. Johnson wearing her performance outfit based on an illustration of Minnehaha (The William Ready Division of Archives and Research Collections, McMaster University Library)

of her most precarious stages was allegedly on top of a billiard table, where she recited her poetry to an audience of miners, changing her outfit during the intermission behind a Hudson's Bay blanket strung up on a line.[37] Her provisional and makeshift stages, much like her actual performances, were fluid and ephemeral. As a reviewer in the *Hamilton Spectator* noted in 1903, her embodied stage presence was one of "perpetual motion."[38] Similar to her poems, which paint landscapes and narratives rife with rushing water and ceaseless movement, her performances rejected containment and inspired mobility. Her dramatic change during the intermission, from her syncretic Native outfit into an evening gown, created the scaffold for her recitations. Through her transformation from a Mohawk woman into an upper-class white lady, she demonstrated that anyone (including her immigrant and working-class audiences in remote settlements) could become a civilized anglophone Canadian. Critics, such as Mary Elizabeth Leighton, suggest that Johnson's embodiment of the ideology of the vanishing Native and her dramatic enactment of assimilation fuelled her immense popularity; however, her two-part performances also revealed her efforts to perform her mixed-race identity by capitalizing on the fluidity of performance.[39] To put it in the terms of Bhabha, she harnessed the subversive potential of mimicry by drawing attention to herself as "*almost the same but not white.*"[40]

The structure of her performances suggests a fluid conversion from Native to white, but in reality the intermission broke these two identities apart. Her bifurcated performances and her two styles of poetry underscored her mixed-race identity as a paradox. The only way Johnson could construct a raced lyric "I" was through impersonation and performance. Her costumed performances "stag[ed] both the process of assimilation and the constructedness of the binary categories that this process assumes."[41] In the second half of her recital, her evening gown and her Victorian nature poems implied that she had assimilated to Anglo-Canadian culture, yet since she changed clothes during the intermission behind closed doors, the conversion process remained invisible to audiences. She made the discursive slippage in Bhabha's account of mimicry tangible, as she slipped in and out of her costumes in what was often a makeshift backstage. Accounts of her actual performances also indicate that she occasionally would appear in her Minnehaha dress in the second act rather than the first, inverting the assimilation fantasy.[42] Her performances engaged the threshold between her two identities.

Late nineteenth-century Canadians generally viewed miscegenation in negative terms and idealized the vanishing Native as a symbol of Canadian heritage (such views provided justification for the settler theft of land and culture from First Nations people). Johnson's performance poetics demonstrates the impossibility of representing mixed-race identity in a way that would be visible (or otherwise apprehensible) to her audiences, because she could never appear on stage as white and Mohawk at the same time. To her contemporaries, her Mohawk heritage would have been incompatible with her identity as a lady. To put it in the lyrical phrasing of the poet Joan Crate, she was perceived to be as "pale as real ladies."[43] However, in performing both identities as separate entities, she sought to make mixed-race identity intelligible. Print publication would prohibit such diverse voices in her poems, yet on stage she had the opportunity to play multiple personas for an audience and make her body the link between them, a common practice in Indigenous oral storytelling traditions.[44]

Reckoning with Longfellow

Johnson's theatrical approach to representing racial identity in her poetics was very unusual. However, other poets also started to pursue stage careers at the end of the nineteenth century. According to Paul Gray, many poets in the United States (almost all of whom were white males) turned to the stage to make a living as part of what he terms the poet-performer movement, which began in the 1870s. Gray helps to contextualize Johnson's innovations. He offers two insights into what precipitated the flourishing of poetic performance in North America. First, construction of the railroads made making a living this way possible, which Johnson's frequent train travel while on tour substantiates. Second, he illustrates how Longfellow and Whittier helped to move poetry off the page and to build a mass audience for poetry. Although Longfellow rarely read his own work aloud, his sound-based poetics, designed for reader performances, laid the foundation for the poet-performer movement.[45]

Johnson's contemporaries were quick to recognize (and even exaggerate) Longfellow's influence on her work, although for them this had nothing to do with recitation. Newspaper reviews of Johnson's first poetry collection, *The White Wampum*, published in England in 1895, frequently interpret her work as part of an emerging New World poetics on the "noble red man" initiated by Longfellow.[46] A reviewer in *The Weekly*

Scotsman observed that "Longfellow naturally occurs to one before many stanzas have been perused."[47] Another reviewer in *The Scotsman* from 8 July 1895, writes, "The noble red man is known to poetry chiefly in the epic of the loves of Hiawatha and Minnehaha: and a reader of Mr. E. Pauline Johnson's book, *The White Wampum* will often be reminded of the incidents in the fine free life of that brave and his Indian sweetheart."[48] Although this reviewer's interpretation of Johnson's relationship with Longfellow may be driven by his distorted and limited knowledge of Indigenous cultures, his claim that these two authors share similarities is accurate. In fact, Johnson herself emphasized Longfellow as an influence. While her initial reception was premised on a link between her poetics and Longfellow's, since her death this troubling aspect of her literary genealogy has drawn little attention from critics.

After her death, critics like John W. Garvin sought to define her work as distinctly Canadian and de-emphasized her US influences.[49] They responded to Johnson's own patriotic ethos in her poem "Canadian Born" by corroborating her statement that "The Yankee to the south of us must south of us remain" (126). Yet despite Johnson's own nationalism, her career depended heavily on cross-border interaction. She toured extensively throughout the United States and she depended on their publishing industry. She also turned to Longfellow and Whittier for literary examples of a New World poetics, and for mentorship, because she struggled to find these things in Canada.

The renewed scholarly interest in Johnson, inspired by feminists and First Nations literary critics, has shied away from unravelling this problematic US white male influence on her work. In their influential study *Paddling Her Own Canoe*, Gerson and Strong-Boag focus on establishing Johnson's autonomy as a Canadian woman artist. Similarly, First Nations women writers such as Beth Brant, Joan Crate, Louise Bernice Halfe, Janet Rogers, and Annharte have claimed Johnson as an influence and refrained from dwelling on her reliance on white men to construct her artistic project.[50] This feminist recovery of Johnson positions her as a significant figure in Canadian history who "reverses the standard White, male gaze."[51] By bringing attention to her engagements with US schoolroom poetry, I hope to build on this important scholarship to understand how transnational exchange facilitates Indigenous women's agency and how their agency can emerge through unexpected channels. As LaRocque points out, we need to more thoroughly understand Indigenous peoples' "responses to untenable colonial situations."[52] Johnson's construction of a public voice defied a world designed to dispossess her of one. Johnson suffered from "a lack of contact with others who shared [her] poetic concerns."[53] As an adult she had few opportunities to exchange ideas with her tribal community and to have them validate her experience of reality. Longfellow's recitation poetics provided her with a pathway to the stage and with a model that allowed her to combine her Anglo-Canadian and Mohawk cultures. Johnson clearly internalized many of the harmful stereotypes in Longfellow's poetry. However, by examining her relationship to his work, we can better understand how colonized people critique dominant narratives, either despite or through such damaging internalizations.

Conventional approaches to analysing literary influence, in terms of anxiety or a tension between homage and rejection, fail to explain how a mixed-race woman such as Johnson contended with the cultural authority of a writer like Longfellow in such a fraught imperial environment.[54] As Lois Parkinson Zamora establishes in her landmark work, *The Usable Past: The Imagination of History in Recent Fiction of the Americas* (1997), Harold Bloom's Eurocentric anxiety of influence model fails to account for literary production in the New World. Writers in the Americas "do not subvert or shun influence but engage and interrogate it; their anxiety is a response not to the danger of inadequate imaginative individuation but rather to a knowledge that legitimate sources of communal identity have been destroyed or are unevenly available."[55] A map of the literature of the Americas that studies only productive cross-cultural exchanges and successful moments of transnational community would exclude a whole range of cultural exchange. Johnson's case reveals the importance of retracing troubling literary genealogies and colonial legacies. Through such a hemispheric approach, we can gain a fuller understanding of how legacies of indoctrination move across borders and become reconfigured, and (at times) resisted. Longfellow's appropriation of Anishinaabe and Haudenosaunee material for *The Song of Hiawatha* also involved cultural theft on both sides of the border – a border produced by colonization and displacement. On the surface, it might seem as though Johnson's professed affection for Longfellow demonstrates the extent of her colonization and her inability to challenge Indigenous stereotypes in her own poetics. However, a more thorough examination disrupts this memory of assimilation, revealing how Johnson advances a submerged critique of the ideology of the vanishing Native through her performance poetics.

In interviews and letters, Johnson frequently referred to the poet as "dear dead Longfellow," making clear her indebtedness to him as a model for how to construct a Native poetics.[56] However, her sister, Evelyn, mentions in her unpublished memoir that Johnson once shared with her a more critical view: "Pauline once remarked that Longfellow had done more harm than good when he wrote his celebrated poem, 'Hiawatha,' as everybody thinks of it as entirely true. The part which Longfellow evidently obtained from history is true, but apparently he himself composed the remainder according to supposition."[57] Based on Evelyn's reporting, Johnson criticized Longfellow for distorting Indigenous history to construct his narrative. He based his poem on the amateur ethnography of the Indian agent Henry Rowe Schoolcraft, who confuses the Anishinaabe god Manabozho with the fifteenth-century Mohawk leader Hiawatha.[58] In her essays, Johnson upholds the real Hiawatha and takes pride in his role in establishing the Haudenosaunee Confederacy among the Six Nations. As she describes it in "The Lodge of the Law-makers,"

> this Commonwealth ... was devised and framed through the brain of the young Onondaga diplomat, Hiawatha, who, conceiving an idea for a universal peace, called together the representative chiefs of all the hostile tribes. It mattered not that war and bloodshed had existed for many decades between the tribes that these envoys represented, the words of Hiawatha were as oil (217).[59]

Johnson praises Hiawatha for his intellect and his oratory skills. She highlights his sharp mind to stress his humanity and to avoid deifying him. Her rational account of his accomplishments and her sister's comments hint that Johnson was perhaps less enamoured by Longfellow's version of Hiawatha than the public record suggests.

Evelyn Johnson's own views of Longfellow may have shaped her recollection of her sister's comments, but the remembrances of Johnson's friend and co-performer Walter McRaye suggest otherwise. He begins his memoir about Johnson by stressing Hiawatha's importance to her and by alluding to Longfellow's historical inaccuracy: "Longfellow, in his poem 'Hiawatha,' makes this great figure a mythical god, whereas he was a very real personage, in fact a politician, which in modern thought is far removed from deity." Later in the memoir, he quotes a newspaper interview with Johnson where she reiterates this point: "Hiawatha – no god, as dear, dead Longfellow pictured him."[60] Again she uses the affectionate "dear" to refer to Longfellow while noting his error and implied disconnection from Native culture. Johnson anticipated the contemporary scholar Alan Trachtenberg's assessment that "the poem had sacrificed its real-life sources for the sake of telling a charming tale whose magic – this seemed the point of the sacrifice – enhanced a political vision." Many scholars, such as Helen Carr, have criticized Longfellow's appropriation and misuse of Indigenous source material and his colonial misrepresentation of Native American history.[61] Longfellow upholds the ideology of the vanishing Native through his fantastical portrayal of Hiawatha, who in the poem assists the settlers in taking over the continent and then canoes to his own death.

While Johnson shared with friends and family her objections to Longfellow's representation of Hiawatha, she never directly disapproves of Longfellow in any of her own writings. This is one of the moments where, as Martha Viehmann suggests, Johnson disappoints us as contemporary feminist scholars. We want her to be more stridently critical of imperialism and Aboriginal cultural genocide than she was.[62] I wish Johnson had been harsher on Longfellow and put in print her feelings about his cultural appropriation. I want her to call him only dead – and not dear. Yet what are we to do with Johnson's "dear dead Longfellow"?

In his influential study *Domination and the Arts of Resistance*, James C. Scott points out that "close readings of historical and archival evidence tend to favor a hegemonic account of power relations." He stresses that critics must decode "the dialectic of disguise and surveillance that pervades relations between the weak and the strong."[63] In the public record Longfellow must appear "dear" to Johnson. It would have been extremely difficult for Johnson, as a mixed-race woman in late nineteenth-century Canada, to challenge Longfellow's immensely popular *Song of Hiawatha*, which helped to validate her own writings about Native identity. Published in 1855, just prior to the Civil War, *The Song of Hiawatha* was an instant bestseller in the United States when it was first released, selling more than thirty thousand copies in the first six months.[64] Immediately following the poem's publication, recitations in classrooms, literary societies, and community events proliferated throughout North America, and continued well into the twentieth century.[65]

The power imbalance between Johnson and Longfellow becomes abundantly clear when one examines reviewers who often characterize Johnson as failing to live up to the mastery of Longfellow and Whittier. Take for example this quotation from a review of her first book, *The White Wampum*, in the British journal *The Sketch* from 24 July 1895:

> Her poems sing their virtues and heroism in a sympathetic fashion, but, though possibly this poetess knows a great deal more about the red-skins

> at first hand than did Longfellow, she describes them in a far more outside fashion than he. In the verses with human subjects, there is none of the strange fascination that creeps on us as we read "Hiawatha." Not that her point of view is more prosaic, but only that her art is less. In nature poetry she is better skilled. Longfellow and Whittier have done more for the red-man she loves and champions.[66]

According to this reviewer, Johnson's Native-themed poetry lacks a magical quality; however, in criticizing Hiawatha's transformation from a human into a god, Johnson points to the falsity at the base of Longfellow's presentation of Indigenous people as magical. As Mary Elizabeth Leighton aptly points out, "The measure of authenticity in this instance, however, seemed to be less an indication of experiential engagement than an ability to construct a representation that accorded with the dominant collective imaginary."[67] The reviewer evokes a central principle of colonial discourse: stereotypical fantasies supplant reality. While the reviewer frames his critique in aesthetic terms, he seems to ultimately object to Johnson's representation of Native characters as actual human subjects, rather than as mythic heroes.

In contrast to Longfellow's fantastical representations, Johnson depicts the voices of real Indigenous subjects addressing social concerns, such as in "A Cry from an Indian Wife," which addresses the impact of the North-West Rebellion of 1885. Through her texts brought to life on the stage, she wrenches Native representation from the domain of the fantastical to move towards a more realistic portrayal of what she characterizes in her poem "The Corn Husker" as "might's injustice" (121). However, her most salient critique of Longfellow appears in her engagement with the motif of canoeing. Because her critics were more inclined to scrutinize her poetry that represented Native voices, she embedded a challenge to Longfellow elsewhere in her canoe poems.

A Recitation Favourite Revisited

The incorporation of "The Song My Paddle Sings" into patriotic schoolroom curricula has further obscured the multiplicity of this symbol in her writing. Johnson, who was an accomplished canoeist, frequently writes about canoeing in both her prose and her poetry. Lyon describes the canoe as "the most frequently recurring object in Johnson's verse," noting that canoes appear far more frequently than "undeniably Native themes."[68] Yet to describe it as an object detracts from her representation of the action of canoeing as a vital and erotic life force. In Longfellow's *The Song of Hiawatha*, the canoe represents Native self-defeat and disappearance. In stark contrast, for Johnson the canoe helps her to conceptualize her performance poetics and to articulate feminist agency and racial hybridity.

Reading "The Song My Paddle Sings" and *The Song of Hiawatha* as intertexts exposes Johnson's intervention in the white masculinist tradition of writing about the Native Other and her efforts to disrupt the ideology of the vanishing Native through performance. It also demonstrates how recitation traditions were pivotal in the development of her poetic voice. Hemispheric approaches to Canadian literature have been less popular than in other parts of the Americas because of "fears of Canadian literary studies being subordinated to a US-centred theoretical paradigm."[69] Recognizing how Johnson advances a submerged critique of Longfellow, one of the most dominant US authors in her period, should perhaps help to ease the anxieties of Canadian scholars who resist the perceived imperializing dynamics of a hemispheric approach. Examining such troubling cross-border connections, rather than avoiding them, provides deeper insight into how subjects negotiate colonial legacies and develop strategies to overcome them.

While the text of "The Song My Paddle Sings" includes no overt racial markers beyond the symbol of the canoe, which only loosely associates it with Native culture, through performance Johnson's racial subtext becomes more explicit. Johnson composed this poem for her second major recital in February 1892, making it one of the first texts she designed for performance.[70] The movement of canoeing played a key role in her construction of her dynamic stage persona and the rapid fluidity that she wanted to create on stage for the multiple voices in her texts.

In the last one hundred years, critics have offered various readings of the canoe in Johnson's verse, interpreting it as symbol for nature, writing, romance, poetic voice, feminism, and even sex; however, they have yet to assess its link to Longfellow's canoes.[71] While her contemporaries detected no real difference between Johnson's canoes and Hiawatha's birch-bark canoes, interpreting them as symbols of Native connection to nature, recent critics recognize that Johnson's canoes tell a different story. Glenn Willmott proposes that the paddle becomes a metaphor for her pen and that through canoeing she negotiates her alienation from her Mohawk culture.[72] More radically, Gerson and Strong-Boag argue that "The Song My Paddle Sings" contains an erotic subtext and feminist message. Through the analysis of sensual lines such as "swelling the song that my paddle sings," they explore how Johnson uses the canoe to emphasize a female subject who desires nature, rather than a male love object (83).[73] While the extent of the erotic content is certainly up for debate, their analysis makes clear that the act of paddling represents empowerment in Johnson's verse. Interpreting this representation of empowered female agency as a direct response to "dear dead" Longfellow makes it all the more subversive. Both Longfellow and Johnson conflate the paddle with the subject in the poem. Hiawatha needs no paddle because of his oneness with the natural environment into which he will eventually disappear. His conflation with the paddle denies him agency. In contrast, Johnson's paddle amplifies her speaker's agency and helps her to envision a rapid momentum for her stage persona.

In her polemic essay "A Strong Race Opinion: On the Indian Girl in Modern Fiction," Johnson identifies the canoe as a common trope in vanishing Native narratives. Written in 1892, during the same period she composed "The Song My Paddle Sings," this essay indicates Johnson's conscious decision to challenge the ideology of the vanishing Native by pursuing a stage career.[74] She takes several nineteenth-century authors to task for their stereotypical representation of what she terms "the regulation Indian maiden" who "secures the time honored canoe, paddles out into the lake and drowns herself" (178–81). Johnson questions why "the regulation Indian maiden" must always die and so frequently by suicide. She emphasizes the "time honored canoe" as a symbol of both traditional Native life and self-disappearance in nineteenth-century fiction. Through her performances, Johnson strove to make racial identity irreducibly present and on the move. She decided to dress in costume shortly after her second major performance in February 1892. Her performances brought "the regulation Indian maiden" to life on stage to challenge her image as a helpless victim who must always die.

Since her essay focuses on female stereotypes in fiction, she does not mention Longfellow; however, the canoe also signifies Native self-disappearance in *The Song of Hiawatha*. From the building of Hiawatha's birch-bark canoe as he prepares to take on the role of hero to his final paddle to his death at the end, Longfellow uses canoeing to develop Hiawatha's identity, allegorize his life journey, and conflate Native life with the natural landscape. Longfellow describes how Hiawatha's oneness with the vessel allows him to move the canoe without a paddle: "Paddles none had Hiawatha / Paddles none he had or needed, / For his thoughts as paddles served him."[75] By making paddles the grammatical subject, Longfellow deflects any sense of Hiawatha's agency. His fantastical connection to the canoe exemplifies his communion with his natural environment.

The mysteriously self-propelled vessel resembles what Misao Dean characterizes as the uncanny motif in Canadian canoe literature, "that of a motionless canoe seemingly suspended in a bubble, surrounded by an indeterminate element composed of reflection, illusion, light, and depth."[76] Confederation Poets, such as Duncan Campbell Scott and Archibald Lampman, invoked the uncanny canoe to represent settler alienation in the Canadian landscape. For Longfellow, the canoe also becomes an uncanny vessel, illustrating that this approach was not unique to Canadian literature. Dean also views Johnson participating in this tradition in her canoe poems "The Idlers" and "Shadow River: Muskoka." However, she never analyses "The Song My Paddles Sings," which does not fit with an uncanny reading.[77] Johnson's emphasis on paddling in this particular poem rejects the drifting, suspended canoe devoid of human action.

Longfellow's magical representation of the canoe culminates in the famous final scene when Hiawatha's birch-bark canoe carries him to his death: "On the clear and luminous water / Launched his birch canoe for sailing" (141). After he instructs his people to "Listen to their [the white men's] words of wisdom," Hiawatha launches his own canoe, which implies that he chooses his own death (141). Yet again Longfellow refrains from making him the subject of the sentence, so that his death appears as natural and inevitable. Longfellow immortalizes Hiawatha through his description of his people watching him sailing to heaven:

> Watched him floating, rising, sinking,
> Till the birch canoe seemed lifted
> High into that sea of splendor
> Till it sank into the vapors
> Like the new moon slowly, slowly
> Sinking in the purple distance.
> (142)

Hiawatha fades into the landscape, becoming part of it. Johnson's critique of Native suicide by canoe would certainly have extended to this famous final (and completely ahistorical) scene.

Johnson's early memorization of lengthy passages from *The Song of Hiawatha* would have complicated her relationship to these lines.

Scholarship on recitation substantiates that the poems you memorize in childhood tend to stay with you into adulthood.[78] Johnson could likely recall many lines from this poem and perhaps even this final scene of Native self-effacement. How does such internalization affect one's critique of a text? Does memorizing a poem provide a person with a sense of ownership over it and therefore make it more open to reinvention, or does the internalization make it more difficult to deflect its ideological weight? These questions involving psychic life are admittedly hard to answer. Nevertheless, it is clear that Johnson's celebration of paddling in "The Song My Paddle Sings" directly responds to Hiawatha's lack of paddling and Longfellow's stereotypical portrayal of him.

Johnson's title articulates the connection to *The Song of Hiawatha*. Both titles include the word *song*, but she distinguishes her title from Longfellow's with the word *my*. Here she underscores lyric agency and self-determination. Unlike *The Song of Hiawatha*'s detached third-person narrator, Johnson adopts the first-person lyric "I," which she brings to life. In contrast to Hiawatha's non-existent paddle, Johnson focuses on the paddle (and the act of paddling) as a symbol of the speaker's agency:

> The river rolls in its rocky bed;
> My paddle is plying its way ahead;
> Dip, dip,
> While the waters flip
> In foam as over their breast we slip.
> (82)

The canoeist must work both against and with the fast current of the river. Later in the poem, the paddler and the canoeist become one: "We've raced the rapid, we're far ahead!" (82). Johnson mimics Longfellow's harmonious relationship between human and canoe, yet without the negation of agency. Through this setting, Johnson designs a poetic voice set in dynamic motion. To emphasize this physicality on stage, Johnson would sometimes carry an actual paddle to enact the movement described in the poem, becoming an Aboriginal woman canoeist on stage.[79] The image of the Aboriginal man canoeing through the wilderness was firmly entrenched in the North American imagination in the nineteenth century through popular texts, such as *The Song of Hiawatha*, as well as through paintings by men like the Canadian artist Paul Kane.[80] Johnson gendered this image and brought the two-dimensional stereotype to life on stage.

The constant rapid movement, the "swirl," "the rapids roar," and "the waters flip," formed an ideal motif for her to enact the performative dynamics of identity (82). As compared to her experience as a mixed-race woman in an Anglo-dominated social environment, in the natural environment of her canoe poems, Johnson represents a subject who gains agency and control. Her water setting also rejects a territorial approach to the environment and the colonial logic of possession. The structure and fast-paced action of "The Song My Paddle Sings" indicate that it was composed for the stage and also explain why it was so quickly taken up as a recitation favourite.

Written in the regular rhythm of tetrameter, a common structure for recitation pieces, the ten-stanza poem's short lines full of repetition and alliteration make it easy to memorize. Combined with the frequent use of sibilance, these techniques grab the audience's attention and underscore the poem as an auditory experience. Formally and thematically the poem resists any sense of stasis:

> And oh, the river runs swifter now;
> The eddies circle about my bow.
> Swirl, swirl!
> How the ripples curl
> In many a dangerous pool awhirl!
> (82)

The dynamic motion of the canoe, through rushing water, provides an excellent script for a performer to bring to life on stage through movement and gesture. This rapid momentum also sets the pace for Johnson's presentation on stage of racial hybridity as a "swirl" of different fluid identities that come to life through her performances.

Although the poem's racial ambiguity made it ideal for incorporation into patriotic curricula that sought to absorb Indigenous identities into Canadian nationalism, for Johnson this ambiguity formed a valuable expression of her mixed-race identity. Her canoe lyrics should be read as racially ambiguous performance scripts. Unlike the majority of her Native-themed dramatic monologues, which clearly impersonate a raced character, such as "A Cry from an Indian Wife," "The Song My Paddle Sings" is a lyric poem with an anonymous speaker. Her canoe verses combine her two poetic modes of Native-themed dramatic monologues and her lyric nature poetry. Through performance Johnson uses her body and her costumes to make the racial and gendered dimensions of the poem explicit. According to most accounts, she typically performed this poem in Native dress, yet she would also sometimes recite it in her evening gown, recoding the lyric "I" as white.[81] Johnson's use of different costumes demonstrates her efforts to destabilize distinct racial categories on stage. Challenging the static representation of canoeing on calm waters in which Native bodies fade away, Johnson's setting for her canoe lyrics in "reckless waves" emphasizes physicality (82). By creating performance scripts based on a strenuous activity, she drew attention to her body and its various transformations on stage. Johnson's dynamic performances opened up the possibility that racial intermixture might be something other than a temporary layover in the process of assimilation. In her childhood recitations of Longfellow, Johnson parroted back his dominant scripts of Native identity. In "The Song My Paddle Sings," she created a script that could potentially disrupt the hidden curriculum of Native disappearance, depending on how the reciter embodied the language.

Examining Johnson's "The Song My Paddle Sings" as a rebuttal to Longfellow's *The Song of Hiawatha* offers educators a different approach to teaching the poem. Asking students to consider why an empowered female canoeist might represent Indigenous self-determination puts stress on Johnson's agency, rather than on her symbolic significance in Canadian culture. The physical approach to recitation that a poem like "The Song My Paddle Sings" invites also anticipates Hughes's approach to rhythmic literacy, which will be discussed in the next chapter. He invited students to *read* with and through their bodies. Unlike him, Johnson never wrote explicitly about education or worked as a teacher; however, her movement-focused verse holds opportunities for student empowerment.

As mentioned at the beginning of this chapter, for many decades Johnson was typically the only Indigenous author in Canadian literature curricula. For example, the Mi'kmaq author Rita Joe names Johnson as the only Native poet she learned about during her schooling. For First Nations students this was often an incredibly formative moment of cultural recognition. The Delaware writer Daniel David Moses describes memorizing "The Song My Paddle Sings" in grade three as a formative moment in his journey to become a poet. The Cree poet Rosanna Deerchild describes her discovery of Johnson's collected poems *Flint and Feather* at the library: "At thirteen and having never seen a positive image of my Indian self, much less a defiant one, this was world opening." She contrasts Johnson with the writer and Indian agent Duncan

Campbell Scott and remarks how "he was killing us in words but Pauline was keeping us alive."[82] Johnson's performance poetics, full of physicality and movement (even on the page), accentuate the kinetic energy of words.

By writing a poem that became a recitation favourite in Canada, Johnson followed in the footsteps of "dear dead Longfellow." Yet her poems offered Indigenous children more empowering scripts to memorize than *The Song of Hiawatha*. Johnson managed to create a broader curriculum for Indigenous students than she had had available to her. By drawing on recitation traditions, she also created a poetics that lives primarily through oral memory and performance, similar to the Mohawk oratory that her grandfather performed for her. Her poetry fits with Paul Zolbrod's description of "the living poetry of Native Americans" in that it "develops by way of a more elastic oral transmission" and "is made to be heard again and again over a lifetime" and "can vary widely with each retelling."[83] Although her poetry became associated with the hidden curriculum of "indigenization," a performance script like "The Song My Paddle Sings" invited readers to make the words come alive in ways that often exceeded the aims of that curriculum.

Creative Memories

Did Johnson anticipate the potential of young reciters to create their own meanings? How did Johnson view the actual act of memorization and recitation? Unfortunately, her archive reveals little on this. However, in one of her most significant short stories exploring mixed-race identity, "The Shagganappi," she includes a telling scene of recitation in which the main character resorts to recalling the Whittier poem "The Red River Voyageur," which he had memorized, to deal with racism. Since Whittier's encouragement of Johnson played a central role in her development as a poet, this reference to him towards the end of her career offers insight into his influence on her work and her intervention in recitation practices. To my knowledge, this is the only explicit reference to memorizing and reciting poetry that Johnson makes in any of her writings. While she repudiates Longfellow through her canoe poems, Johnson enfolds Whittier's poetry in her own writing, suggesting that he is the more enduring influence. Her affinity for Whittier makes sense because she had a personal relationship with him, and his ardent embrace of abolition and less patriotic view of the United States were likely palatable to her.[84]

The title "The Shagganappi" comes from the main character Fire-Flint Larocque's nickname, a Cree word, which refers to his "buckskin" complexion. By exploring the psychic life of this mixed-race Metis boy, Johnson rejects one-dimensional stereotypes of Native characters popular in fiction of the time.[85] Longer than most of her magazine stories, "The Shagganappi" originally appeared in her short story collection of the same name, published just after her death in 1913. The schoolboy theme likely indicates that she intended it for publication in the American magazine *Boys' World*, where she published many of her stories during this period. Gerson and Strong-Boag speculate that its length made it less suitable for magazine publication, and they also suggest that *Boys' World* may have rejected it because of its "unreserved political message."[86]

The story depicts Larocque's struggles contending with the forces of Anglo-assimilation at a prestigious all-white boarding school.[87] Written during the rise of enforced residential boarding schools for Native children, Johnson's setting at an elite white boarding school forms an uncanny and sanitized double of the actual social realities of North American Native education during this period. By not targeting the system of residential schools directly, Johnson softens her political critique, perhaps to make it suitable for publication in a children's magazine while still being able to draw attention to the insidious force of assimilation in education. Overall, she promotes racial tolerance and encourages her young white readers to accept Indigenous children as their equals. By the end of the story the mixed-race protagonist eventually gains the acceptance of his white peers by risking his life to save the most popular boy in school, Hal. His classmates acknowledge that "his skin is tinted – it is tinted, not tainted" (271). Johnson's biographer notes that the prose she wrote towards the end of her life for *Mother's Magazine* and *Boys' World*, while she was battling breast cancer, earned her substantial pay when she was financially strapped.[88] While finances clearly motivated Johnson, her focus on children and their education anticipated the intimate relationship between performance poetry and education that would emerge later in the twentieth century. Like Hughes and Bennett, she anticipated the important role that youth education would play in changing social attitudes and prejudices.

"The Shagganappi" describes the predicament of Larocque's mixed Cree and French ancestry on its opening page: "If he could have called himself 'Indian' or 'White' he would have known where he stood in the great world of Eastern advancement, but he was neither one nor the other – but here he was born to be a thing apart, with no nationality in all the world to claim as a blood heritage" (262). In the late nineteenth century, people generally believed that a nation was based on a shared racial heritage, which made the mixed-race subject "a thing apart" from the rest of society.[89] By describing how this alienates the mixed-race subject, Johnson brings attention to the dehumanizing effects of discrimination. As contemporary author Zadie Smith notes in her autobiographical essay about her Jamaican-British identity, mixed-race subjects must deny the space between cultures that they are forced to occupy.[90] Johnson dramatized this denial in her two-part poetry performances by appearing on stage in two racially distinct outfits. She underscored how one could not appear to be both white and First Nations at the same time in late nineteenth-century Canada but instead had to choose to be one or the other. Yet her bifurcated performances destabilized this ideology. Even though she divided her two identities on the stage, she managed to play both parts of herself.

However, "The Shagganappi" presents a different racial vision than the divided one, which she performed most of her life. Johnson presents her new perspective on racial integration through the authoritative voice of a fictionalized governor general of Canada who helps Larocque get into the white boarding school. Rather than criticizing the government's enforcement of residential schooling, she idealizes governmental power. By making it come from the British monarchy's benevolent representative in Canada, she also upholds British imperial power as the ultimate authority in Canadian society.[91] In stark contrast to the Indian Act laws of the time, which strictly defined First Nations status in all-or-nothing terms, the governor general in the story expresses his disdain for the term *half-breed* and urges Larocque to see the special value of his mixed-race background: "Few white people can claim such a lineage. Boy, try and remember that as you come of Red Indian blood, dashed with that of the first great soldiers, settlers and pioneers of this vast Dominion, that you have one of the proudest places and heritages in the world; you are a Canadian in the greatest sense of that great word" (263). Johnson upholds the mixed-race subject as the ideal Canadian identity, challenging the prevailing anti-miscegenation views of the period. Rather than present the mixture of races as a weakness of Canada, she argues that it is a strength that will help Canada's rise to power. Gerson and Strong-Boag point out that this represents a shift in Johnson's perspective, since throughout her career she idealized the pure Indian and expressed ambivalence towards her own mixed-race identity.[92] However, through her protagonist in "The Shagganappi" she argues for racial amalgamation while rejecting the complete assimilation promoted by government policies. Albert Braz concurs that in this story, "Johnson implied that, rather than being a sign of degeneracy, racial mixing was the ultimate marker of inter-Americanness, of citizenship."[93]

For this study, Johnson's revised racial politics is significant because recitation figures prominently as a strategy for integrating both parts of Larocque's mixed-race identity. She reveals how memorization and recitation in education open up possibilities for a student's identity construction, rather than restrict them. In "The Shagganappi," recitation becomes a method for the mixed-race subject to take control of the process of racial amalgamation and resist racial hierarchies, lending insight into her own use of this practice in the development of her performance poetics. Through her fictional scene of recitation, she shows how the practice can activate the creative capacity of memory, transforming both the past and the present to disrupt the all-encompassing culture of assimilation.

On his first morning at the school when Larocque enters the college chapel, the other schoolboys cannot "resist furtive looks at the newcomer" (266). In Frantz Fanon's terms, Larocque (as the racial other) undergoes the alienating experience of being the object of a white gaze, and of being aware of his "to-be-looked-at-ness."[94] Johnson describes the white schoolboys as jealous of this "Indian's" appearance of "wonderful self-possession," and they resent his ability to "come among them as if he had been born and bred in their midst" (266). In drawing attention to the students' resentment of Larocque's presence, Johnson exposes the hypocrisy of colonization, and how white people never questioned their right "to come among" Native people and take their land. Their jealousy drives the desire for "indigenization." Applying Fanon's theory to Canadian racial politics, Goldie aptly sums up how Native presence threatens Euro-Canadian identities. The white students see "the Indian is Other and therefore alien. But the Indian is indigenous and therefore cannot be alien. So the Canadian must be alien. But how can the Canadian be alien within Canada?"[95] The boys' envy of his "wonderful self-possession" and their inability to "resist furtive looks" also underscore the (somewhat threatening) pleasure they experience witnessing what Coco Fusco describes as "the spectacle of Otherness."[96] In depicting Larocque's entrance into the chapel, Johnson represents an awareness of the ways in which performance does not just happen on the stage but frequently structures our encounters in everyday life. Larocque's marked racial body leaves him no choice but to play the part assigned to him by the white gaze whether he intends to or not (something Johnson surely experienced as well). He cannot help but be "the Indian" in this scene, which Johnson makes clear by referring to him as such at the beginning of the paragraph (266). Through insisting on Larocque's self-possession, Johnson rejects the idea that his mixed-race identity makes him "a thing apart" but instead insists on his rightful inclusion in Canadian society.

While Johnson makes clear that Larocque's body marks him as other in this scene, she also shows him resisting this designation and holding on to a sense of self by reciting lines from John Greenleaf Whittier's poem "The Red River Voyageur" (1859). Through the act of recitation, Johnson reveals that his "wonderful self-possession was the outcome of his momentary real indifference" propelled by his memory of this poem that transports him from this scene of objectification (266). When he enters the chapel and hears the bells, this reminds him of his church at home on the Prairies and "the last time he had knelt in a sanctuary" (266). This brings to mind Whittier's poem, which describes those particular bells in the Red River Valley. Rather than saying his prayers, he recalls "the first words of English poetry he had learned to memorize" (267). Despite the poem's Anglo-American perspective, it actually helps to protect him psychologically from the white gaze in this moment. By calling Whittier's poetry "English" rather than American, Johnson emphasizes a general education in a transnational anglophone culture, rather than specifying nationality.

By describing "The Red River Voyageur" as the first poem "he had learned to memorize," she indicates that, similar to her own childhood, her protagonist learned many English poems. To a certain degree, it makes sense that he would recall this particular poem that commemorates the geographical origin of his Metis people in the Red River Valley in Manitoba. The poem depicts the heroism of a fur trader (who were known as voyageurs and who were often Metis) canoeing north on the river. Whittier's poem builds on the tradition of the "pious voyageur" popular in Canadian literature from this period, making the voyageur's life into a Christian allegory for every man's journey to heaven.[97] In Johnson's efforts to valorize mixed-race identity, she turns to an immensely popular poem related to the topic to give authority to her position. This recitation favourite, which James C. Scott might define as "a public transcript" in that it is "accommodationist [in] tone" and "provide[s] convincing evidence for the hegemony of dominant values," shapes Larocque's own memory of his racial identity and his home, thus revealing the all-encompassing dynamic of racial hegemony.[98] However, by depicting this as an internal scene of recitation, Johnson demonstrates how the subjugated use of creative memory alters the public transcript to reflect their own realities, even though this often remains invisible to one's audience.

While Larocque's audience in the chapel perceives him as a primitive "Indian," Johnson makes clear to her intended audience of young readers that his status as a civilized subject is beyond question by describing his internal poetry recitation – a recitation that reveals both his competence in Western culture and his ability to appropriate this culture on his own terms. Johnson interrupts her narrative to quote in their entirety stanzas five through seven from "The Red River Voyageur":

> Is it the clang of the wild geese?
> Is it the Indian's yell,
> That lends to the call of the north wind
> The tones of a far-off bell?
>
> The voyageur smiles as he listens
> To the sound that grows apace.
> Well he knows the vesper ringing
> Of the bells of St Boniface.
>
> The bells of the Roman mission –
> That call from their turrets twain
> To the boatman on the river
> To the hunter on the plain.
> (quoted in Johnson 267)

This middle part of Whittier's ten-stanza ballad focuses on how the church bells motivate the voyageur to continue his journey through cold "north wind[s]" on the Red River. Johnson selects the stanzas, which represent an active and determined subject. The lines "to the boatman on the river" and "to the hunter on the plain" emphasize solidarity between the hunter and the voyageur, similar to the cross-racial solidarity Johnson imagines in the story. The voyageur at first mistakes the church bells for an "Indian's yell" and the "clang of wild geese." Typical of white settler Native-themed poems, "the Indian's yell" is depoliticized and objectified as a sound of nature. The final stanza of the poem (which Johnson avoids enfolding in her story) reveals the tones of the far-off bell as a symbol of death, thus associatively linking the Indian's yell with death as well.

In the conclusion of the poem, Whittier upholds the dominant ideology of the vanishing Native by implying that the "wild Assiniboins" are dying out as part of a natural and inevitable process, but Larocque avoids reciting these lines.[99] Four out of the ten stanzas refer to the theme of death that Whittier makes explicit in the final stanza through allusions to "the Angel of Shadow," as well as a reference to "our mortal journey" in stanza eight. The church bells of St Boniface invoke death, which the final lines of the poem reveal "In the bells of the Holy City, / The chimes of eternal peace!"[100] The voyageur's paddling up the Red River, similar to Hiawatha's final canoe ride, becomes an allegory for the journey to heaven. However, Johnson's recontextualization of the middle three stanzas in her short story, which make no reference to the final destination as death, deflects the theme of the vanishing Native in the poem and the idea that the mixed-race subject will eventually die out as part of the inevitable process of full racial amalgamation. As in many of her own canoe poems, she emphasizes the active element of the voyageur's journey along the river.

Johnson makes clear that her protagonist Larocque ignores the explicit death theme in the poem, which emphasizes children's power to reinterpret memorized poems to suit their own purposes. Larocque deflects the religious emphasis of both the poem and his own morning prayers in the chapel through his secular interpretation of the poem. After the citation of the three stanzas from Whittier's poem, Johnson describes how Larocque focuses on the line about the hunter, which reminds him of his father:

> "To the hunter on the plain" said Shag's thoughts, over and over. Perhaps the hunter was his trapper father, who with noiseless step and wary eye was this very moment stalking some precious fur-bearing animal, whose pelt would bring a good price at the great Hudson's Bay trading-post; a price that would go toward keeping his son at this Eastern college for many terms. (267)

In her description of Shag repeating the lines "over and over," Johnson dramatizes the interpellative power of memory. His own memory at this point, activated through recitation, allows him to gain a more empowering perspective on the present. She also demonstrates the power of repetition to shape one's own memory. The circular pattern of repetition allows him to disrupt the poem's hold over him and transform the poem's meaning by focusing on the lines that resonate with him. Through his fixation on these particular lines, he deflects the voyageur's journey as a metaphor for death. Rather than view the hunting line as a relic of the past, Larocque connects it to his father's current livelihood as a trapper, emphasizing that he might be hunting at "this very moment." Larocque's material concerns about whether his father's trapping will earn enough to pay his school tuition offset the religious grandiosity. Similar to Johnson's own poetic responses to Longfellow and Whittier, Larocque takes Whittier's poem out of the fantastical/spiritual realm to address material reality. Through Larocque's concern about his father's ability to make a living, Johnson subtly refers to the loss of hunting lands in the late nineteenth century and the financial pressures on Metis and First Nations people to provide for their families and the decline of the fur trade industry. Johnson witnessed such realities on her tours out west and would have been aware that many First Nations families suffering from starvation would have considered boarding school tuition the least of their worries.[101]

Johnson narrates the majority of the scene in the chapel in the past tense but then switches to the present as she describes how Whittier's "lines were drifting through his [Larocque's] mind now" to illustrate how memorization and recitation alter our space–time perception (267). The word *now* functions like an interjection, dramatizing how memory works as an active and immediate force in the present. In Larocque's recalling of the poem, it becomes an active text open to reinterpretation. By using the word *drifting*, Johnson conveys that the lines resist being firmly entrenched in Larocque's psyche, as recitation manuals suggest, but float through his mind, making them flexible for new meaning.

The scene concludes when the end of morning prayers interrupts Larocque's memory of his father and he realizes that the man before him is his professor "whose studious eyes now required glasses to see through, and whose hand was white and silken in its touch" (267). Through the juxtaposition of his father's strength with his professor's frailness, Johnson inverts the ideology of the vanishing Native by aligning whiteness with impending death. Larocque considers "how hopelessly lost this little man would be should circumstances turn him forth to gain his livelihood at hunting and trapping," upholding the value of his father's knowledge and agency (267). However, he also concludes that his father "would hardly be more incongruous teaching in this college," recognizing that his father's knowledge would be unacceptable in this Christian school setting (267). By refusing to say his prayers and reciting the Whittier poem (stripped of its religious emphasis) instead, Larocque manages, in this moment, to resist the impending force of Christian assimilation and value his mixed-race identity.

Unlike Johnson's own vocal performances on stage throughout her career, Larocque's poetry recitation happens internally. By making it silent, she explores the psychological interiority of the subject, something that vocalized recitation always renders somewhat invisible to the audience. In the gulf between the stance of a performer and the audience's perception of that stance, Johnson displays the inner workings of memory. Although Larocque remains silent, through her description of his objectification when he enters the chapel Johnson makes clear that his recitation has a performative dimension. His classmates watch and interpret his body while he recalls Whittier's poem. On the surface, Larocque appears to be saying his prayers with his classmates, yet Johnson reveals that he is actually reciting Whittier's poem, which he, in turn, secularizes in his interpretation. Through this scene, Johnson underscores a complete break between his audience (the boys in the chapel), who cannot resist objectifying him, and his view of his own subject position dramatized by his internal recitation. Through Larocque's private recitation, which on the surface appears as "mere indifference," Johnson emphasizes the significance of meanings that are private and imperceptible to one's audience. Writing towards the end of her own lengthy performance career, she presents a provocative example of the slippage between performer intention and audience reception.

In "The Shagganappi," Johnson reveals how memorization and recitation can be used to disrupt the enormous power of "the public transcript" over one's own memory. She reveals how the creative capacity of memory destabilizes the assimilation process, leaving it open to ambivalence and creating opportunities for disruption. Larocque's reinterpretation of "The Red River Voyageur" also gives her own young readers permission to reinterpret poems that they memorize, anticipating the more radical reading strategies that Langston Hughes and Louise Bennett would develop through recitation later in the twentieth century. Johnson's unprecedented performance career demonstrates how verse recitation culture provided an entry point into writing for disenfranchised subjects. Yet writing alone was insufficient for Johnson.

Only through performance could she enact the threshold between her two racial identities. Johnson's performances critiqued the victim stereotype of "the regulation Indian maiden" (even though her critique may have remained largely imperceptible to many of her audience members who were bent on witnessing the stereotypes they believed in). She worried about the historical inaccuracy of Longfellow's *The Song of Hiawatha*. Rather than make truth claims about history to correct misperception, she embodied the line between fantasy and reality on stage. Wearing her different costumes, she destabilized any clear sense of racial authenticity. Perhaps Atwood correctly suggests that Johnson is merely a postmodern performance artist born in the wrong century. But was Johnson an elocutionist? Was she a recitalist? These identities played a pivotal role in her artistic project. They allowed her to go on stage disguised as a reader and as an imitator of "great poets" like Longfellow and Whittier, so that she could author her own versions of personal and collective memory.

Chapter Two

Langston Hughes's Rhythmic Literacy

Let's Make a Rhythm.

Langston Hughes, *The First Book of Rhythms*

If I ever get in the school books then I know I'm ruined.

Langston Hughes, Letter to Carl Van Vechten

On 2 November 1966, at East Orange High School in New Jersey, a riot allegedly broke out after a student recited black poetry at a school assembly. According to an article in the *New York Times*, the following lines from a poem called "Black Man," by an unnamed author, incited the students to begin yelling, acting out, and threatening a boycott: "You fought for freedom on many shores, / At home in America freedom ain't yours."[1] It is not surprising that, weeks after the formation of the militant Black Panther party, a seemingly minor moment of social unrest would have elicited concern and been covered as a national story in the newspaper. The threat of insurrection in a small New Jersey town composed mainly of Caribbean immigrants would have played to the fears of the average, white *New York Times* reader. The principal dismissed the black teacher from his position as the adviser of the student council for selecting verses to be read by students from an anthology of black poetry. As compared to Pauline Johnson's childhood recitations of Longfellow, in this 1966 incident, student recitation departed from an assimilationist agenda and began to facilitate direct resistance.

In a letter, Langston Hughes's longtime friend Arna Bontemps shares his excitement with him about the disturbance at East Orange High

School. He tells Hughes, "it is good to know that kids react explosively to you-all's poetry."[2] Even though the high school principal denied "'exaggerated reports' that there had been anything like 'a riot or a rumble' after the assembly," Bontemps reads between the lines of the newspaper article to celebrate young readers performing black poetry as a means of social dissent.[3] The principal "pointedly distinguished between 'the printed word,' which might not be objectionable, and 'the manner in which it is presented.'"[4] He tried to avoid attacking black poetry directly by blaming the students' performances. However, he inadvertently highlighted how recitation's hidden curriculum of indoctrination falters, because readers gain control over a text's meaning through performance, something that Hughes capitalized on throughout his career.

This public disturbance of reading encapsulates Hughes's lifelong project to inspire communities of young readers with his poetry and to foster reading as performance (especially at predominantly black schools like this one). Hughes's politics went through many transformations throughout his life as he struggled to understand how a racist mindset in the United States could be overcome. Regardless of his shifting ideological affiliations, he increasingly recognized that social change must be tied to literacy education. Through the design, production, and circulation of his poetry, he encourages his young readers to make social connections through their textual practices and to make a "rumble" with their poetry performances. This chapter examines the specific role he envisioned for poetry in literacy education by analysing the relationship between his childhood experiences with recitation and his two most innovative pedagogical projects: *The Negro Mother and Other Dramatic Recitations* (1931), a chapbook poetry recitation manual that he distributed to children on his reading tour through the South in 1931, and *The First Book of Rhythms* (1954), based on his experiences teaching poetry at John Dewey's Laboratory School in 1949. I track the development of what I call Hughes's "rhythmic literacy" and how it took shape through his reinvention of poetry recitation. By drawing on this tradition, he encourages students to perform his poetry, rather than read it alone in silence. Both of these projects underscore why his target audiences were black students like the ones at East Orange High School.

In certain ways, he achieved his goal, since he is one of the most taught poets in US classrooms. Students frequently memorize and recite his poetry today, especially in predominantly black schools. Yet

3. Hughes performing at the Horton Branch Library, Winston Salem, NC, 1949 during Negro History Week. (Beinecke Rare Book and Manuscript Library, Yale University; Permission: Langston Hughes Estate)

his own vision for black literacy education through poetry often gets forgotten. Recitation favourites, like Hughes's "I, Too," about "the darker brother" claiming a spot at the dinner table, become scripts for students to perform a racially inclusive national community and to embody a civil rights narrative of progress.[5] Yet for Hughes the line "I, too, sing America" made a deeply ambivalent claim to citizenship.[6] He composed the poem while stranded in Genoa, where he lost his passport. Racist officials at the US embassy in Italy made it difficult for him to get the document replaced.[7] The simultaneous resonance of this line as strongly patriotic and deeply critical of the United States often becomes muted in the deployment of the poem in elementary school curricula. Like Johnson's "The Song My Paddle Sings," Hughes's "I, Too" gets appropriated into a national narrative that it aimed to question. Hughes seems to have anticipated this outcome when he declares in a 1925 letter to Carl Van Vechten, "If I ever get in the school books then I know I'm ruined."[8] Although this statement suggests that Hughes rejected education, his commitments to children's literature and his work as a teacher prove otherwise. His desire to never be included in "school books" reveals his distrust of institutionalized education. He turned to poetry recitation to reinvent literacy practices that could escape institutional control.

On the surface, Hughes's modernist blues poetics seem to have little in common with Johnson's Victorian canoe lyrics. Yet these popular national poets shared more than it appears, including fondness for Longfellow's *The Song of Hiawatha*. Both used performance to make racial difference intelligible, and recitation pedagogies played a formative role for both of them as they cultivated their poetic voices. Hughes developed the subversive potential of recitation that Johnson began to explore at the turn of the twentieth century. For Hughes, recitation became an explicit strategy to make performance poetry into a collaborative art, creating a space for his readers to also take to the stage. Studying Hughes alongside Johnson reveals how recitation provided an entry point into a public dialogue for people who come from cultures that place value on performance. Hughes's work also demonstrates the pedagogical direction that performance poetry took in the twentieth century. Many people believe that he prioritized performance because his renderings of jazz rhythms and vernacular voices in print were better suited for oral delivery. But there is another side to Hughes's performance poetics. The stage also played a crucial role in his experimental literacy politics.

Readers of All Ages and Abilities

In *Forgotten Readers: Recovering the Lost History of African American Literary Societies* (2002), Elizabeth McHenry illustrates how the focus on oral traditions in African American studies has obscured the examination of black subjects as readers in the nineteenth and twentieth centuries.[9] This definitely proves to be the case with Hughes scholarship; the words, music, blues, jazz, orality, folk, speech, and dialect are everywhere, but literacy and reading are rarely mentioned. Yet Hughes's innovation extends beyond modernist aesthetics to education. His critique of the relationship between schooling and domination, and his efforts to provide black children with more liberating literacy models, anticipate Freirean critical pedagogy. Rather than view reading as a solitary act, he envisions communal literacy practices that draw on black vernacular speech.

During most of Hughes's life, literacy was ideologically intertwined with the rights of citizenship. Even though African American men were enfranchised in 1870 and African American women were enfranchised in 1920 (through the women's suffrage movement), literacy tests were a prerequisite for voting until the Voting Rights Act in 1965. Hughes's commitment to promoting literacy in black communities cannot be separated from this political reality. He cultivated his audience through public talks, readings, and teaching. In his search for an inclusive audience, he made his poems accessible to people of a broad range of literacies and performed his work so he could reach those who were unable to read, or who were learning how to read. Hughes also began writing at a time when literacy rates in black communities were dramatically on the rise. According to US census figures, in 1880, only 30 per cent of the black population could read, as compared to 1910 when it jumped to 70 per cent.[10] He hoped to activate the potential of these new readers with his poetry and education projects.

Hughes's desire to have widespread appeal and to be considered as a "serious" poet were often at odds. By the onset of modernism these two things were seen as mutually exclusive. People began to believe that popularity lessened the value of one's art and that appealing to new readers made one's work too simple for sophisticated intellectuals. Northrop Frye encapsulates this view in his 1968 essay "Silence in the Sea," about E.J. Pratt:

> But the idioms of popular and serious poetry remain inexorably distinct. Popular poems tend to preserve a surface of explicit statement: they are

> often sententious and proverbial, like Kipling's "If" or Longfellow's "Psalm of Life" or Burns' "For A' That," or they deal with what for their readers are conventionally poetic themes ... Affection for such poets is apt to be anti-intellectual, accompanied by a strong resistance to the poetry that the more restricted audience ... finds interesting.[11]

Frye neglects to mention that this distinction between "popular" and "serious" poetry did not emerge until the late nineteenth century. In Longfellow's era, one could appeal to both children and intellectuals without this threatening one's literary value. Although Longfellow's subsequent reception was hurt by these assumptions, during his lifetime he was not judged for his mass appeal.[12] Like Longfellow, none of the poets in this study wanted "a restricted audience" of intellectuals, and they each turned to performance to build diverse audiences. For Hughes especially, his experiences with white patronage during the Harlem Renaissance compelled him to reach readers of all ages and abilities. In my analysis of his inclusive recitation experiments, I focus on how accessibility amplified, rather than detracted from, the formal complexity of his poetics.

Hughes's children's literature has received less critical attention than his modernist experiments with blues and jazz because his children's books make him seem like a popular poet, rather than a serious one.[13] This is quite comparable to the situation of Louise Bennett. Critics have not "taken seriously" Hughes's seemingly "simple" poems that are straightforward enough for a child to read.[14] This attitude is compounded by Bennett's and Hughes's use of the vernacular as a symbol of the strength and creativity of black people. Many reviewers (both black and white) dismissed Hughes's second book, *Fine Clothes to the Jew*, for its use of dialect, assuming that the poems were mere transcriptions of black speech.[15] While contemporary critics obviously recognize the literary value of his dialect poems, his focus on black oral culture has steered them away from his concerns with reading. Yet Hughes's experiments with vernacular expression relate to his desire to teach reading through poetry. In the next chapter, on Bennett, I will more thoroughly examine the relationship between the vernacular, recitation, and reading, but for now I want to highlight that Hughes's children's literature relates to his other poetic projects that engage with vernacular expression.

Hughes's commitment to literacy has also remained understudied because his children's literature has been interpreted as the most conformist of his literary production. Since he published the majority of his children's books in the 1950s, after the McCarthy subcommittee interrogated him in 1953, his work for children has been classified as an attempt to redeem himself as a loyal American.[16] Hughes's recitation legacy reinforces this patriotic interpretation. However, recent scholars have challenged these reductive interpretations of Hughes's children's texts and begun to assess their complicated politics. For example, Julia Mickenberg argues that leftist writers such as Hughes who were blacklisted because of McCarthyism often found a way to subtly promote leftist ideals in their children's books. Because of the assumption that children's literature is a conservative genre, these meanings often went undetected. Similarly, Jonathan Scott suggests that rather than represent his socialist politics thematically, Hughes enacts them formally in his 1950s children's books.[17]

To fully understand the politics of Hughes's children's literature, we need to study what he hoped his young audience would do with his books. His texts are rife with ideological contradictions, especially in terms of African Americans' relationship to US nationalism. He did not intend for literary critics to debate or resolve such contradictions; they exist for his young readers to embody. Hughes uses poetic form to teach new and emerging black readers how to navigate these contradictions through their own performances, just as they must learn how to navigate similar contradictions in their everyday lives.

Giselle Anatol argues that Hughes seeks out children as his readers because he views them as a disempowered group in American society.[18] The many young speakers in Hughes's poems evince his preoccupation with young black people as agents of social change, such as the "darker brother" from the poem "I, Too."[19] Such poetic personas embody Freire's belief that the purpose of education should be to cultivate a student's political agency.[20] Children typically have very little authority to make definitive readings. To counteract this, Hughes encourages poetry performance to give children the power to make their own meanings from what they read and, by extension, what they experience. Like Johnson's young protagonist Larocque (discussed in the previous chapter), Hughes imagines students gaining control over their textual interpretations through performance.

Hughes's understanding of the essential role that youth can play in the building of community is conveyed in the last line of his poem "Youth": "We March!"[21] He strategically places this poem near the end of his first book-length collection of children's poetry, *The Dream Keeper and Other Poems* (1932). This final line calls on his young readers to come together and form communities of dissent like the students at East Orange High School.

The Big Sea as a Literacy Narrative

Like Johnson, Hughes's investments in poetry recitation and education can be traced back to his childhood experiences. He makes clear in his first autobiography, *The Big Sea*, which spans the first thirty years of his life, that as a young African American male he felt little agency when reading. Interpreting this text as a literacy narrative reveals why Hughes places emphasis on reading as performance. The title invokes the big sea as a reference to life in general, but it also becomes a metaphor for the development of Hughes's literacy and the big sea of Anglocentric textuality, which Hughes must learn to navigate to become a writer.

Through the creative retelling of his own experiences, he illuminates Brian V. Street's concept of "ideological literacy" and "the central role of power relations in literacy practices."[22] Hughes reveals how black youth struggle to maintain their cultural identities as they learn how to read in US society. He experienced this at both white and black institutions. He completed his undergraduate degree at Lincoln University, a historically black university. In his 1934 essay "Cowards from the Colleges," he expresses dissatisfaction with his education there and with southern black colleges in general, accusing them of "doing their best to produce spineless Uncle Toms, uniformed and full of mental and moral evasions."[23] According to him, students must be the agents of change (just as they are in Freirean critical pedagogy): "Frankly, I see no hope for a new spirit today in the majority of Negro schools of the South unless the students themselves put it there."[24] For this to happen, students must learn how to critically read both their environment and their schoolbooks.

To establish the big sea as a metaphor for empowered reading, Hughes opens his autobiography with the following epigraph:

Life is a big sea
full of many fish.
I let down my nets
and pull.

He echoes this in the closing lines of the book: "literature is a big sea full of many fish. I let down my nets and pulled. I'm still pulling."[25] By replacing "life" with "literature," he frames his autobiography as a literacy narrative. He compares the acts of reading and writing to fishing to draw attention to their embodied and mobile dimensions. The image of pulling the nets illustrates how one becomes engulfed by language and how one must gain control of the language in which one is immersed. Reading becomes a process of reaching out to explore what is available and then selectively drawing in what is useful.

The title *The Big Sea* refers to both the epigraph and the opening scene, which begins in medias res with Hughes as a young man working as a sailor on a boat headed from a New York port to Africa. He commences his life story as a big sea of books that he must actively reject to become a writer:

> Melodramatic maybe, it seems to me now. But then it was like throwing a million bricks out of my heart when I threw the books into the water. I leaned over the rail of the S.S. *Malone* and threw the books as far as I could out into the sea – all the books I had had at Columbia, and all the books I had lately bought to read. ... Then I straightened up, turned my face to the wind, and took a deep breath. I was a seaman going to sea for the first time – a seaman on a big merchant ship. And I felt that nothing would ever happen to me again that I didn't want to happen. I felt grown, a man, inside and out. Twenty-one. (3)

Hughes, frustrated by the racism of both the curriculum and his fellow students, dropped out of Columbia University after his freshman year.[26] By throwing his books overboard, he rejected his socialization in white culture and literacy. Instead of continuing at school he travelled to Africa for the first time and searched for a connection to his ancestors: "You see, books had been happening to me. Now the books were cast off back there somewhere in the churn of spray and the night behind the propeller. I was glad they were gone" (4). He strives to make a personal connection with his readers through his casual, second-person address, bringing oral dynamics into print. Rather than being lost in a sea of books, he claims the identity of a sailor and asserts control over his own destiny.[27]

The only author of any of the books thrown overboard whom he names is the journalist H.L. Mencken (4). Although he avoids mentioning the title, it is likely that Hughes was referring to Mencken's widely read linguistic history *The American Language* that had just been published in 1919. Given Mencken's Eurocentric approach to defining American English, Hughes likely would have been critical of it. In his study, Mencken only briefly mentions the African American vernacular, and he characterizes it as a simplified version of American English with no link to African languages. In a later edition of *The American Language*, Mencken claims that "the Negro dialect, as we know it today, seems to have been formulated by the [white] song writers for minstrel shows."[28] Since Hughes bases his poetic project on an African American English that has roots in Africa as well as slave resistance in the United States, Mencken becomes an ideal symbol for the white world of letters that Hughes must reject.

After this opening scene, Hughes describes his childhood experiences with poetry recitation. During his time at a predominantly white elementary school in Lincoln, Illinois, he began to write poetry when his classmates elected him as the class poet to recite at graduation: "In America most white people think, of course, that *all* Negroes can sing and dance, and have a sense of rhythm. So my classmates, knowing that a poem had to have rhythm, elected me unanimously – thinking, no doubt, that I had some, being a Negro" (24; italics in the original). As Meta DuEwa Jones points out, "the white students' apparent belief that '*all* Negros can sing and dance' is rooted in the demeaning racial stereotypes fostered in part by American minstrelsy."[29] Like Johnson, whose audiences expected that she play the role of Indian, Hughes realized at a very young age that white audiences would expect him to perform blackness in a circumscribed way. What to do about such an expectation (not only for himself but also for other young black children) became a driving force in his literacy projects; in his chapbook, *The Negro Mother*, he invites his young black readers to confront minstrel characters directly on stage by embodying them, and later, in *The First Book of Rhythms*, he presents rhythm as a model for the interconnectedness of living things, rather than as a marker of racial identity. He comments that he had never thought of becoming a poet before and he even stresses that he didn't particularly like poetry (24). By staging the birth of his poet identity in a racially fraught classroom setting, he emphasizes poetry as a pedagogical medium intertwined with racial difference. From within the interpellation of the racist stereotype, Hughes rejects it and indicates that the discourse of poetry has the potential to teach racial difference in more positive terms.

Why did Hughes dislike poetry as a child? Like countless other children of his generation, he was forced to memorize and recite it. However, in addition to his formal schooling, Hughes experienced a distinctly African American version of the elocution movement in black literary societies. In her study of African American readers in the nineteenth century, McHenry examines how these societies engaged in a range of activities to promote literacy and to provide opportunities for black people to participate in literary production and reception. Such groups demonstrate Joanna C. Street and Brian V. Street's point that scholars need to study how "other literacies exist alongside the dominant, school-oriented versions."[30] As they establish, "Much, then, of what goes with schooled literacy turns out to be the product of Western assumptions about schooling, power, and knowledge rather than being necessarily intrinsic to literacy itself."[31] McHenry argues that a non-institutional approach is especially crucial when studying black readers because their access to literacy in formal education has been limited.[32] African American literary societies embraced recitation because it made literary and public speaking training available to people outside of academic institutions.[33] Similar to Johnson, they benefited from the decreased elitism in the elocution movement in the late nineteenth century. Dramatic reading also appealed to them because it "fostered an environment in which a truly democratic 'sharing' of texts could take place, and it ensured that cohesive groups could be formed from individuals with widely divergent literacy skills."[34] According to McHenry, "Many early nineteenth-century literary societies endorsed a broader notion of oral literacy that did not valorize the power of formal or individualized literacy over communal knowledge."[35] In other words, one could *read* a written text by listening to an oral performance of it. This communal and orally driven literacy model played a formative role in Hughes's later literacy projects.

bell hooks describes how poetry recitation remained prominent in African American communities well into the twentieth century:

> As young black children raised in the post slavery southern culture of apartheid, we were taught to appreciate and participate in "live arts." Organized stage shows were one of the primary places where we were encouraged to display talent. Dramatic readings of poetry, monologues, or plays were all central in these shows. Whether we performed in church or school, these displays of talent were seen as both expressions of artistic creativity and as political challenges to racist assumptions about the creative abilities of black folks. We performed for ourselves as subjects, not as objects seeking approval from the dominant culture. In our all-black schools and churches, performance was a place of celebration, a ritual play wherein one announced liberatory subjectivity.[36]

hooks characterizes poetry recitation as an empowering "live art" that she participated in as a young girl in the 1950s and 1960s. She illustrates how black communities reinvented this Euro-American practice as a powerful form of self-expression. Without the dominant society watching, poetry recitation lost its emphasis on mimicry, even if the majority of the texts recited were still from the Anglo-American recitation canon. Yet poetry recitation's influence on twentieth-century black art has remained largely unexplored. Although Hughes writes of poetry recitation in less glowing terms than hooks, the fact that he devotes so many pages in his autobiography to the topic illustrates that growing up immersed in these "live arts" shaped him as a performance poet.

Hughes attended the Inter-State Literary Society, which his grandfather Charles Langston founded in 1891.[37] He describes being dragged to meetings with his mother and being forced to perform Greek recitations such "Lasca" and "The Mother of the Gracchi":

> On one such occasion, she had me and another boy dressed in half-sheets as her sons – jewels, about to be torn away from her by a cruel Spartan fate. My mother was the star of the program and the church in Lawrence was crowded. The audience hung on her words; but I did not like the poem at all, so in the very middle of it I began to roll my eyes from side to side, round and round in my head, as though in great distress. The audience tittered. My mother intensified her efforts, I, my mock agony. Wilder and wilder I mugged, as the poem mounted, batted and rolled my eyes, until the entire assemblage burst into uncontrollable laughter. (25)

Here Hughes learned an important lesson about the power of embodied reading. To convey his displeasure, he resisted the seriousness and formality of his mother's recitation, and appropriated the performance through mockery. This playfulness anticipated Hughes's casual poetic style. He conveyed his interpretation of his mother's recitation through his bodily gestures, thus performing his "reading" with his body. In the last sentence of the quotation, Hughes's physical gestures and the poem become grammatically confused with the action of the poem – as he "mugged," the poem "mounted." The audience's "uncontrollable laughter" indicates that his embodiment of the poem trumps his mother's words. He saw how an audience often pays more attention to a performer's body than they do to her language.

He also learned to associate poetry with bodily experience in a different way when his mother gave him what he calls "the worst whipping

I ever had in my life" for ruining her performance (25). He humorously adds that through this punishment he "learned how to respect other people's art" (25). While his embodiment of the poem was a form of dissent on stage, through his punishment poetry became associated with bodily control. Beating was a common punishment for insufficient recitation during this period, which reinforced the physicality of the practice.[38] Yet his punishment for disrupting his mother's performance failed to shake his resistance to poetry being used as a disciplinary force:

> Nevertheless, the following spring, at a Children's Day program at my aunt's church, I, deliberately and with malice aforethought, forgot a poem I knew very well, having been forced against my will to learn it. I mounted the platform, said a few lines, and then stood there – much to the embarrassment of my mother, who had come all the way from Kansas City to hear me recite. My aunt tried to prompt me, but I pretended I couldn't hear a word. Finally I came down to my seat in dead silence – and I never had to recite a poem in church again. (25–6)

Like many children, Hughes was "forced against [his] will to learn" a poem, but he feigned amnesia on stage. To stress that he resisted internalizing the poem, he neglects to give the name of it in his autobiography. He demonstrates how children gain agency as readers through their bodies. Poetry performance engenders a hyper-awareness of physicality: "the actuality, of performance was often attended by symptoms of the fear of failure – clammy palms, shaking legs, and pounding hearts."[39] Regardless of whether one enjoys reciting a poem or not, one becomes aware of one's body in an entirely different way on stage. In these early experiences reciting in African American literary societies, Hughes learned how to manipulate the power of embodied reading on stage.

Reciting poetry as a child definitely soured Hughes's attitude towards the genre, although he acknowledges that a couple of poets captured his imagination: "The only poems I liked as a child were Paul Lawrence [*sic*] Dunbar's. And *Hiawatha*." (26). His preference for Dunbar makes sense, since Hughes's depiction of vernacular black voices builds directly on Dunbar's folk poetics, but here is Longfellow again. The sentence fragment "And *Hiawatha*" avoids naming him directly, suggesting that, like Johnson, Hughes liked the protagonist more than the poet. What are we to make of Hughes's affection for this poem? How does his relationship to it compare to Johnson's? Is it merely another testament to its ubiquitousness in school curricula? One might be tempted to pass off his casual mention of *The Song of Hiawatha* as a childhood fancy; however, in his essay "Ten Ways to Use Poetry in Teaching" (1951), he proposes it as an ideal poem for children to recite, indicating that he believed as an adult that the poem had pedagogical value.[40]

Hughes and *Hiawatha*

Many critics have explored Dunbar as Hughes's literary predecessor along with Walt Whitman; however, his relationship to Longfellow has yet to be explored.[41] Certainly, Longfellow's influence is less pervasive than Whitman's or Dunbar's, yet especially when considering Hughes's children's literature we cannot discount him as a model. *The Song of Hiawatha*'s themes of reading, community, and race are all topics that Hughes deals with in his poetry, although from a different vantage point. Hughes's interest in recitation in and of itself underscores a link to Longfellow's poetics. While we cannot know exactly what Hughes's experience of *The Song of Hiawatha* may have been (he leaves us fewer clues than Johnson), his enduring fondness for the poem stresses how individual reader reception complicates literary histories that omit Longfellow from the picture.[42] Understandably, scholars have shied away from assessing how *The Song of Hiawatha*, a poem rife with cultural appropriation, may have inspired one of the greatest African American poets of the twentieth century, whose work is championed for its anti-racist politics. Yet to understand Hughes's education activism we need to look more closely at how *The Song of Hiawatha* informed Hughes's use of literature to teach children about reading and race relations.

Pauline Johnson notes that *The Song of Hiawatha* caused a lot of "harm," and this harm extends to African Americans.[43] Published just prior to the Civil War, its immense popularity can be explained partly by its racial themes. The release of the poem in 1855 coincides with the height of minstrelsy's popularity, from 1846 to 1854.[44] According to Tavia Nyong'o, this is the reason black elocutionist Mary Webb's recitations of the poem drew a large audience. In a period of intense racial conflict about the end of slavery, the poem repeated the colonial narrative of peaceful conquest over Native Americans as a displacement of whites' anxiety over the role that free African Americans would play in the national community.[45] How much Hughes would have detected this racial subtext as a child is questionable, but he likely recognized that race relations (although presented in a biased way) were a predominant theme.

How would *The Song of Hiawatha* have been presented to Hughes when he went to school? According to Angela Sorby and Virginia Jackson, in early twentieth-century classrooms, many teachers taught *The Song of Hiawatha* as an allegory for literacy. As Sorby explains, "selections from *Hiawatha* had been used as rote schoolroom recitations beginning in the 1850s, but toward the end of the century the poem became extraordinarily popular among progressive educators as an interactive reading text for elementary schoolchildren."[46] Influenced by evolutionary theory, progressive educators believed that a young child's development mimicked the stages of civilization. Longfellow's narration of how Indigenous people become literate citizens provided a mirror for a child's learning process and reinforced a Western model of literacy, where one must move from a primitive (and childlike) orality to a mature literacy. As Sorby puts it, "*The Song of Hiawatha* makes learning to read a process of assimilation into American culture."[47] As I previously discussed, Hughes critiques the relationship between literacy and assimilation in his own education. Reading *The Song of Hiawatha* might have been one of his earliest encounters with this. Rather than bury literacy's ideological dimensions in the hidden curriculum, in this poem it becomes an explicit theme – revealing how learning how to read is not just a skill-based pursuit but an essential part of one's Americanization. In the prologue of *The Song of Hiawatha*, Longfellow instructs the audience to interpret the poem as an elegy for an oral culture, inviting the reader to first listen as she wanders through a graveyard:

That like voices from afar off
Call to us to pause and listen,
Speak in tones so plain and childlike,
Scarcely can the ear distinguish
Whether they are sung or spoken; –
Listen to this Indian Legend,
To this Song of Hiawatha!
(4)

Longfellow equates primary orality with immaturity through the phrase "tones so plain and childlike." The "voices from afar off" suggest that this oral song comes from the distant past. As I discussed in the last chapter, Longfellow reinforces the ideology of the vanishing Native in the conclusion when Hiawatha dies, and this theme gets established at the very beginning of the poem. Longfellow begins by asking his audience to listen for traces of this lost oral culture in the landscape, in "the groves of singing pine-trees," and then he suggests that the poem has been written down:

> Pause by some neglected graveyard,
> For a while to muse, and ponder
> On a half-effaced inscription,
> Written with little skill of song-craft,
> Homely phrases, but each letter
> Full of hope and yet of heart-break,
> Full of all the tender pathos
> Of the Here and the Hereafter; –
> Stay and read this rude inscription,
> Read this Song of Hiawatha!
> (4)

The instruction "Read this Song" underscores the theme of literacy. The "homely phrases" written with "little skill" mirror the young child's transition from an oral to a literate state. Longfellow underscores how the action that takes place in the rest of the poem belongs to a distant past. Despite presenting the mastery of literacy as the ideal, the poem also evokes nostalgia for primary orality as a relic of the past. Such nostalgia also explains why the poem became so popular in elocution contests.

Walter Ong establishes how the elocution craze in the late nineteenth century, while firmly a product of print culture, also expresses a "yearning for the old orality," untainted by writing technologies.[48] For a reader like Johnson, who learned Mohawk oral culture through her grandfather's songs and stories, the idea that Indigenous culture had already disappeared must have seemed less convincing (yet the nostalgia for it may have had a validating effect). Hughes may have also been able to relate the poem to his experiences of black orality, which would have been very much alive in his life. The emphasis on teaching this poem through recitation also diminishes Longfellow's insistence that to become literate, orality must pass away. When students perform this poem on stage, they embody the culture that is supposed to be represented as dead. This might have been another instance where Hughes experienced the power of performative reading and its ability to contradict the textual meaning of a poem. It also demonstrates how recitation practices can help to sustain and even reinvigorate an oral tradition, even though in this instance this is based on a disturbing appropriation of Native culture.[49] Moreover, Longfellow suggests that oral culture is suitable (and even preferred) poetic material because it already comes in "song" form. His appropriation of oral culture and his translation of it into written form provide an example, albeit a problematic one, for Hughes to imagine how he could transform black American folk culture into black literature. This approach to *The Song of Hiawatha* also makes performance part of the process of learning how to read, something that Hughes emulates in his literacy projects.

In her study of the performance history of *The Song of Hiawatha*, Theresa Strouth Gaul argues that the use of reading to build community parallels the theme of "social unity" between different Indigenous nations that culminates in the arrival of the whites, who ensure that a peaceful community will continue after Hiawatha's death.[50] The rhetoric of Longfellow's *Song of Hiawatha* makes readers feel (through the act of reading itself) part of a national collective, premised on a shared preliterate Native culture through the figure of Hiawatha. Although the poem makes African Americans an invisible part of the US story, Hughes may still have identified with the feeling of national collectivity that the poem inspired through a man of colour.

Scholars have begun to explore how the racial hierarchy in the United States encourages immigrant ethnic groups to follow in the footsteps of white settlers by appropriating Indigenous motifs as a means of Americanization. For example, in his study of Jewish representations of Native identity, Stephen Katz suggests that Native characters "serve as a means for writers to imagine the national self projected through others."[51] Yet Katz argues that even through their appropriations some Jewish writers form alliances with Native Americans and destabilize settlers' destructive cultural fantasies of indigeneity. Hughes had a similarly conflicted relationship to *The Song of Hiawatha*. In the 1950s, he suggested that educators use Longfellow's poem for a "Poetry Costume Party in which folks come dressed as 'The Ancient Mariner,' or 'Hiawatha' and recite each his own poem – which gives an added incentive to the memorizing of poetry."[52] This indicates that Hughes promoted the dominant practice of "playing Indian" that underwent a resurgence during the Cold War.[53] Yet his identification with Hiawatha as a child also seems to have been motivated by a sense of solidarity with a man of colour.

In his poem "Let America Be America Again," Hughes encourages collectivity between African Americans and Native Americans, as well as other minority groups. He recognizes that the so-called "American Dream" has never been available to either group when he writes, "I am the Negro bearing slavery's scars. / I am the red man driven from the land."[54] The African American relationship to indigeneity is complicated by the entangled histories of the Middle Passage and slavery, which intertwine with the dispossession of Indigenous peoples. For Hughes, it gets even more convoluted because he had Native blood through multiple lines in his family tree. Hughes may have felt a personal connection to the figure of Hiawatha through his own Native American ancestry. In *The Big Sea*, Hughes fondly remembers his maternal grandmother, who was part Cherokee, as "a proud woman – gentle, but Indian and proud" (17). His descriptions of his family in his autobiography reveal how he defined blackness in hybrid terms, provocatively declaring, "You see, unfortunately, I am not black. There are lots of different kinds of blood in our family. But here in the United States, the word 'Negro' is used to mean anyone who has *any* Negro blood at all in his veins" (11; italics in the original). He claims he is "not black" for rhetorical effect and to make a critique of the one-drop rule that defined anyone with any amount of black ancestry as legally black, making them subject to Jim Crow laws. These laws hindered the forming of alliances between African Americans and Native Americans, even though they share similar experiences of oppression. Many Native Americans in the South denied their African American ancestry and discouraged intermarriage to hold on to their already fragile tribal affiliation and to escape segregation.[55] Such racial tensions became obscured by the dominance of the white/black dichotomy in the United States.

Hughes made it his mission to create literature that could teach children to unlearn racism. In his canonization as the great Harlem Renaissance poet, this mission became contained within the black/white dichotomy and black essentialism, yet for Hughes unlearning racism was a much larger project. His understanding of race as fluid, hybrid, and socially contingent encouraged him to teach children to perform race rather than essentialize it. Maybe he felt an inkling of this when he performed *The Song of Hiawatha* as a child. According to US laws, he could not be identified as Native American; perhaps by reciting this poem he could perform both his blackness and his Indigenous identity at the same time. Just as Johnson used performance to make racial hybridity intelligible in Canada, Hughes also turned to performance to redefine blackness in the United States, but for him this was a collaborative project that he undertook with his young audience.

Hughes's lifelong commitment to reaching an audience of children extends back to the beginning of his career. At nineteen, he published for the first time in *The Brownies' Book*, a children's magazine begun by

W.E.B. Du Bois in 1919 and edited by Jessie Fauset. Du Bois started the magazine to offer African American children positive representations of black culture that were non-existent in children's literature of this period.[56] Steven Tracy argues that Hughes's production of children's literature stemmed from his experiences of racism as a child and his desire to provide children with socially validating representations that he was unable to find when he was young.[57] His work in *The Brownies' Book* – two short stories and a couple of Mexican children's games that he learned about while visiting his father in Mexico – also illustrates his desire to build an audience that would engage in action and community rather than solitary textual contemplation. The games offered children ways to play and interact with one another, rather than merely to read, anticipating his emphasis on play and performance in his later work.

Elocution in the Jim Crow South

Despite Hughes's dislike of poetry recitation as a child, he promoted this practice on his tour to the South in 1931. After his disillusionment with elitism and white patronage during the Harlem Renaissance, he decided to go on a reading tour, one of the purposes of which was to make literacy more accessible to black children in the Jim Crow South.[58] He self-published *The Negro Mother* to sell on his tour. Hughes started the Golden Stair Press with Prentiss Taylor to publish the chapbook because of the difficulties he experienced with his editors at Alfred Knopf, who marketed his books primarily to white readers and who were unwilling to stock his books in black bookstores.[59] The cheaply priced chapbook contains dramatic monologues with instructions in the margins for how to perform them to inspire readers to stage their own performances of his poetry.

In one of the only in-depth studies of Hughes's chapbook, Elizabeth A. Davey argues that it exemplifies his work to build a black audience throughout his career. He believed "that a mass black audience for black literature would be built through public readings, rather than private consumption of books."[60] Davey acknowledges the influence of nineteenth-century verse recitation on Hughes's chapbook, yet she limits her study to the significance of the Golden Stair Press. Rather than examine his tour and chapbook in terms of their engagement with print culture, I consider how they contribute to the development of his pedagogy.

His recitation manual was shaped by his experiences as a child in his grandfather's literary society, where he witnessed people engaging with texts primarily through performance and public discussion, rather than through silent reading. In his initial extended experiment with the form, memorization and recitation became methods of distribution for his poetry, and ways to inspire children towards a more vocal and empowered form of reading. Nurhussein also points out that he undertook this project in a moment when US education began to stress silent reading over reading aloud. I share her view that *The Negro Mother* should be studied in terms of its "rhetoric of literacy" and its combination of oral and literate modes. For her, this rhetoric "allows silent reading of poetry to exist with still some trace of performance."[61] Yet it goes further than this. In his recitation manual, Hughes rejects the shift towards silent reading in institutionalized education and espouses an orally infused model of literacy that upholds the value of what hooks characterizes as African American "live arts."

In his second autobiography *I Wonder as I Wander*, Hughes explains how he wanted to make literacy more accessible for black subjects in the Jim Crow South after he returned from his trip to Haiti and Cuba in 1931. His idealized image of Haiti as the first free black republic in the Americas was shattered when he witnessed the extreme poverty of the black underclass. On his way back from his trip, he visited the black education activist Mary Bethune. She invited him to read at her school, and this performance gave him the idea for his tour.[62]

He recognized how Jim Crow laws prevented access to literacy education and even reading materials. In *I Wonder as I Wander*, he writes about his own difficulty finding copies of the black national paper *The Chicago Defender* in the South. He also tells a story about trying to buy a copy of the *New York Times* in the white waiting area of a train station because no newspaper stand existed in the black waiting area, and then being ordered out of the white section by a policeman who forced him to leave the train station.[63] Hughes's vivid description of his determination to procure a newspaper by crossing white lines of segregation shows how he sought to empower readers to fight for their own access to literacy.

He left for his seven-month reading tour on 2 November 1931, with his friend and driver Radcliffe Lucas. They set out in a Model A Ford sedan packed full of books and drove across the Mason-Dixon Line. Packed in his car were copies of *The Negro Mother*, as well as single broadsides of poems from the chapbook for those who could not afford to purchase the book, along with his first book, *The Weary Blues* (1926), which he arranged with the publisher Knopf to sell at the reduced rate of a dollar. He also shared the work of other black authors through a small exhibition of black literature displayed at his readings. He drove all over the South performing at black colleges, schools, and churches. Surprisingly, Hughes managed to make a profit from book sales and speaker fees even though his primary audience was the black population hardest hit by the Depression.[64] Since he booked the majority of his tour engagements using the *Negro Year Book*, a catalogue of black schools and colleges, the majority of his audience would have been students. He also placed ads in black newspapers and magazines, such as *The Crisis* and *The Amsterdam News*, to encourage black readers in southern communities to contact him to arrange readings, thus employing readers themselves to help him create his audience. The ad in *The Crisis* offered a free copy of *The Negro Mother* in exchange for a one-year subscription to the magazine, illustrating how Hughes promoted both his own work and other publications to foster a black public sphere.[65]

At first glance, the chapbook's reliance on the tradition of schoolroom poetry recitation led by writers like Longfellow seems disconnected from Hughes's formal experiments with black music. Critics point to his 1920s blues poetry as a key influence on Black Arts poets, such as Amiri Baraka, for how to fashion a black poetics free from the domination of white American culture.[66] However, his reading tour and his self-produced chapbook also anticipated the Black Power principle of self-determination. He took every aspect of cultural production – including distribution – into his own hands and travelled through the dangerous Jim Crow South to advocate for a poetics for the people.

Hughes's targeting of young students at black schools and colleges in the South in the 1930s anticipated the significant role that black students would play in the civil rights movement.[67] His recognition that the "Dark Youth of the U.S.A." (the title of one of the chapbook poems that he produced as a broadside to distribute on his tour) would become a powerful force in black liberation was realistic in terms of the population in the South, where, according to a US census in 1930, there were 2,817,137 black youth between the ages of ten and twenty-five, and 57.1 per cent of the southern black population was under twenty-five.[68]

Hughes encouraged young people to perform poetry as a way to provoke them into action. He believed that his chapbook would provide black students with an alternative to the white recitation canon. As Carl Van Vechten explains in a note to Gertrude Stein, "Langston one day bemoaned to me the fact that Negro elocutionists had nothing to recite like Kipling, or The Boy Stood on the Burning Deck. So he wrote these."[69] Hughes's intended audience for this text is key for understanding how he critiques the minstrelsy tradition through his appropriation of recitation. In fact, he never republished anything from the chapbook in his subsequent books, underscoring that his chapbook poems were specifically composed for a black southern audience.[70]

The twenty-page chapbook includes six short poems with instructions for how a person should recite them. Each poem is written in the voice of a black character: a soldier, a young student, a mother, a rich man, a poor man, and a clown. Hughes engages with black stock characters in order to subvert them in the content of each poem.[71] For example, rather than the black mammy, he offers a strong, empowered black mother who has led the way to freedom for her children. He presents a black clown who refuses this designation at the conclusion of the poem:

> Say to all foemen:
> You can't keep me down!
> Tear off the garments
> That make me a clown!
> …
> I was once a black clown
> But now –
> I'm a man![72]

Hughes waded into risky territory with this chapbook; he composed poems that basically invite black children to embody minstrel stereotypes in order to disrupt them. To what extent was Hughes's mimicry strategy successful? By only publishing these poems in a book with explicit instructions on how to perform them, he indicated that the subversion of black stereotypes only becomes fully realized when the poems are recited. Hughes's navigation of the murky terrain between minstrelsy and elocution is bound up in his historical moment. As Dwight Conquergood explains, "Elocution existed in dialectical tension with minstrelsy" in the nineteenth century: "Whereas blackface minstrelsy was a theatrically framed mimicry and parody of blackness, elocution can be thought of as the performativity of whiteness naturalized."[73] Yet at the turn of the century, the lines between these two performance genres became increasingly blurry as elocution became more entertainment-oriented and less educationally focused. Recitations of dialect poetry began to draw large audiences, and the distinction between elevated elocution and racist parody began to collapse.[74] Davey identifies how Hughes's project depended on this slippage.[75] He offered children scripts that invited them to subvert minstrel stereotypes by recasting them formally in the style of elocutionary recitations. Like Johnson's performances in Native costume, Hughes took on black stereotypes to reverse them. For him, readers needed to participate in this work along with him, suggesting that subversive mimicry requires collective (and repeated) action to ultimately dislodge stereotypes. Yet it would be an overstatement to argue that Hughes's first recitation project became a model for subversive mimicry. As with Johnson's mimicry, its ambivalence potentially endangered the critique. Since Hughes approached recitation in this particular way only once, with a clearly delimited audience, he seems to have been aware of the risks involved. His chapbook and tour offered him an opportunity to experiment with recitation and mimicry, helping him to figure out ways to engage his young black audience in his future projects.

In this early experiment, Hughes provides explicit instructions to ensure that readers perform the poems in ways that subvert (rather than reinforce) stereotypes. As he learned as a child, bodily gesture dominates audience interpretation. Nurhussein notes that he "is anachronistically rigid and prescriptive in his instructions for performance."[76] This stems from his wish that children embody these poems in the way he imagined. His notes in the left-hand margin, entitled, "The Mood," describe how a performer should recite the poem and what music should accompany it. While his instructions reflect elocution pedagogy's directive approach, Davey points out that including them in the margins breaks from the nineteenth-century recitation tradition.[77] In the poem "The Black Clown," he instructs his readers about the music and emotions that they should embody:

But now a harsh
and bitter note
creeps into
the music.
Over-burdened.
Backing away
angrily.[78]

These dramatic cues resemble his use of italicized instructions in the right-hand margin in his later experimental work *Ask You Mama: 12 Moods for Jazz* (1961). These musical instructions, rather than the literal directions in *The Negro Mother*, take a figurative tone:

Bop
blues
into
very
modern
jazz
burning
the
air
eerie
like
a neon
swamp-
fire
cooled
by
dry
ice.[79]

Nurhussein points out that even the notes in *The Negro Mother* "don't, however, quite qualify as stage directions."[80] She argues that they become like "parallel poems," drawing attention to the gap between oral and written communication because they exist only for the silent reader, and she goes on to claim that "the silent form of *The Negro Mother*'s apparatus ends up overshadowing the book's voiced (and implicitly oral) poetic text as whole."[81] Yet this overlooks how Hughes imagines a new form of literacy through oral performance. Through his notes, he imagines what a reader might do on stage, clarifying his understanding of the politics of performance. Although he dispenses with this instructive model in his later recitation projects, where he emphasizes reader improvisation over authorial intention, choreographing actual reader performances during the act of composition helps him to imagine how to formally inspire a different approach to reading and racial performance in his texts.

"Learning by Doing"

More than twenty years later, Hughes presents his most fully developed model of collective literacy using rhythm to underscore interconnectedness in his children's reader *The First Book of Rhythms*. In this project, he conceptualizes all reading – even when silent – as a performance. His First Book series, commissioned by the publisher Franklin Watts, marked his return to children's literary projects in the early 1950s. The majority of the books in the series – *The First Book of Negroes* (1952), *The First Book of Jazz* (1955), *The First Book of the West Indies* (1956), and *The First Book of Africa* (1960) – were designed to educate children on black diasporic cultural themes. Despite Hughes's desire in 1925 to never be in schoolbooks, he produced this series to make curricula more inclusive and to feature African diasporic history in newly racially integrated US classrooms. Perhaps he felt more optimistic about institutionalized education than he had in previous decades due to the *Brown v. Board of Education* decision in 1954.

While the themes explored in *The First Book of Rhythms* have no explicit connection to reading, poetry, or racial empowerment, a contextualized analysis of the book provides insight into Hughes's pedagogical perspective on how to use poetry to promote literacy. He uses rhythm as an allegory to represent the kind of embodied active reading that he desired for his poetry, as an alternative to rote-learning methods and recitation for teaching reading. The concept of rhythm, which he defines as a "measure of time or movement by regular beats coming over and over again in a harmonious relationship" differs from the black cultural themes of his other First Books.[82] However, the small amount of scholarship on this book identifies how Hughes "elaborates a challenge to white racial oppression" through form.[83] In Scott's insightful Marxist analysis, he interprets the book through Gramsci's theories of education as "dynamic conformism" to argue that the book promotes "dialectical thinking and acting in the world."[84] Building on Scott's interpretation, I illustrate how Hughes's formal innovations grew out of his earlier investments in poetry recitation and illuminated the kind of reader that he envisioned for his own poetry.

In his afterword to the 1995 edition of *The First Book of Rhythms*, Robert O'Meally argues that Hughes challenges the racist stereotype that African people understand rhythm better than other ethnic groups without ever stating it directly: "by defining rhythm as originating not in 'race' but in the patterned shapes and movements of nature (the stars, leaves, winds, and rivers for example), in the pulses of the human body, and in learned cultural practices."[85] Hughes invites his readers to make (and perform) new patterns of meaning based on their experiences of rhythm. While he provides an extensive catalogue of rhythms to prove that everything has a rhythm, he never refers directly to reading as rhythm, which reflects his phenomenological pedagogy. The form and content of the book are designed to enact a form of learning by doing rather than by explanation, so that reading is experienced as rhythm (a feeling that readers of Hughes's poetry are familiar with) through the interactive text.

The lessons in this unique fifty-page book teach children how to recognize and decode rhythms in their environment through interactive exercises, as well as through explanations of a diverse array of rhythms: seashells, rivers, leaves, washing machines, furniture, airplanes, garden hoses, printing presses, language, music, dance, curling hair, skipping rope, electromagnetic waves, handwriting, and sweeping. Robin King's illustrations in the 1954 edition of the book begin as lines, squiggles, and shapes in the first few pages and then develop into images as the book progresses to enact the creative energy of rhythm. The book's short chapters – "Some Mysteries of Rhythm," "Broken Rhythms," "Athletics," "Sources of Rhythm," "Rhythms May Be Felt – and Smelled," "Machines," "Unseen Rhythms," "Rhythms in Daily Life," and "How Rhythms Take Shape" – present different ways to experience and think about rhythm.

Prior to writing this book, Hughes spent a semester in 1949 teaching at the Chicago Laboratory School, an experimental school for children from kindergarten through grade twelve. Founded on John Dewey's method of experiential education – an important precursor to critical pedagogy – the school provided Hughes with a unique learning environment to put his ideas about the pedagogical possibilities of poetic language into practice. He designed and taught an interdisciplinary writing workshop for city youth. His eighth-grade students were primarily first- and second-generation migrants from the South.[86] As he did during his tour in 1931, he aimed to teach black children new literacy practices, but this time he did this in a classroom environment, merging the role of poet and teacher into one. He used rhythm as a uniting theme to explore different modes of artistic production and interpretation. He led discussions on rhythms in human body movement, speech, nature, music, visual arts, and poetry. Children were assigned homework that involved creatively documenting rhythms they had observed in their environments.[87] He taught children to see rhythm as a relational force that connects everyone and everything together. As he puts it in *The First Book of Rhythms*, "*All* the rhythms of life in some way are related, one to another. You, your baseball, and the universe are brothers through rhythms" (42; italics in the original). Through rhythm, "People and races and nations get along better when they 'row together'" (43).

The First Book of Rhythms offers insight into Hughes's representation of jazz, blues, and black vernacular speech rhythms in his poetry to inspire new forms of literacy. In his experimental long poem *Montage of a Dream Deferred*, written in 1948, just prior to his poetry workshop at the Laboratory School, Hughes employs the improvisational framework of bebop to place more responsibility on the reader to co-create meaning. The reader must use her own rhythm to create connection between the series of disjunctive voices, which depict Harlem as a "community in transition."[88] The frequently anthologized fragment "Theme for English B" reveals Hughes's preoccupation with the development of a student-centred black pedagogy. The poetic persona, a black college student, questions the relationship between his Western education and his African American culture, and expresses his desire to transfer oral modes onto the page in the line "we two – you, me talk on this page." The young speaker worries about how his "page for English B" will be read by his instructor. He wants his "older – and white" teacher to "learn from" him.[89]

The musician Wynton Marsalis suggests that Hughes based his model for rhythm's interconnectivity on a jazz ensemble where all the players must keep the rhythm, unlike other genres of music where the drummer alone takes on this responsibility.[90] Extending this metaphor to textual production, it could be said that Hughes conceptualized the relationship between writer, reader, and text as a jazz ensemble, where everyone participates in the making of meaning without enforcing a consensus of meaning. Unlike in his 1931 chapbook, where he prescribes in the marginal notes what type of musical rhythm should accompany the poem and what the performer should do – acting like a conductor, rather than a band member – in this project he allows the reader more authority. Jazz rhythm (as opposed to metrical verse rhythm) presents a model of democratic collectivity, without implying the need for hierarchy or unison.

Fred Moten's discussion of the "interactive rhythmic feel" of Afro-diasporic music in his essay "The New International of Rhythmic Feeling(s)" illuminates Hughes's approach to recitation. He draws on jazz musician Charles Mingus's concept of "rotary perception" to theorize rhythm as a model for cross-cultural relations and negotiations. In Mingus's own words:

> If you get a mental picture of the beat existing within a circle you're more free to improvise. People used to think the notes had to fall on the center

> of the beats in the bar at intervals like a metronome, with three or four men in the rhythm section accenting the same pulse. That's like parade music or dance music. But imagine a circle surrounding each beat – each guy can play his notes anywhere in that circle and it gives him a feeling he has more space.[91]

The "rhythmic feel" of many of Hughes's poems evokes this participatory jazz model of improvisation. Mingus's circular model of rhythmic collaboration helps us to spatially conceptualize the relationship between reader and writer that Hughes cultivates and his departure from the metrical verse tradition. He encourages reading rhythmically around, rather than on, the beat.

In the opening sentence of *The First Book of Rhythms*, Hughes invites his readers to draw the shape of a rhythm on the page. The first chapter, entitled "Let's Make a Rhythm," emphasizes a collaborative textual relationship between reader and writer, embodying Dewey's educational ideal of "learning by doing." By immediately inviting his readers to become involved, Hughes encourages them to bring their own sense of rhythm to a text. First he suggests, "Take a crayon or pencil and a sheet of paper and start a line upward. Let it go up into a curve, and you will have a rhythm. Then make a wavy line, and you will see how the line itself seems to move. Rhythm comes from movement" (2–3). By inviting his readers to pick up a pencil on the first page, Hughes makes reading active rather than passive. His statement that "rhythm comes from movement" locates this movement in his readers' bodies. He gives readers experiential tasks to feel and simultaneously perform reading as movement. He continues to address the reader directly: "you can make a rhythm of sound by clapping your hand or tapping your foot," and "you can make a body rhythm by swaying your body from side to side or by making circles in the air with your arms" (4). He draws his readers' attention to the book in their hands as a material object when he suggests, "try beating a slow steady rhythm with your fingers softly on the table, or on the edge of this book" (10). Hughes provides a step-by-step approach to engage all of one's senses, including touch, in the act of embodied reading, and make it into a performance:

> Now make a large circle on a paper. Inside your circle make another circle. Inside that one make another one. See how these circles almost seem to move, for you have left something of your own movement there, and your own feeling of place and roundness. Your circles are not quite like

the circles of anyone else in the world, because you are not like anyone else. (4)

He instructs his readers to draw shapes to represent the rhythms of their bodies. Through the repetition of circles, he encourages children to embrace their own uniqueness. By asking his young readers to draw shapes rather than letters and words, he also encourages readers with developing literacies to feel empowered to participate in textual production. This also demystifies writing by showing how letters are just shapes. Hughes avoided stressing grammar in his approach to teaching writing and instead asked students to follow their own sense of rhythm. He encouraged children to feel confident in their individuality and to view their own embodiment as a source of agency – a "roundness" in the world that gives them place.

Elsewhere in the book he discusses the rhythm of printing presses, illustrating how for him different kinds of textual production are forms of rhythm. The rhythmic repetition of the prose in this passage encourages his readers to experience rhythm in the act of reading. His simple, direct sentences speak personally to each reader. When they follow his instructions to draw the shapes, they enact the idea that "one rhythm affects another rhythm" as bodily rhythms and textual rhythms blend together (14). As in his own childhood recitations, Hughes capitalizes on the power of embodied reading.

The second chapter, "The Beginning of Rhythm," explicitly tells readers that rhythm starts in their bodies: "Your rhythm on this earth began first with the beat of your heart. The heart makes the blood flow. Feel your heart. Then feel your wrist where your pulse is. That is where you can best feel the rhythm of your blood moving through your body from your heart" (8). Again, his experiential instructions in this passage foster body awareness while one is reading. Through these instructions, he shows students how their internal body movements interact with the world around them to offer an embodied way of relating to the world. Hughes suggests learning to read through the rhythms of one's heartbeat, which Robson identifies as something that happens in recitation: "The compulsorily memorized poem inserted itself into individuals and established its beat in sympathy with, or in counterpoint to, their bodily rhythms."[92] As a child, Hughes rarely felt a rhythmic harmony with the poems he was forced to recite, which explains why he gives priority to one's bodily rhythms in his literacy model. Elocutionary manuals instruct a reader to follow the metre of the poem; however,

Hughes leaves more room for free play. Formally, the sentence breaks punctuate the rhythm of his prose with his reader's activity to convey the interconnectivity of rhythms. The fragment "feel your heart" provides readers with space for this instruction to register physically as well as cognitively. While traditional methods of "learning by heart" promote the idea that the body is the primary place to store knowledge, Hughes privileges the body not as a repository of knowledge – or, as Freire would put it, a "bank" – but as an agent of knowledge through the heart, which one can act out through performance.

After establishing readers' experiences of rhythm in their bodies Hughes goes on to explore rhythms in the natural environment. He encourages children to experience the world around them as a composition of rhythms. He begins with the rhythms of nature in seashells, rivers, oceans, trees, birds, nests, and leaves. He describes seashells as made from the rhythms of the ocean: "Each shell is molded into a rhythmic shape of its own by the all the rhythms and pressures that bear upon it from the sea" (26). The apparent simplicity of the sentences condenses a poetic complexity. The book proceeds by interconnected analogy, illustrating the meaning of rhythms through its formal structure. In doing so, Hughes creates a convergence between signifying and enacting. Readers experience text as rhythm through the style and form of the sentence fragments. Punctuation, specifically the period, functions to set the tempo of his prose. He uses plain vocabulary and short, direct sentences that build on one another through repetition. By using repetition as a form of elaboration, he maintains an interactive rhythm with his readers. Rather than stressing recitation as faithful imitation, Hughes enacts recitation with a difference, making his text accessible for new readers, who can develop their reading skills through repetition.

Central to Hughes's idea of rhythm is the idea that human production and labour, both artistic and technological, can be traced back to the generating energy of rhythm. For example, he suggests that sweeping is done most efficiently when one keeps a steady pace, because "rhythm makes it easier to use energy" (33). By extension, reading itself, as a form of labour, becomes easier to accomplish when a reader's rhythm freely interacts with the rhythm of a text. By aligning the manual labour of everyday acts like sweeping with the intellectual labour of reading (and artistic production), Hughes de-emphasizes reading's status as an elite activity and suggests that it should be accessible to all.[93]

In terms of artistic production, Hughes privileges poetry as a form well suited to harness the power of rhythm. In his lecture, "Ten Ways to

Use Poetry in Teaching," given at the College Learning Association in 1951 and based on his months at the Laboratory School, he explained how poetry can be used to teach students how to interpret rhythm: "The rhythms of poetry give continuity and pattern to words, to thoughts, strengthening them, adding the qualities of permanence, and relating the written word to the vast rhythms of life." Poetry offers a dialectic model of learning: it "can be used to bridge the often imagined gulf between literature and life" in the classroom.[94] In "Rhythm and Words," a chapter from *The First Book of Rhythms*, Hughes suggests that poetic language engages the rhythmic potential of words as a source of social connection. He explains, "rhythm is very much a part of poetry. Maybe that is because the first poems were songs" (34). He emphasizes how poetry increases the force of words: "Just as the feet of soldiers marching in rhythm carry men forward, so the rhythms of sermons or speeches or poems carry words marching into your mind in a way that helps you to remember them" (36). Poetry helps one to internalize language structures, which makes it a useful genre for literacy instruction. Yet instead of espousing the disciplinary use of rhythm (as regular metrical form) in memorization and recitation, Hughes invites readers to bring their own rhythms to a text to give them more agency. Moving beyond the limitations of a staged reading, Hughes conceptualizes all reading, even when silent, as a performance. To escape literacy as indoctrination, Hughes suggests that one relate to it as a collaborative rhythmic process, rather than a set of skills that one must master.

Although *The First Book of Rhythms* might seem like a completely different kind of project than his 1931 chapbook, they both take inspiration from poetry recitation. In fact, Hughes frequently used poetry recitation in his 1949 poetry workshops at the Laboratory School. In "Ten Ways to Use Poetry in Teaching," six out of his ten suggestions involve using some form of recitation or reading aloud. He presents recitation as a fun and collaborative activity, rather than as a prescriptive practice. He encourages children to study folk poems and invites them to make up their own to recite. He also suggests working as a group in a choral speech or verse choir to recite poetry together.[95] His most playful suggestion is to hold a "Poetry Quiz Party" where students read aloud a poem and then the class must guess what country it is from, who the author is, and the title. If they cannot figure out the title, he encourages teachers to "let the members of the class give it a title of their own choosing."[96] These various interactive exercises illustrate how Hughes encouraged his students to be creative in their performances. His suggestions for recitation avoid rote memorization by inviting students to be more original in their interpretation and presentation of the poems.

Hughes's rhythmic literacy draws on communal oral practices and anticipates Freire's focus on literacy as a mode of cultural politics essential to the process of decolonization in the 1970s. Freire maintains that students need to be able to learn using models from their own cultures, which he calls "emancipatory literacy." For him, this involves teaching a critical form of reading that interprets the text in its social environment.[97] Hughes's chapbook, *The Negro Mother*, and his experimental children's reader, *The First Book of Rhythms*, are emblematic of his efforts to inspire rhythmic literacy, a mode of active embodied reading as a form of social change.

To exemplify Hughes's goals for his poetics, this chapter began with a story about black poetry causing "a rumble" in a high school in the town of East Orange, New Jersey, in 1966. Although black poetry may have been perceived as a threatening force in education in the 1960s, East Orange is now home to an elementary school called the Langston Hughes School of Publishing and Fine Arts. In addition to Hughes ending up in textbooks, schools across the United States have been named after Hughes, demonstrating his status as a national cultural icon. This parallels the naming of schools after Longfellow in the late nineteenth century.[98] Although the naming of schools after Hughes surely indicates racial progress, and stems from his own efforts to promote poetry as a pedagogical form, it also marks an apex in the institutionalization of black poetry. Does this canonization undermine his work's potential to cause "a rumble"?

Contemporary educators might benefit from a consideration of Hughes's rhythmic literacy to prevent his poetry from being used to teach children to "sing the nation-state" in the tradition of Longfellow.[99] Hughes was deeply committed to expanding the possibilities for reading and representing race through performance poetry. So where does a prominent national poet like Hughes fit in the explosion of African American cultural production in the early twentieth century? Many remember him for his groundbreaking work to create a poetics based on black folk culture and music; however, he should also be remembered for his contributions to education activism.

Chapter Three

Miss Lou Pedagogy and Mimic Women

I had grown up as a young child performing the works of Louise Bennett on stages all over Jamaica in the annual festival. I had read and performed works from other women writers in Jamaica, but Miss Lou had not only drawn on the characters, experiences and languages of the people, she had also managed to give the people's poetry back to them in a way that made the nation celebrate itself. No other woman poet had taken on the popular stage, no other had broken so totally out of the literary and academic circles of recognition, indeed, had forced them to accept her and so opened the way for all of us who now work in our own language with ease.

Jean "Binta" Breeze, "Can a Dub Poet Be a Woman?"

Of the three main poets in this book, Louise Bennett's recitation legacy is the most pervasive in her country. Aside from Bob Marley, no other artist's words have permeated the national consciousness so thoroughly. Most Jamaicans who grew up on the island can recite at least a part of a Bennett poem by heart because they were assigned to memorize her work in school. For many children who grew up in the 1960s and 1970s, this was often the only time they were permitted to speak Jamaican Creole (and praised for it) in school.[1] If children were not exposed to Bennett in the classroom, they may have watched her children's television show *Ring Ding* on Saturday mornings, listened to her weekly radio monologues on *Miss Lou's Views*, seen her perform in the annual Christmas pantomime, or watched one of her many public performances. At the national finals of the Jamaica Festival's Speech Competition, one is guaranteed to hear her poems being recited by students. Like Johnson and Hughes, Bennett has had buildings named after her, including the

Gordon Town All-Age School, now called the Louise Bennett-Coverley All-Age School. Bennett lived for many years in Gordon Town, a small community just outside of Kingston, Jamaica, and she frequently visited this school, as well as many others across the island, to perform her poetry. Her commitment to educating children also extended to the diaspora. While living in Toronto for the last twenty years of her life, she played a significant role in the Canadian Caribbean community, mentoring many emerging writers. In 2007, Harbourfront Centre, a non-profit cultural organization in Toronto, opened Miss Lou's Room, which features a permanent Bennett exhibit and hosts school visits where children learn about storytelling and her contributions to Jamaican culture.

In the epigraph, the dub poet Jean "Binta" Breeze personally addresses the formative influence that reciting Bennett's poetry at the annual Jamaica Festival had on her development as an artist.[2] First held in 1962 to celebrate Independence, the annual festival features many different arts and culture events. Of all of these events, the Speech Competition attracts the most entries every year.[3] Students begin by competing in their own schools and then move on to local and regional contests. The top recitations from these competitions advance to the national finals. Breeze underscores Bennett's unparalleled legacy and the empowering effects of reciting Bennett's Creole poetry at the festival. Other Caribbean dialect performance poets came to local prominence in the 1950s and 1960s, yet Bennett is the only one to be cherished as a national icon while being applauded internationally.[4]

What makes Bennett's recitation legacy so strong and the speech contest so popular? The orality of Jamaican culture drives both of these to some extent. In his entry on "Poetic Contests" in *The New Princeton Encyclopedia of Poetry and Poetics*, Earl Miner notes that speech contests "remain vital in third-world and popular culture," which he attributes to the role of verbal competition in African oral traditions.[5] Yet the act of recitation, especially in an evaluative context, also evokes indelible marks from a colonial past. The categories of the Speech Competition – Standard English Poems/Prose; Jamaican Dialect Prose; Dub Poetry; Speaking Ensemble; Public Speaking; Story Telling; Caribbean Dialect Poems; and Sonnets, Psalms and Shakespeare – reflect Jamaica's colonial past as well as its post-colonial present. Bennett's poems are competition favourites in the Caribbean Dialect Poems category, because she promoted poetry recitation throughout her lifetime. She knew that her performances alone would not be enough to transform the colonized

Jamaican public sphere. She needed her audience to help her reclaim public discourse.

While people recognize Bennett's commitment to education, her innovative Miss Lou pedagogy remains understudied. Most Jamaicans affectionately refer to Bennett as Miss Lou. More than a stage name, her nickname encompasses a communal identification with the peasant woman voice that she embodied in her poetry and the imaginative world that she created through her performance career. This chapter examines Bennett's pioneering efforts to use performance poetry to decolonize literacy education. Her recycling of colonial elocution in her 1940s poetics played a pivotal role in the development of anglophone Caribbean poetics and underscored the necessity of subverting colonial power from within to develop new cultural forms. My argument revolves around an analysis of Bennett's rarely discussed 1942 poem "Sammy Intres," which responds to the history of memorization and recitation in British colonial education in the West Indies. In addition, I examine how she put her educational aspirations for Creole poetry reading into practice in her media projects for the Jamaica Broadcasting Corporation.

Throughout her career, Bennett played an impressive array of roles, including poet, archivist, folklorist, radio commentator, television host, musician, social welfare agent, foster mother, actor, and children's entertainer. The range of her audience is equally diverse, cutting across class, generation, and race in Jamaica. A cursory glance at Bennett's career suggests that she increasingly rejected print culture in favour of oral performance, yet a more thorough examination reveals how Bennett merged writing and performance to encourage audience participation. Similar to Johnson, Bennett saw herself primarily as a writer at the beginning of her career. She published much of her early poetry in newsprint, first in her weekly column in the national paper, the *Jamaica Gleaner*, and then later in the anti-colonial weekly *Public Opinion*. However, as her career progressed, she turned to performance as she cultivated her Miss Lou persona. Bennett explains the transition in an interview with Mary Jane Hewitt: "You know, at the beginning of my career, I thought of myself as more quietly writing rather than being a person of the stage. Then through writing and performing, I realized that performance was one big way of getting across this thing."[6] Performance helped her to build a more inclusive audience and reach those in the lower classes who held varying levels of literacy. To establish her career she went to London in 1945 on a British Council fellowship to study drama at the Royal Academy of Dramatic Art. Upon her return, she took on one of her most significant cultural roles in Jamaica, as the director of the annual Christmas pantomime, transforming it from a British form into a Jamaican tradition.[7]

She also met Langston Hughes around this time, when she lived briefly in New York in the early 1950s. In an interview with Daryl Dance, she describes her friendship with Hughes:

> I knew Langston Hughes very well. Yes, he was a good friend … I met Langston Hughes first in 1953, but I had known about him before all that, but I met him personally and we became very good friends. I used to visit – whenever I would go to New York, Langston would have a sort of "little thing" and have people, you know, people in the theatre come and that sort of thing, and I would do my verses and so. And I have even a picture inside with us doing a radio program together, WWRM, with Alma John, you know. And he used to send me everything he wrote, he would send me you know … He would always send me something, but we did talk a lot about what he was writing, and what he was doing and we had a lot of mutual friends, you know. I liked him.[8]

It is likely that Hughes sent her *The First Book of Rhythms*, since it came out in 1954, a year after they met in New York. One wonders what she thought of his approach to embodied reading for children. Perhaps his work helped her understand the potential of performative reading. She also had the benefit of seeing an example of refashioned poetry recitation to help her craft her own version. Bennett and Hughes shared many similarities – they both critiqued institutionalized literacies and promoted black communal literacy practices through recitation. However, Bennett's approach to recitation, which she began to develop before their first meeting, was quite distinct from his. Through rhythmic improvisation, Hughes's embodied reading aimed to cultivate harmony, whereas Bennett's highlighted discord. Her poems bring the embodied conflicts that underpin colonial mimicry to the forefront for her readers to both laugh at and confront. As Jahan Ramazani points out, the gulf between British English and Creole is a frequent source of comedy in Bennett's poems.[9] She invites her readers to activate a creolized clash of rhythms, gestures, and voices in their performances and to capitalize on the physical and social contours of reading to resist indoctrination. Bennett's gendered critique of "schooled literacy" and her emphasis on using recitation to empower women distinguish her work from Hughes's as well.[10]

Even in her turn to oral performance later in her career, she never ceased to promote reading through the recitation of poetry, especially among children. Bennett's use of print, as well as television and radio, illustrates how she educated her audience through a range of media outlets because institutionalized education resisted her Creole politics. Like Johnson did more than fifty years earlier, Bennett struggled to gain acceptance as a performance poet. The literary establishment in Jamaica rejected her poems in Creole as "real" poetry because they failed to meet their idea of British literary standards.[11] And, like Hughes, her experiments with vernacular expression and performance shaped her reputation as an oral poet and have caused scholars to overlook the role of literacy in her poetics.

Educating Women and Children

When Bennett first published in the early 1940s, many of her middle-class readers feared that her dialect verses would promote illiteracy. What often gets overlooked in analysis of these early debates is that she intended her poetry to do the exact opposite – to promote literacy. To challenge her critics, Bennett wrote one of her most famous poems, "Bans a Killin" (1943), which defends the legitimacy of Jamaican Creole as a language "dah equal up wid English."[12] She singles out and makes fun of "Mas Charlie," a middle-class Jamaican man who wrote a letter to the *Jamaica Gleaner* newspaper complaining about Bennett's poetry column and claiming that he wanted to "kill dialect." Her mocking pun on "self" and "shelf" in the final lines playfully demonstrates how Jamaicans hurt themselves when they reject Creole:

> An mine how yuh dah read dem English
> Book deh pon yuh shelf,
> For ef yuh drop a 'h' yuh mighta
> Haffi kill yuhself![13]

People trying to emulate a "correct" British accent often overemphasize the letter *h*, which makes this especially funny.[14] This pun also enacts precisely the kind of clash between textuality and Creole pronunciation that Bennett encourages her readers to participate in.[15]

In Bennett scholarship, her engagement with oral traditions has dominated the conversation. Brathwaite positions Bennett as a forerunner of nation language poetry, which he stresses exists "in the tradition of the spoken word."[16] Mervyn Morris acknowledges that "Bennett's art is both oral and scribal," but he encourages scholars to treat her poems "like dramatic literature" and to analyse them as scripts for performance, rather than as templates for a creolized literacy.[17] Many critics praise Bennett for writing in Jamaican Creole, but they focus primarily on a unilateral movement from oral to written work. For instance, in his chapter on Bennett and the oral tradition in his foundational book *West Indian Poetry*, Lloyd Brown claims that for Bennett, "publication has really been an after-thought, of sorts, in terms of her function and achievement as an artist in an oral medium."[18]

In contrast, I examine how her decision to write down Creole was not just an "after-thought," or a method of conservation and documentation, as Hewitt has argued, or "a legitimizing process," as Carolyn Cooper has argued.[19] More importantly, she offered a method to activate new modes of bilingual literacy that invites readers to draw on their embodied Creole knowledge. Through her reader-centred performance poetics, Bennett staged what Walter D. Mignolo characterizes as the conflict between language as an object controlled by grammar and "languaging (bilanguaging) imbedded in her body."[20] Bennett recognized that this conflict between internal and external language often erupts when a student memorizes a poem in a colonial environment.

Her education poetry anticipates later anglophone Caribbean literature that critiques the oppressive effects of British colonial education, and argues for new curricula that focus on Caribbean language and culture, such as Earl Lovelace's *The Schoolmaster* (1968), Brathwaite's *History of the Voice* (1984), Jamaica Kincaid's novels *Annie John* (1985) and *Lucy* (1990), and Olive Senior's poem "Colonial Girls School" (1985). However, Bennett's work differs significantly from these later texts because her critique is neither tragic nor defiantly oppositional; instead, she turns to rearticulation and comedy in the tradition of the Jamaican pantomime. Humour relieves tension between the contradictions of local knowledge and colonial knowledge, while also leaving them at play for a reader to negotiate at both the thematic and linguistic levels, so that she can make her own meanings from her colonial education.[21]

"Sammy Intres" demonstrates the humorous elements of Bennett's education poems and her focus on women's concerns about children's welfare. Originally published in her first book, *Jamaica Dialect Verses* in 1942, this poem appears in Bennett's *Selected Poems*, a book designed for the classroom. It is included in the education section, "TECK TIME WID HIM, YAW, TEACHER," along with "Bed-Time Story" and "New

Scholar." Much like her poems set on tramcars and in markets, these 1940s classroom poems illustrate how Bennett disrupts the social hierarchies of public space.[22] The title of the section comes from a line in "New Scholar," which is about a mother taking her child to his first day at a new school. The mother instructs the teacher to "No treat him rough, yaw, Teacher."[23] Like "Sammy Intres," this poem explores the contrastive relationship in a colonial setting between mothers and teachers as figures of female authority in childhood development. The other poem in the section, "Bed-Time Story," also deals with the blurring of public and private knowledge for comic effect. It depicts a mother trying to put a crying baby to sleep by reciting English nursery rhymes that are interspersed with local gossip about a sex scandal. All three dramatize the fraught relationship in colonial Jamaica between intimate familiar knowledge and schoolroom knowledge. They illuminate Cooper's point that Bennett resists how "upward social mobility in Jamaica requires the shedding of the old skin of early socialization: mother tongue, mother culture, mother wit – the feminized discourse of voice, identity and native knowledge."[24] Like her Aunty Roachy radio persona, Bennett's education poems assert the feminine discourse of gossip as a source of authority to challenge colonial power. Through these poems Bennett demonstrates how "matters of the intimate are critical sites for the consolidation of colonial power" and also potential sites for its subversion.[25]

"Sammy Intres" is Bennett's only poem that directly engages with memorization and recitation practices in West Indian education. By making recitation the focus, the poem invites students to be self-reflexive about what it means to recite a Bennett poem – instead of one by a white author like William Wordsworth or Henry Wadsworth Longfellow – in post-colonial Jamaica. Consisting of nine stanzas, it features a woman who stands in her doorway conversing with her friend about her son's progress in school. Like the majority of Bennett's female dramatic personas, the woman speaks in Creole; however, this speaker, rather than reference Jamaican folk culture, translates from English into Creole lines from Longfellow's Latinate poem "Excelsior" (1841). Since working-class women have the highest illiteracy rates of any social group worldwide, Bennett's presentation of a peasant woman reading indicates her commitment to an inclusive feminist literacy politics.[26] Through the lines of the Longfellow poem, the woman speaker reinvents his text to talk about her son, who has been assigned to memorize this poem in school. Rather than reciting Longfellow faithfully, the woman speaker inserts her own interests, effaced by the colonial society that she inhabits, into the text of the poem. Through this dramatization of reading, Bennett makes a critique of poetry recitation in colonial schools while also refashioning its embodied and performative potential. When Bennett's woman speaker in "Sammy Intres" embarks on memorizing and reciting Longfellow's "Excelsior," she recalls a long history of these practices in the West Indies that extends back to the beginning of the nineteenth century. Before analysing this poem, I will briefly review this history as well as Bennett's educational experiences with recitation. My contextualized close reading of "Sammy Intres" involves a number of detours – history and formal analysis are interwoven – to establish how the poem becomes a blueprint for Bennett's literacy politics.

Recitation in Colonial Jamaica

In the period leading up to the Slavery Abolition Act in 1833, the British government began to implement literacy education through rote learning as a form of social control. The abolition of the slave trade in 1807 and the increasing insurrection of enslaved groups in the different colonies signalled that the abolition of all slavery practices in the British Empire would happen soon. With the Haitian Revolution (1791–1804) as the only Caribbean model for a shift from slavery to freedom, the British government desperately wanted to avoid such a violent revolt in their colonies and to salvage a post-emancipation labour force. Historian Olwyn Blouet argues that this desire caused a dramatic shift in the perspective on education in colonial policy. Rather than being seen as a threat, education became an integral part of the so-called civilizing mission. In contrast to the United States, where teaching enslaved people to read was illegal, and was often punished severely, in the West Indies colonial officials began to implement it as a way of "maintaining social and moral order" and ensuring "Christian conversion."[27] In 1823, the British government passed amelioration proposals to ostensibly improve slavery conditions. It legislated Christian education for enslaved peoples. Many interpreted this act as an unsuccessful attempt to quell the anti-slavery movement, rather than as an actual humanitarian improvement. As Blouet explains, "Missionaries, abolitionists, British government officials, and some planters hoped that education would replace the whip."[28] The methods of instruction for reading followed those current in Britain, where rote learning predominated. During slavery, missionary groups taught literacy almost explicitly for the purpose of Bible study. Students were taught to memorize and recite Bible passages as a form of internalizing moral instruction. In the pre-emancipation period, memorization and recitation emerged in West Indian education as a "safe" way to teach reading without leading to radical consciousness or revolt; this fraught history reverberates in "Sammy Intres."

The British parliament introduced universal elementary education in the West Indies as part of emancipation. A two-tiered system, designed to maintain social hierarchies, quickly developed and continues to this day. Most students attend all-age primary schools, where they receive a limited basic education, and a select few (usually from light-skinned, upper-class families) go to elite secondary schools (both government and private) that more closely resemble the British model.

In one of the first comprehensive studies of West Indian education written post-Independence, Shirley C. Gordon quotes a circular dispatched by the British Colonial Office to the West Indies, dated 26 January 1847, which outlines the guidelines for the curricula in the all-age primary schools. It specifies English-language instruction as the second most important subject after Christian instruction: "To diffuse a grammatical knowledge of the English language as the most important agent of civilization for the coloured population of the colonies."[29] This mandate makes transparent the role of British English as a means of colonial control and cultural assimilation. Yet historical records indicate that this goal was rarely achieved at all-age primary schools. As V.S. Naipaul's novel *The Mimic Men* illustrates, only those at the elite schools were trained to become "mimic men."[30] An annual report from a colonial inspector of education in Jamaica from 1895 concluded that most students leave school no better equipped in English than people who never attended.[31]

"To diffuse a grammatical knowledge" as a form of domination, both types of schools began to rely on literary texts, especially poetry.[32] West Indian schools followed the British model, where reading was often taught and tested through the memorization and recitation of poetry. Ruby King and Mike Morrissey characterize "the nineteenth-century primary school curriculum" as "a diluted version of working-class education as it was provided in England."[33] In the late nineteenth century, Thomas Nelson's *Royal Readers* became the standard text in most primary schools throughout the British Empire.[34] These readers included "Poetry for Reading and Recitation" by the usual suspects – Alfred Lord Tennyson, Robert Louis Stevenson, Felicia Hemans, and Longfellow.

Robson explains how standardized testing increased the popularity of poetry memorization and recitation in UK school curricula because it provided a convenient way for examiners to evaluate reading, by making it into a performance that could be easily judged.[35] Students were expected to memorize and recite a certain number of lines of poetry depending on their grade level. In "Sammy Intres," Bennett implies that Sammy failed his recitation test of "Excelsior."

The frequent references to poetry recitation in anglophone Caribbean literature substantiate that it was common in both types of colonial schools in the twentieth century. Scenes, such as the one in Kincaid's *Lucy* (discussed in the Introduction) where the heroine becomes haunted by nightmares of daffodils after being forced to recite Wordsworth's "I Wandered Lonely as a Cloud," are symbolic of the damage inflicted by colonial education and reveal the hidden curriculum of assimilation motivating these practices.[36] Brathwaite references Hemans's "Casabianca," a frequently assigned poem, in *History of the Voice* to underscore how recitation contributes to colonization, stressing that it limits the development of a distinct Caribbean literature.[37] In her poem "Colonial Girls School," Senior, who attended Montego Bay High School for Girls, also stresses how the curriculum, which entailed "months, years, a childhood memorising / Latin declensions," caused students to lose their identities and "willed our skins pale" and "muffled our laughter."[38] Yet there is a slightly different story to tell about poetry recitation in twentieth-century Jamaica that deviates from this "mimic men" narrative.

Despite its evaluative colonial history, recitation helped to introduce many Jamaican poets, including Bennett, to the pleasures of poetry. Just as African Americans refashioned recitation to merge with their "live arts" traditions in the late nineteenth century, Jamaicans also began to adapt recitation practices for their own purposes in the early twentieth century.[39] As this book has demonstrated, poetry recitation, despite being attached to dominant institutional agendas, became a malleable form due to its embodied nature. As creolization theorists have demonstrated, Caribbean island societies excel at cultural mixing and repurposing, perhaps more so than any other societies in history.[40] Bennett and many other poets participated in creolized versions of poetry recitation in their formal schooling and in their communities. These different versions of recitation were distinct but overlapping, as demonstrated by the annual Jamaica Festival's Speech Competition entry categories. This intertwined inheritance can be seen in Breeze's childhood experiences as well. In addition to reciting Bennett's vernacular poetry at the festival, her experience with recitation, and praise for the practice, extends to texts from the Euro-American canon. She speaks fondly about her mother teaching her poems as soon as she could talk and performing them at church, giving the example of the Tennessee author Will Allen Dromgoole's recitation classic "The Bridge Builder."[41] Her mother would teach her to memorize the lines of poems by saying them aloud to her. Breeze indicates that when these classroom practices spread outside of an institutional setting and merged with Jamaican oral traditions, their disciplinary power greatly diminished. In Breeze's case, recitation nurtured her oral memory, strengthened her bond with her mother, and encouraged her to explore the embodied dimension of performance in her own poetics.

Even in the classroom, some students claim to have enjoyed recitation. In her literacy narrative, the Jamaican poet and education activist Glasceta Honeyghan remembers that her "old half-tumbled-down schoolhouse was full of horror," yet she acknowledges that poetry recitation "brought an artistic sweetness to school life."[42] The dub poet Linton Kwesi Johnson (hereafter referred to as LKJ), while critiquing poetry recitation, also claims that he found it pleasurable in school. In an interview with Mervyn Morris, he describes his experiences in Jamaican schools in the 1950s, prior to his migration to England at age eleven: "I quite enjoyed it when I was out here in Jamaica, but in those days they taught you parrot fashion … and the whole class said it. "O wind a-blowing all day long, / O wind that sings so loud a song." Yet he suggests he "had no poetic models to draw from" when he started to write.[43] LKJ's ambivalence towards recitation reveals much about its contradictory history. He claims to have no poetic models but then acknowledges that he liked poetry in Jamaican schools, even though the phrase "parrot fashion" sounds dismissive. He provides a quotation from Robert Louis Stevenson, a popular poet in schoolroom readers, as an example, repeating the apostrophe to wind to compare recitation's insubstantial influence to the ephemerality of wind.[44] Although LKJ sees recitation as inconsequential, poets' affinity for recitation reveals that these internalizing practices have had far-reaching effects on the development of anglophone Caribbean poetics. LKJ's enjoyment also may have been determined by his teacher's approach to recitation. Based on his description, his teacher may have emphasized communal performance (a strong feature in Caribbean oral traditions) over individual examination. Admittedly, it is difficult to determine to what extent individual teachers creolized recitation practices and deviated from the colonial agenda, but it certainly must have happened at times. Because LKJ, Breeze, and Honeyghan all recited Bennett's poem as children, these Creole examples may have lessened their direct contact with the colonial history of these practices.

Unlike poets born in the second half of the twentieth century, Bennett learned recitation primarily through the Euro-American tradition; however, she still experienced a creolized version of it.[45] In an unpublished interview with Hewitt from 1975, Bennett describes how the first poems that she wrote were influenced by memorizing and reciting Victorian verse in school:

> HEWITT: That first poem that you wrote – there's a world of difference there, between it and your dialect verse – when did the transition take place?
>
> BENNETT: (*Laughter*). Quite different! Oh, you want to know the influence of all that? That was the sort of thing we used to recite in school. When I was at my fifth birthday party, I think, I recited "Lady Clare," and on my sixth birthday party, I recited "The Burial of Sir John Moore," and "The Burial of Moses." (*recites remnants of it*). And everybody clap and say, "My, look and the little girl look at her size and she reciting these things!" So this was quite a thing, and recitation was quite a thing in school in those days.
>
> HEWITT: And it was a tradition to recite at your birthday parties?
>
> BENNETT: Oh, yes, Man! To recite, Man!
>
> HEWITT: Not just you, but everybody?
>
> BENNETT: Jamaicans! And people would come and other children would come and recite. It was almost like a competition – who could out-recite the other. You heard them at every birthday party.[46]

In her questions, Hewitt draws a rigid distinction between Bennett's earlier Victorian verse and her dialect poetry, yet these two forms overlap much more than Hewitt acknowledges. Bennett's response reveals the popularity of recitation outside of the classroom in twentieth-century Jamaica. Her description of the informal recitation competitions at birthday parties provides insight into how the Speech Competition at the annual festival developed as schoolroom poetry reading merged with Jamaican oral practices. Such practices often involve playful rivalry and verbal dexterity through "the compressed allusiveness of proverb, the enigmatic indirection of riddle and the antiphonal repetitions of oral narration."[47] Like Breeze, Bennett indicates that when schoolroom recitation merged with Jamaican social life, it took on different meanings as Western- and African-descended oral modes combined. As the poet Donna (Aza) Weir-Soley describes, in her Jamaican village oral performance "was our only form of entertainment – on moonshine nights everyone in the extended family would gather outside to tell stories and perform, so I guess I was just imitating what I saw."[48] Her words highlight how creative imitation plays a central role in the communal experience of Jamaican orality. As early as age four, she recalls joining in these performances by reciting poetry. Honeyghan describes a similar experience, noting how poetry recitation provided her with a form to combine her village's oral practices with her colonial education in her literacy development: "The most extraordinary discovery, however, was when I recognized the connection to my own world – the stories told to me, the poems I memorized and performed. There was a relationship between the familiar, the voice of the village, and the unfamiliar, the situation in books."[49] Poetry recitation did not cause Honeyghan to have daffodil nightmares like Kincaid's protagonist Lucy. Instead it helped her to resolve the rift between her colonial education and her village life.[50] Hewitt implies that Bennett's recitation of Victorian poets ceased to influence her when she began writing verse in dialect; however, the blurry boundaries between village practices and schoolroom recitation reveal the difficulty of separating these two forms in tracing her poetic development. "Sammy Intres" is such a key text in Bennett's oeuvre precisely because the poem explores the relationship between formal schooling and community education and dramatizes a direct confrontation between Western recitation practices and Jamaican oral traditions, thus providing insight into how they merge in the formation of her poetics and her approach to literacy.

In "Sammy Intres," Bennett explores the impact of forced memorization of anglophone literatures to disrupt its power over her voice. Rather than the "parrot fashion" (to borrow LKJ's phrase) she learned in school, her parody builds on the creolized version she experienced in her community, to create space for new voices to emerge, including her own and those of her readers. Standardizing and controlling language through recitation were central aims of the hidden curriculum in colonial schools, yet Bennett dramatizes how the embodied dimension of performance necessarily creates linguistic multiplicity and transformation. Written when she was in her early twenties, the poem can be read as a response to Longfellow, as well as to her education in colonial Jamaica.

The poem also includes a veiled reference to Bennett's actual high school, Excelsior High School in Kingston, which she attended from 1936 to 1938. Longfellow's "Excelsior" may have been a familiar poem in the school curriculum, used to convey the ethos of its name and to foster school spirit.[51] Bennett valued her education there because the curriculum emphasized more Jamaican content than her previous school. She switched to this school from St Simon's College because she wanted to learn more about Jamaica. Both were elite private schools based on the British system; however, Wesley Powell, the innovative headmaster at Excelsior, chose to include more Jamaican culture. According to an interview with Michael Reckord, after her first week Bennett told her mother: "I love Excelsior. Mr. Powell encourages us to dance and sing and recite – all the things I like to do."[52] The headmaster established Friday social afternoons that involved students creating "a performing arts programme consisting of dance, song, poetry and speeches."[53] This is where Bennett first began to perform her own Creole poetry rather than recite the work of others. The line "dance and sing and recite" encompasses both Jamaican oral traditions and poetry recitation in the same category, illustrating how these different performance traditions mixed together for Bennett. The different versions of recitation that she experienced at school and in her community began to blur together even more while she was at Excelsior, rather than divisively split as Hewitt suggests. The fact that "Sammy Intres" explores the intersection between Jamaican folk traditions and Western recitation through Longfellow's "Excelsior" seems more than coincidental.

Bennett also displays her familiarity with Longfellow's "Excelsior" in an earlier poem that she composed about her first day of school there. The poem mimics the declarative "Excelsior!" from Longfellow's poem at the end of the first stanza:

> It was a warm September day.
> Along North Street I made my way.
> I stopped at the gate and heaved a sigh.
> One word caught my eye:
> Excelsior![54]

Her rhyming couplets and "Standard English" in this early piece illustrate how she copied the style of British Victorian poetry before she got the support at Excelsior to begin writing and performing in Creole. Yet even in this early poem, Bennett revises the original meaning of Longfellow's "Excelsior," which upholds Eurocentric knowledge through the Latin motto, to signify her excitement about her new Jamaica-focused education.[55] By returning to "Excelsior" in "Sammy Intres," she also indicates that her initial Victorian poems and her dialect verses have more in common than scholars often assume.

Bilingual Literacy in "Sammy Intres"

With Bennett's personal education history, as well as the role of recitation in West Indian schooling, in mind, let me now return to an examination of the poem. The confusion over the meaning of the word *interests* creates the central humorous conflict in "Sammy Intres." The speaker decides to try to memorize Longfellow's poem "Excelsior" because her son's teacher tells her that she should be more concerned with her son's interests. The mother assumes that Sammy is interested in the Longfellow poem because he "learn it off by heart," without realizing that he would have been assigned to memorize the poem in school.[56] The teacher complains that Sammy failed to memorize the poem to pass his exams. Yet Sammy may have actively resisted learning the poem because it did not relate to his interests, just as Langston Hughes did as a child when he was forced to recite poetry at church. By using the vernacular version of the word *intres,* Bennett stresses that what one is taught in most Jamaican schools reflects the interests of the British ruling power and the local elites, rather than the child's personal interests. This distinction highlights the alienating effects of education on the mother–child relationship.

Through Sammy's exam failure, Bennett also critiques the emphasis on rote learning and standardized testing in Jamaican schools, which persists to this day. As Mark Figueroa writes in his report for the Commonwealth Education Partnership in 2007, "In the Caribbean, our students are required to be far too passive; they are trained to be risk averse and are forced to engage in endless rote learning in a school system that is oriented more towards passing exams than learning and developing life skills."[57] He expresses concern that the Caribbean Secondary Education Certificate (CSEC) exam restricts pedagogy and encourages teachers to teach for the test. To gain entrance into secondary school, students must also complete an exam. In the colonial era, this gatekeeping exam prevented many poor children from attending secondary school because they were unprepared to pass an exam based on foreign "interests" that necessitated fluency in British English. Bennett implies that Sammy may be on this trajectory due to his inability (or refusal) to recite "Excelsior." Shondel Nero argues that standardized testing, as one of the main holdovers from the colonial system, prevents the development of innovative approaches to Creole in the classroom and perpetuates the prestige of "Standard English." As she describes, "poor children from Jamaican Creole (JC)-speaking backgrounds are disproportionately tracked into overcrowded, low-resourced, underperforming primary schools, which means they are less well-prepared for, and perform poorly on, standardized tests that lead to admission into traditional academic high schools."[58] Bennett never directly identifies what type of school Sammy attends or his age; however, his mother's social class, indicated by her Creole speech, and Sammy's poor performance on his exam imply that he likely attended an underperforming primary school.

Through Sammy's mother, Bennett critiques rote learning and anticipates a more dialogic approach to literacy that draws on Creole practices. Even though the foreign form, content, and style seem to make "Excelsior" unsuitable for an expression of the mother's interests, she manages to successfully revise it to suit her needs in her conversation with her friend Miss Della. The lack of a possessive in the title questions whether a young student in a colonial school can have agency over his own interests.[59] The word *intres* is invoked doubly to signify what one likes or prefers as well as what is in one's best interests. Colonial mimicry makes it difficult for a student to determine what's in his best interests, often making it appear as though acting like a British person is the best strategy for success. Bennett questions who has the agency to decide what is in a child's best interests through the conflict between the mother and the teacher. This encapsulates a broader critique of colonial rule as meddling in the interests of others. Bennett also makes fun of the teacher's reprimand to the mother that she should be more concerned with her son's interests. Even though the mother misunderstands what the teacher means by interests, her conversation with her friend illustrates her concern for her son. Through the deliberate misinterpretation of interests, Bennett subtly resists the colonial myth that it is neglectful working-class mothers who are responsible for underachieving youth in Jamaica, rather than a flawed education system.[60]

The mother relays her decision to memorize the poem to her friend Miss Della, who has just dropped by her house and is "jus in time fi hear" her recite the poem. The speaker explains, "So me write it out fi study it – / Me jus benna go start" (7). Bennett adds this detail about the mother's learning process to emphasize that she can read and write. The mother tells Miss Della, "Me was talkin to Sam teacher / Todder day right at dis door" (7). The doorway setting represents the boundary between public and private space. Sammy's mother stands on guard at her door trying to prevent colonial knowledge and authority, figured by Longfellow's poem and her son's schooling more generally, from entering her domestic space under any terms but her own.

The woman speaker's appropriation of the Longfellow poem dramatizes the intertextual conversation between Bennett and Longfellow. While the mother seems unable to grasp Longfellow's poem, Bennett uses the mother's voice to deliver a gendered critique of "Excelsior" as a blueprint for "schooled literacy." As the previous two chapters have illustrated, performance poets have had to reckon with Longfellow's legacy of popular verse, often more so than with high modernism.[61] Belinda Edmondson notes that, unlike many Caribbean writers, Bennett avoids referencing the big hitters of the British canon, such as Wordsworth, Shakespeare, and Milton, and instead cites Victorian verses that circulated throughout the colonies through recitation.[62] These more renowned authors would have been common in the curricula at elite secondary schools, but less so in the primary schools where students would have learned nursery rhymes and popular Victorian verse.

By invoking Longfellow, Bennett playfully draws a distinction between her experimental poetry pedagogy and the overt moral didacticism of schoolroom poetry, like his. "Excelsior" exemplifies the type of poetry used for traditional elocution lessons, which Bennett critiques. It promotes the "civilizing mission" of the English language through liberal individualism and the belief in great men who must aspire to achievement through cultural pursuits. As Angela Sorby argues, "Excelsior" epitomizes the message of Longfellow's poetics, which encourages readers "to perform (and perhaps to negotiate) their roles as middle-class strivers."[63] The poem lays bare the ideological underpinnings of literacy practices in Western society and how liberalism constructs reading as an individualistic pursuit. "Excelsior" depicts a boy striving for cultural elevation, symbolized by his literal attempt to climb a snowy Alpine mountain, and his gender also reinforces reading and education as masculine. Bennett's recontextualization of this metaphor in the tropical climate of Jamaica draws attention to how difficult it is for a young child to successfully mimic this model of cultural ascent.[64] By prioritizing a woman's voice in this poem, Bennett reveals how Jamaican girls have even less access than boys to this model.

The title "Excelsior" also points to Latin language learning as a way to achieve success, thus upholding a European hierarchy of languages that effaces Creole – which, as Carolyn Cooper stresses, is associated with the feminine in Jamaican culture.[65]

Bennett's focus on Longfellow also differs from other Caribbean writers, such as Kincaid and M. NourbeSe Philip, who have focused on Wordsworth and his daffodils to critique colonial recitation. By selecting a US author, Bennett raises the issue of who is allowed to claim ownership of European culture in the Americas. While Longfellow sought to cultivate a unique American poetics rooted in the US environment, he was obsessed with the imitation of European poetic forms and with cultural appropriation. Unlike many of his famous poems, "Excelsior" is one of his more resoundingly Eurocentric texts in both form and content.[66] In an uncanny doubling, Bennett's own (often conflictive) merging of Creole rhythms with the English ballad form parallels this central conflict in Longfellow's poetics. Bennett has also been critiqued for relying too much on European models for her dialect poetry. For example, Brathwaite argues that "the tyranny of pentametre" can still be heard in her verse.[67] Yet the clash between vernacular speech rhythms and the English ballad form engage the colonial tensions of her historical moment and play a key role in the literacy politics of her poetics. Bennett intentionally stages the collision of cultures to draw attention to the disjunction between them, and to the effects of colonial rule on everyday life. The confusion over being in control of one's interests can also be read as Bennett's post-colonial critique of Longfellow, who fails to depict his own culture and environment in this particular poem. He becomes the failed "mimic man," unable to imitate a European voice. By making a mockery of Longfellow's Eurocentric representation of cultural ascent, Bennett undermines his privilege, as an Anglo-American man, to claim a direct link to European modernity in the Americas, a privilege Bennett, as an Afro-Jamaican woman, was not afforded.

The intertextuality of "Sammy Intres" also demonstrates how, for Bennett, mimicry became a compositional strategy as well as a performance technique. Playing on the theme of "interests," the woman speaker continues her dialogue with Miss Della by recombining and revising lines from Longfellow's poem to suit her own interests as she talks about her child's progress in school. Below, quatrains four through seven from the poem by Bennett appear on the left, and the first four quatrains from Longfellow's poem appear on the right:

De shades of night was fallin fast
As o'er – yuh hear me cross?
Sam teck exam an not even –
An Alpine village pass.

A youth who bore mid snow an ice
– Not even one wud bout –
A banner wid de strange device –
When results gwine come out.

Excelsior! His brow was sad –
Ef him pass – his eye beneath –
Teacher seh nex year him wi teck –
A falcon from its sheat!

Den ow is fi-yuh lickle gal?
Me hear har – clarion rung –
Me hear har singing wid – de accent
Of dat unknown tongue.
(7)

The shades of night were falling fast,
As through an Alpine village passed
A youth, who bore, 'mid snow and ice,
A banner with the strange device,
Excelsior!

His brow was sad; his eye beneath,
Flashed like a falchion from its sheath,
And like a silver clarion rung
The accents of that unknown tongue,
Excelsior!

In happy homes he saw the light
Of household fires gleam warm and bright;
Above, the spectral glaciers shone,
And from his lips escaped a groan,
Excelsior!

"Try not the Pass!" the old man said;
"Dark lowers the tempest overhead,
The roaring torrent is deep and wide!"
And loud that clarion voice replied,
Excelsior![68]

Bennett's subversive mimicry depends on mockery. She avoids mimicking "Excelsior" in a line-by-line fashion, instead choosing to recombine and play with the ordering of Longfellow's lines. In the reconfigured lines, the mother's concerns for her son are reflected in her recitation. Moreover, even though Bennett includes much of the language and many of the themes from the original poem, the mother's interests (which are primarily expressed through her speech rhythms) overtake Longfellow's text. Bennett playfully draws attention to the semantic doubleness of language by punning on words in the original poem, such as the mother's use of the word *pass*. Sammy's mother replaces the alien Alpine mountain pass in "Excelsior" with the more local and maternal concern about whether her son will pass his school examinations. As previously mentioned, Sammy may have had to recite "Excelsior" to gain that pass, making his mother's pun on Longfellow's "Alpine pass" as a way to describe Sammy's academic achievement all the more salient. Bennett disrupts the driving rhythm of Longfellow's poem by avoiding the declamatory "Excelsior!" at the end of each quatrain.

"Sammy Intres" and "Excelsior" share a similar structure, with some important variations. Both poems are nine quatrains long. However, Bennett replaces Longfellow's couplets with the abcb rhyme scheme of the ballad stanza. Robson argues that the rhymed quatrain ballad stanza was a popular form for poems intended for recitation because the succinct structure helps make poems easy to memorize:

> Usually organized as one divided sentence, or two sentences with a natural pivot or place for breath, the quatrain is long enough to paint a discrete scene; to express a contained thought; to feature dialogue in the form of question and response; or to describe a narrative movement; but not long enough to permit much complicated elaboration. And while rhymed couplets close in upon themselves and offer no convenient bridge to the succeeding lines, an alternate rhyming scheme helps lead us forward.[69]

While Longfellow's poem uses rhyming couplets punctuated at the end of every quatrain by the declarative "Excelsior!" Bennett departs from Longfellow's rhyme scheme by having only the second and fourth lines of each quatrain rhyme. As Katherine Verhagen Rodis points out, "disturbed rhythm" becomes "one of Bennett's (frequent) manifestations of vernacular politics."[70] Her alternating rhyme scheme propels the dynamic interactions in the poem. As she traverses through Longfellow's original poem, she recontextualizes and rewrites it.

Sammy's mother makes it clear in her discussion of her son's weak progress in school that he is not interested in striving for "excelsior" like the young boy in Longfellow's poem, although she still hopes that her son will pass his exams. The mother gives up on learning the poem after she misses a line: "Excelsior! Tap, me lef out / One whole line, yuh know!" (7). Again, Bennett makes fun of the original poem; the speaker invokes "excelsior" as an expletive, rather than as a goal to strive for. She also deflates the intensity of Longfellow's melodramatic tail rhyme by repositioning "excelsior" at the beginning of her stanza, giving the pause created by the stanza break more emphasis. The gaps between the lines that rhyme, as well as the elongated stanza break, create space for the rhythms of Creole to take over in her poem.

After giving up on memorizing it, the mother tears it up and throws it out the door: "Me dah go tear i up, Missis, / An fling i outa door!" Then she asks her friend to share with her all the gossip from her "yard":

> Pop tory gimme, Della – all
> De labrish from yuh yard.
> Me cyaan study pickney intres
> Ef a so it a go hard.[71]
> (8)

Throwing the poem out of her door represents the eviction of colonial knowledge and authority from her domestic space. Bennett makes fun of the ridiculous – and fatal – perseverance portrayed in Longfellow's poem. The speaker and her son resist striving for the "excelsior" of triumphal individualism that Longfellow depicts. By ending with the mother pressing her friend to share gossip, Bennett implies that the dialogue continues beyond the space of the poem. While both poems represent subjects who fail to accomplish their goals – the boy dies trying to climb the mountain and Sammy's mother fails to successfully memorize "Excelsior" – Sammy's mother perseveres in her "labrish." The emphasis on women's gossip presents communal exchange as an alternate form of achievement as compared to an individual work ethic.[72]

In his journey up the mountain, the young boy in "Excelsior" resists the following temptations: "household fires" that "gleam warm and bright," the advice of an old man and a peasant, and the invitation of a "maiden" for him to "rest / thy weary head upon this breast."[73] When Bennett's woman speaker tears up "Excelsior" and throws it out the door, she reverses what the boy in Longfellow's poem refuses: the domestic space, oral culture, local knowledge, and feminine comfort. Bennett privileges the local feminine knowledge of gossip over the foreign masculine knowledge conveyed in "Excelsior." Her attack on liberal individualism is aimed at both the British ruling power and the Jamaican middle class, who often upheld and applied such values to the struggle for Independence. The mother resists the internationalization of the poem by performing it on her own terms, making it into a form to use for her own labrish and then throwing it out the door. Bennett demonstrates in "Sammy Intres" how performative reading can increase a reader's agency, which is instructive in terms of how to deal with the operations of colonial power. While one cannot completely resist internalizing colonial power structures, Bennett's speaker demonstrates that within the framework of reading, performance provides a mode to deflect or transform its force.

Through Sammy's mother, Bennett also shows how schoolroom recitation will remain complicit with its colonial history unless children are encouraged to read dialectically and bring their own "interests" to their performances and textual interpretations. The conflict of "interests" in the poem, created by the power dynamics of colonial rule, also questions how much a reader, under any circumstances, can bring her own interests to a text through the process of interpretation. "Sammy Intres," with its deliberate misreadings through puns and embellishment, gives Bennett's readers permission to bring their own interests and interpretations to her poems. Similar to Freire's "problem-posing model," Bennett advocates for a student-centred approach to learning based on dialogue.[74] The poem depicts interactions between the woman speaker and her friend Miss Della, and between the speaker and Longfellow's "Excelsior." These interactions also indirectly gesture to interactions between the mother and her son as well as the mother and the teacher. The poem's *mise en abîme* structure, which stages an animated scene where the speaker engages in reading and interpreting Longfellow's poem through performance, becomes a mirror for a reader's own engagement with Bennett's poem, especially if a reader chooses to recite the poem aloud. All of these various exchanges, both textual and interpersonal, foreground the process of reading as an interaction between text and reader.

Bennett represents reading a poetic text as far more than memorized reiteration; it is instead a creative act, embodied, performative, and produced through a series of interactions that constitute a liberating form of literacy. A traditional understanding of poetry reading as memorization and recitation suggests that reading is fundamentally imitative and devoid of meaning production. However, by having the woman speaker reinvent Longfellow's lines for her own purposes, Bennett proposes that a reader does not merely ventriloquize the author without variation but rather has agency to bring her own concerns or interests to her interpretation. In doing so, she provides readers with an opportunity to disrupt the learning of literacy "with the transmission and mastery of a unitary Western tradition based on the virtues of hard work."[75]

The traditional classroom approach to poetry memorization often combines oral memory with literacy skills, and relies on repetition. As the speaker in "Sammy Intres" demonstrates, despite a poem's final delivery in oral form, in the classroom a teacher would often make one "write it out fi study it" to help with the memorization process (7). Sorby explains the power of these classroom rituals:

> Readers in schools were taught to read poems in specific ways … but they were also invited to interpret poems through acts of repetition. This resulted in an experience of poetry that was highly institutional, grounded in specific incorporated social bodies, but also deeply internalized, grounded in individual bodies and in readers' earliest memories of language-learning.[76]

The corporeal experience of repetition heightens the tension between indoctrination and creativity in the act of reading. Memorizing a poem by writing it out encourages a highly analytic relationship to the text because it prompts one to dissect every word, while the process of internalization also encourages an embodied and intimate relationship to it. Traditionally in elocution pedagogies, this learning process aims to unify one's written language with the way one speaks, to make "dat unknown tongue" conform to dominant language norms. However, Bennett's dramatization of memorization and recitation in "Sammy Intres" enacts the opposite. In the translation of "Excelsior," she draws attention to the disjunction between Creole and British English and makes English into the "foreign tongue," rather than Latin in the original "Excelsior." As in her poem "Bans a Killin," Bennett promotes a dynamic interaction between Creole pronunciation and the written text. The speaker's creolization of the Longfellow poem makes the written text conform to her accent. This functions as a demonstration of how readers can use their own "tongues" to animate the written page. Bennett invites readers to bring their oral embodied relationship to language into their textual relationship and to inflect their reading with the rhythms of their own accents. She suggests a mode of reading where one rewrites the poem according to one's local patois and sense of transcribing it. Rather than use recitation to standardize speech, Bennett reappropriates poetry recitation from elocution pedagogies to encourage new bilingual literacies.

Gender and Subversive Mimicry

One might be inclined to interpret the speaker's embrace of "labrish from yuh yard" at the conclusion of the poem as a rejection of literacy in favour of orality; however, this simplifies her complex negotiation of oral and literate practices and reinscribes the association of femininity with orality and masculinity with literacy that Bennett aims to break down. Education scholars Joanna C. Street and Brian V. Street explain how women's literacy practices are often discounted:

> The uses of literacy by women; its association with informal, nonreligious, and nonbureaucratic practices; its affective and expressive functions; and the incorporation of oral conventions into written usage – all are features of literacy practice that have tended to be marginalized or destroyed by modern, Western literacy with its emphasis on formal, male, and schooled aspects of communication.[77]

Studying different colonized societies, they illustrate how when Western literacy gets introduced it gets "added to the communicative repertoire that already exists in the receiving societies" and people "adapt and amend it to local meanings, concepts of identity, and epistemologies."[78] Yet often these alternative practices remain invisible or are perceived as inferior literacies when measured against "the standard of schooled literacy."[79] To interpret the mother's half-hearted recitation of Longfellow's poem as a sign of her inferior literacy is to miss Bennett's gendered critique of colonial mimicry.

The mother clearly knows how to read, as evidenced by the fact that she writes in the poem, but the foreignness of Longfellow's language and the irrelevance of "Excelsior's" themes in Jamaica make the poem hard for her to memorize. By drawing attention to this unfair playing field, Bennett exposes how the hidden curriculum of colonial poetry recitation sets up students, especially girls and those at underfunded all-age primary schools, to imperfectly master a British voice. As Homi K. Bhabha emphasizes, for colonial mimicry to consolidate imperial power the mimic needs to reveal his difference. A reciter's small pronunciation deviations make him appear "*almost the same but not quite,*" yet to reject the performance assignment altogether, like the speaker (and perhaps her son), asserts cultural difference to threaten colonial authority.[80] While Bhabha focuses on the failure of the colonized subject to successfully mimic colonial discourse, in this particular poem Bennett makes an open mockery of imitation; she critiques the text itself rather than the failed mimic. Through Sammy's mother, Bennett capitalizes on what Bhabha describes as "the *menace* of mimicry ... which in disclosing the ambivalence of colonial discourse also disrupts its authority."[81] As a recitation text, "Sammy Intres" provides readers with a loose script to act out the disruptive ambivalence of mimicry.

In Ramazani's insightful analysis of "Sammy Intres," he draws attention to how Bennett's subversive mimicry relies on mockery, making a distinction between "earnest [colonial] mimicry" and "ironic post-colonial mimicry."[82] He notes that many of Bennett's speakers often use "gossip- or labrish-based knowledge, produced and exchanged in the female realm of the Jamaican yard" to unmask the male colonial mimic, citing as an example Mas Charlie, the *Gleaner* reader in "Bans a Killin," who objects to Bennett's dialect verse.[83] When an audience laughs at a recitation of "Bans a Killin," they affirm Mas Charlie as a misguided fool who cannot see what is good for his own country. Yet the mother in "Sammy Intres," rather than unmask another mimic, takes on the task of mimicry herself, and the comedy derives in part from her exaggerated failure as a mimic. As Ramazani puts it, she "recites rhymes either that she cannot grasp or that accidently comment upon her gossip in ways that escape her."[84] However, he points out that she resists becoming a colonial victim, because she ultimately mocks the colonial establishment that upholds this type of poetry as superior to Jamaican folk culture. I would also add here that Bennett's approach to unmasking colonial mimicry in "Sammy Intres" reveals how women often excel at subversive mimicry in colonial settings.

The gendered language used in post-colonial scholarship on mimicry – Naipaul's phrase "mimic men" and Bhabha's chapter "Of Mimicry and Man" in *The Location of Culture* – is not an accident. The colonial power structure typically only rewards boys for becoming "mimic men" by giving them positions as bureaucrats or low-level colonial officers in the local elite. Bennett suggests that women – because they rarely achieve the marginal benefits of colonial mimicry – are less beholden to its power and therefore more willing to disrupt its authority.

Like Pauline Johnson, Bennett dressed in costume for her performances to accentuate her gendered critique of colonial mimicry (see figure 4). Through her costumed performances, Bennett reversed the stereotypes of Jamaican working-class women as illiterate and revealed the damaging effects of this malignant fiction on Jamaican collectivity.[85] Her mother designed Bennett's signature outfit in the 1930s based on the traditional Jamaican dress of a peasant woman, replete with a head-tie and a quadrille dress made out of colourful red plaid madras cotton. Many believe that this pattern originated from a blending of brightly coloured African kente cloth and Scottish tartan.[86] The quadrille dress, named after the European dance form that was reinvented in the Caribbean, is now recognized as the national costume. Its syncretic origins illustrate the creolization of Jamaican identity. Bennett's Miss Lou persona

4. Miss Lou wearing her signature performance outfit (The William Ready Division of Archives and Research Collections, McMaster University Library. Permission: The Louise Bennett Coverley Estate)

5. Miss Lou performing in front of a live studio audience on *Ring Ding* (The William Ready Division of Archives and Research Collections, McMaster University Library. Permission: The Louise Bennett Coverley Estate)

became inseparable from her stylized image based on this outfit. As she recited her poems on topical themes in the 1940s, her nineteenth-century costume blurred the colonial past with the present. More importantly, by dressing in costume for her performances, Bennett drew her audience's attention to her own mimicry – she made it clear that she was imitating a character, rather than playing herself. Yet her performances had nothing to do with imperial imperatives. Rather than imitate the standard British voice, she imitated working-class black women's voices in her poems. In the colonial version, mimicry reinforces the colonized subject's inferiority, yet Bennett's imitation celebrated cultural difference. She asserted mimicry as a creative force, integral to creolization, rather than as a derivative weakness.

Bennett's playful approach to mimicry provides a model for her readers to imitate in their own recitation of her poems. Compared to Johnson's white settler audiences in Canada, Bennett's post-Independence Jamaican audience was much more receptive to the pedagogy of her performances (except, of course, for the Mas Charlies out there). Leading by example, Bennett invited her audience to enjoy, embody, and embellish the dismissed voice of another. Watching Bennett perform live on stage or on television underscored recitation (and by extension, reading) as an explicit act of ventriloquy.

Othermothering in Bennett's Media Projects

Bennett's media projects for the Jamaica Broadcasting Corporation in the 1970s – her children's television show *Ring Ding*, and her radio program *Miss Lou's Views* – further illuminate the centrality of education in her performance poetics, and the pedagogical role she envisioned for her labrish poetics to teach new forms of reading and interpretation. Through her emphasis on children, she used her art to educate new readers, who themselves could foster a more inclusive public sphere as they grew up. Her work's appeal to children, its use of Creole, and its representation of working-class women all, unfortunately, indicate why it hasn't been taken "seriously" by critics.[87]

Bennett promotes a form of activism similar to what Patricia Hill Collins, in an African American context, calls "othermothering": "By seeing the larger *community* as responsible for children and by giving othermothers and other nonparents 'rights' in child rearing, those African-Americans who endorse these values challenge prevailing capitalist property relations." Collins also notes that "the co-operative nature of child-care arrangements among bloodmothers and othermothers" is common in the Caribbean and other black diasporic societies.[88] Bennett hints at such a cooperative approach in "Sammy Intres" when Sammy's mother and her friend Miss Della talk about their children, even though their conversation is relayed through Longfellow's poem.

Many of Bennett's female personas talk about children, either their own or those of their friends or relatives. Feminist scholarship has established the link between Bennett's women speakers and her critique of patriarchal power; however, her emphasis on childrearing has received less attention.[89] Her women characters' labrish about children promotes an ethic of maternal care that the community shares. Through her emphasis on mothers and othermothers, she demonstrates how learning how to read happens not just within formal schooling but also in the yard. Bennett describes this in one of her radio monologues: "An pickney welfare is a great future heritage to we all, for if we doan look after pickney now, den naw gwine got nobody fi look after we an look after Jamaica an look after we worl affairs later on, a oh!"[90] In addition to advocating for this approach in her career, she took on this responsibility in her personal life. Although she was unable to have her own children due to a hysterectomy in her early twenties, she fostered many children in her home in Gordon Town, and she was also a stepmother to her husband's son, Fabian, from his previous marriage. As Morris describes it, "For nearly three decades, their household absorbed a steady stream of other people's children whom they brought up with Fabian, some staying a few months or a few years, and some longer."[91] Her approach to othermothering as a form of community education fully developed in her children's television show *Ring Ding*. As a former participant on *Ring Ding* recalled, "You had your mother, and then you had Miss Lou. And sometimes the two were interchangeable."[92]

Ring Ding started as a spin-off of *Sesame Street*.[93] Bennett was invited to do short segments to introduce *Sesame Street* to Jamaican children, and her introductions were so popular that the Jamaica Broadcasting Corporation asked her to do her own television show, which aired from 1970 to 1982.[94] While there is no media archive of the show because the JBC had few resources, and therefore recorded over the tapes with other shows, *Ring Ding* should be recognized for its contribution to the development of children's educational television in the 1970s, particularly for its promotion of a decolonized literacy.[95] As the creative director and host of the show, Bennett encouraged children to value their African-descended oral culture and compelled those learning to read to bring their embodied knowledge of Creole into their language.

The impact of *Ring Ding* on children growing up in Jamaica in the second half of the twentieth century can be seen in the huge response from her fans from across the Jamaican diaspora to her death in 2006. Because the recordings were not archived, people's memories of the show offer one of the few resources that we have to consider its role in Bennett's education politics.[96] In the following letter to the editor in the *Jamaica Gleaner*, reader Audrey McLaren responds to Bennett's death by writing about the influence *Ring Ding* had on her as child:

> Miss Lou has been my mentor from the days of *Ring Ding*. I was not fortunate enough to be among the many children who joined her each Saturday

> morning for what I call a session of cultural awareness. Apart from the fact that my parents were Seventh-day Adventists, my mother's beliefs were Eurocentric, hence she had very little tolerance for patois and anything of African ethnicity. This is where my ingenuity came in. In order to be an active participant of this renaissance that was taking place in Jamaica, I faked illness numerous Saturday mornings in order to be excused from church. The television would then become my "chapel" until *Ring Ding* ended. After that, I would spend some time praying that when my mother returned from church, she did not touch the top of the television set – it was hot! It was from these Saturday morning sessions with the television set that I learnt about my cultural heritage and started to develop an appreciation for my Afro-Caribbean heritage. It was from Miss Lou that I learnt not only to read and write patois, but that respect is due to a language that evolved out of our blood, sweat, tears, longings, struggles, and most important, out of our need to be a recognized people with dreams, aspirations and roots ... Without her, I would not be the positive, self-confident person I am. Although she is no longer here in the flesh, she has left us such a great legacy, that like Paul Bogle and Marcus Garvey, will empower us forever.[97]

McLaren is now a teacher, poet, and education activist who lives in Ontario. Her editorial comments indicate that Bennett had a formative influence on both her education activism and her poetry. Her poetry publications, *I am the Djembe* and *Bareface Pickney*, pay tribute to Bennett's legacy of using Creole to explore and foster children's consciousness. She is one of the founding members of the Jeffrey Town Education Association, a non-profit group in Toronto that rebuilt the elementary school in Jeffrey Town, Jamaica. McLaren describes how *Ring Ding* taught her many things, including how to "read and write patois." Her comments indicate that even within the visual/oral medium of television, Bennett promoted children's reading habits. McLaren's description of how she had to actively pursue her Creole education behind her mother's back also exhibits the kind of student-directed learning that Bennett promoted. McLaren suggests that having the opportunity to learn how to read in her native language made her a more self-confident person.

Bennett's radio program *Miss Lou's Views*, broadcast by Radio Jamaica (run by the JBC), is another example of how she turned to media to educate her audience. On the air between one and three times a week, from 1966 to 1982, Bennett would express her views on Jamaican culture and society by invoking her invented persona of Aunty Roachy. Speaking in Creole, Bennett's voice would echo across the airwaves to challenge British English as the dominant language for media communication on radio and television in Jamaica. Despite the cultural movement to accept Creole as a symbol of national identity, there were still many people who challenged the use of the language in public life and who rejected Bennett's use of Creole on the radio. In fact, the JBC did not permit her to converse in Creole on *Ring Ding* unless she was singing folk songs or reciting poems.[98] As one writer wrote in the Jamaican newspaper the *Star* in December 1971, "Admittedly … the greater part of our population uses the dialect but that should not be good grounds for our radio stations to stuff so much raw 'Patois English' into our ears daily. Take for example *Miss Lou's Views* – such a program should be scrapped as it tends to perpetuate ignorance in Jamaicans."[99] The reviewer's fear that Bennett's use of the oral language would "perpetuate ignorance" is an example of the widespread rejection of her educational aims.

Her monologues both critiqued and instructed Jamaican society. As in her poems, the didactic tone of her moral lessons wielded authority not through a Longfellow type of driving exclamation but through humour and playfulness. She delivered the wisdom of her invented persona Aunty Roachy, whom she would call on in her broadcast as a source of authority. Bennett's characterization of her as an aunt, rather than as a mother, exemplifies her promotion of "othermothering." Through this radio persona, Bennett expanded on her use of female personas as a pedagogical tactic in her poetics. Similar to Langston Hughes's invented persona of Jesse B. Semple, who expressed his views on African American society once a week in his *Chicago Defender* newspaper column, Aunty Roachy functioned as a black vernacular intellectual.[100] However, Bennett's Aunty Roachy intervened in these male-dominated discourses to claim power for women's authority in Caribbean culture. Carol B. Duncan proposes that Bennett "makes subversive use of the mammy stereotype" in her portrayal of Aunty Roachy as a community mother figure who "represents an older time and the wisdom of elders in Miss Lou's pronouncements."[101]

In Bennett's radio monologue "The School's Challenge," broadcast in October 1976, she relays Aunty Roachy's disapproval of the presentation of Jamaican culture in exclusively oral terms in schools. Through her description of Aunty Roachy's response to an episode of the popular quiz show for children "The School's Challenge," she urges schools to include more Jamaican literature in their curricula. Aunty Roachy expresses pleasure that a child could answer questions about both Jamaican and English proverbs. However, "Auny Roachy shivel up wid shame" when a student fails to answer the examiner's question about who wrote the book *New Day*.[102] Vic Reid's novel *New Day* is a contemporary classic story of Jamaican resistance to colonial rule. Aunty Roachy questions why children do not read more Jamaican literature in school:

> An Aunty Roachy holler, "Dem haffi know, we haffi learn dem! Jamaica pickney of all rank and pedigree haffi start learn bout Vic Reid an Claude McKay an Clare McFarlane an Roger Mais, an dinky an ring ding an kumina an all we Jamaica proverbs an riddle-dem, an all dem Jamaica heritage, same like how dem know bout de works of Shakespeare and Hitler and all dem foreign smaddy-deh, a oh!"[103]

Bennett groups together oral and literate forms of Jamaican culture to challenge a hierarchal separation between them. She emphasizes authors like McKay and Reid to insist on a literary culture made in the Jamaican language. While children's knowledge of Jamaican oral culture has been promoted in post-colonial Jamaica, she draws attention to how they lack knowledge about Jamaican literature. For her, this perpetuates the assumption that Jamaican culture is predominantly oral in nature, and distinct from a Western literary tradition. She humorously groups Hitler and Shakespeare as "foreign smaddy-deh" to imply a similarity between British colonialism and European fascism. By suggesting that Hitler and Shakespeare are in the same category, she aligns political and cultural domination to insist on the violence of cultural control. Shakespeare represents precisely the kind of colonial literary education that Bennett rejects in her poetry.

The Aunty Roachy persona frees Bennett to express more radical views than if she were to present them as her own. However, under the title *Miss Lou's Views*, the sentiments, ideas, and perspectives are simultaneously identified as Bennett's own, even when she attributes them to Aunty Roachy.[104] Aunty Roachy functions like an alter ego or a split subjectivity. Bennett begins most monologues with the command "Listen, no!" to get the audience's attention and then acknowledges that she is reciting what her Aunty Roachy told her using the line, "My Aunty Roachy seh dat …" before she presents the subject of her satirical commentary. This citational structure resembles that of her poems, which feature one woman reporting on the labrish of another woman.

By having one woman's voice call on the authority of another, she presents a shared economy of feminine knowledge, quite different from the model of colonial recitation, which calls on the authority of European authors. Her use of one voice speaking through another, both in her poems and in her radio show, demonstrates the influence of poetry recitation on Bennett's poetics. Through performance, she makes reading into an act of mimicry. Whereas in colonial mimicry one often feels subjected to "the interests" of another when forced to learn a poem, Bennett's personas intentionally align their voices with the voices of other women to produce communal knowledge.

Brathwaite insists that "reading is an isolated, individualistic expression. The oral tradition on the other hand demands not only the griot but the audience to complete the community."[105] It is strange that, as a theorist of cultural intermixture, he addresses oral and literate modes in such discrete terms. By using oral performance dynamics, Bennett critiques the Western ideology of "schooled literacy" and engenders reading as a form of social expression. Poetic personas in Bennett's texts do not merely serve as documentary social realism but instead become scripts of social voice for their readers to embody and perform. Through her poetry and her media projects, she underscores how communities produce meaning and, by extension, knowledge. She challenges the ideology of liberal individualism and calls for a more communal and dialogic approach to education.

Miss Lou Pedagogy Today

For the most part, Bennett advanced her Miss Lou pedagogy outside of institutions. However, I want to end this chapter in the contemporary classroom because ultimately Bennett aimed to decolonize the Jamaican education system. While Jamaican Creole is widely recognized in society today – it can be heard on the radio and even in parliament – the role it should play in the classroom is still controversial.[106] Although Bennett depicts a very different 1940s colonial world in "Sammy Intres," her emphasis on Creole as a vehicle for learning (rather than as a symbol of identity) remains relevant to contemporary debates about Creole use in education. Bennett first published "Sammy Intres" at a time when illiteracy, perpetuated by the socially stratified education system, began to be recognized as a serious societal problem in Jamaica. In 1943, less than 1 per cent of Afro-Jamaicans were admitted to secondary school. For the mixed-race population, the attendance rate was marginally better at 9 per cent.[107] When Jamaica gained official self-government in 1944, improving education became a primary focus, and many changes have been made to raise literacy rates since Independence in 1962. In 1974, the People's National Party government created the National Jamaica Literacy Board, which established adult literacy programs and targeted reading curricula in schools. While great strides have been made, the underachievement of Creole speakers in Jamaican schools continues to be a problem. A 1983 UNESCO report urged educators in Jamaica to address why almost 50 per cent of twelve-year-old students entering secondary education were not literate.[108] In their 1988 study of Caribbean textbooks, King and Morrissey establish how colonial values persist in anglophone Caribbean curricula.[109] Even more alarming is Lena Mccourtie's analysis of the Annual Reports of "Her Majesty's Inspectors" for colonial schools in the late nineteenth century. She reveals how Creole speakers in all-age primary schools in the 1890s and the 1990s faced similar obstacles – teachers were untrained in Creole linguistics and students lacked adequate support.[110] In 2008, the illiteracy rate in Jamaica was 20.1 per cent.[111] One of the main obstacles has been the tendency to treat Creole as a liability rather than as a potential asset in literacy acquisition.

Linguists have proved that for pupils to learn the dominant version of a language they must draw on their vernacular understanding. This approach is aptly characterized as "transitional bilingualism." Many education scholars in Jamaica have advocated for such an approach. For example, in her manual *From Jamaican Creole to Standard English: A Handbook for Teachers* (2003), Velma Pollard proposes that elementary school teachers develop students' English fluency by adapting their intuitive knowledge of Creole grammar to English structures. However, creating policies and implementing this approach has proved difficult in Jamaican schools.[112] Nero notes that standard language ideology has created a huge disconnect between linguistic theory and educational practice.[113] In 2001, the government drafted a national language education policy to help address illiteracy; however, the policy was never accepted in parliament because it characterized Jamaica as a bilingual society and advocated for schools to adopt a transitional bilingualism approach.[114] As Bennett recognized in an interview in 1975, "Everybody is bilingual – even those who will not admit they are."[115]

While transitional bilingualism continues to be contested in Jamaican education, reciting Bennett's poetry gives students some access to it. Advocates of this approach, such as Beverley Bryan, stress that students must first be taught to recognize the two languages as separate linguistic systems; however, since Creole exists on a continuum with Standard Jamaican English, students often have difficulty distinguishing between them. Bryan recommends that teachers offer students opportunities to "role play as one of the most useful ways of contrasting the two languages" in the early grades.[116] Bennett's poems, which often deliberately juxtapose the two systems for comedic effect, give students the chance to experiment with different types of Creole voices. At the beginning of this chapter, I questioned why reciting Bennett's verse is so popular in Jamaica. Despite the lack of official implementation in schools, Bennett's poetry provides students with an opportunity to learn literacy through transitional bilingualism. However, in "Sammy Intres" Bennett pushes this pedagogy even further by representing a woman who, rather than translate Creole into "Standard English," engages in the opposite practice and transforms an English text into a Creole grammar. She anticipates the more radical pedagogy of "full bilingualism" advocated by scholars such as Hubert Devonish, the director of the Jamaican Language Unit and Unit for Caribbean Language Research at the University of the West Indies.[117] In the transitional approach, Jamaican Creole acts as a temporary bridge, but learning Standard Jamaican English remains the central goal. Devonish, on the other hand, believes that students should be taught to read and write in both Standard Jamaican English and Jamaican Creole. Rather than view the classroom as a space that reinforces social norms, he and his co-researcher, Karen Carpenter, believe that "the classroom can be used as a catalyst to bring about changes at the societal level."[118]

On Bennett's final visit to Jamaica in 2003, she was an honorary guest at the launch of the Jamaican Language Unit. To celebrate the opening of the unit, Bennett sponsored a primary school literary contest for works written in Jamaican Creole. This contest inaugurated the Jamaican Language Unit's four-year bilingual education project for primary school students, where students were given reading and writing instruction in both Jamaican Creole and Standard Jamaican English in grades one through four. The research findings proved conclusively that students taught in both languages had a higher competence in both as well as in other subjects such as mathematics and science.[119] Unfortunately, Bennett died in 2006, so she did not get to witness the achievements of this program. As a belated response to many of her early critics in the 1940s, who feared that her Creole performance poetry was detrimental to the Jamaican population's literacy, this study provides concrete evidence of the value of Creole reading practices.

The poet Donna (Aza) Weir-Soley suggests that the time has come "to demystify and demythologize" Miss Lou.[120] I hope this chapter has helped to dispel the myth of Bennett as an oral poet and encourage more teachers and scholars to study the educational aspects of her poetics. In terms of the story of this book, she illustrates how recitation's colonial history provides unintended openings for Afro-Jamaican identities to emerge. Her experiences with verse recitation in her community and in her formal schooling encouraged her to make recitation a central part of her poetic practice. She reinvented this colonial mode of reading and merged it with Jamaican oral practices to stage a contiguous overlap of women's voices, jostling for space and for recognition in the wider social body. Her poems represent the involuntary intimacies of colonialism between strange cultures, ideas, objects, bodies, and texts. However, within these crevices of uncomfortable contact, self-conscious mimicry becomes a disruptive force to reject the colonizer's scripts and to create new language ideals.

Chapter Four

Recitation Legacies in Dub and Indigenous Poetics

The poetry of dub poets and I believe the poetry of Indigenous artists have played forward the more iterative to being mostly concerned with being generative, less about copying, being like, imitating, shadowing, and getting approval from media-constructed mainstream society, and are as much a poetics of resistance, revival, renewal, and transformation.

Lillian Allen, "Poetics of Renewal: Indigenous Poetics – Message or Medium?"

What do contemporary dub and Indigenous poets have in common? According to the Toronto-based Afro-Jamaican artist Lillian Allen, they both challenge metanarratives and damaging histories.[1] They often achieve these aims by prioritizing performance. In the epigraph, she also stresses that they are less beholden to colonial mimicry than previous generations were. Their art creates "resistance, revival, renewal, and transformation."[2] In the same essay, she expresses a kinship with the Mohawk-Tuscarora spoken-word artist Janet Marie Rogers's sound-based poetics. Allen's friendship with Rogers began at the Spoken Word Program at the Banff Centre for the Arts in 2009. Allen also wrote a back-cover blurb for Rogers's latest collection, *Peace in Duress* (2014). Her supportive comments reflect the community and mentorship common to small-press publishing. Just below Allen's comments on the back of the book, the Secwepemc poet Garry Gottfriedson, one of Rogers's most important teachers, offers praise as well.[3] By selecting an Afro-Jamaican poet and a First Nations poet, Rogers deviates from the emphasis on Indigenous separatism in Native literary studies.[4] Instead, Allen's advocacy situates her book in a broader *politicized* spoken-word community. In her blurb, Allen highlights Rogers's memory poetics: "For her, memory is a pen, a tool of vindication creating a new literature that breathes with nature and roars when it does ... Rogers's poetry marks the terrain with sounds braided in history and soars like the songs of a politically tuned cosmic map-maker who dares to delve into personal journey." Allen suggests that Rogers's poetry creates a history of the voice similar to her Jamaican dub poetry.

The dub poetry movement, which began in the 1970s in Kingston, Jamaica, and in Toronto and London, England (two cities with large concentrations of Caribbean immigrants), builds directly on Langston Hughes's rhythmic literacy and Miss Lou's Creole pedagogy. In addition to Allen, some of the prominent figures of the movement include Linton Kwesi Johnson (LKJ) and Jean "Binta" Breeze (both based in the United Kingdom); Mutabaruka, Michael Smith, and Oku Onuora (who remained in Jamaica); and Clifton Joseph, Afua Cooper, and d'bi young, members of the Dub Poets Collective in Toronto. According to Allen, "the dub poetry movement in Canada boasts more major practitioners than either Jamaica, Britain, or the U.S. and this, ironically makes dub poetry as essentially Canadian as it is a worldwide black phenomenon."[5] Using Allen as his primary example, Phanuel Antwi notes that Canadian dub poets stress grassroots activism and feminist politics more so than dub poets based in the UK and the Caribbean.[6] In Canada, Indigenous poetics is also a vibrant and diverse field, representing numerous tribal identities. Rogers, along with many other Indigenous authors, claims E. Pauline Johnson as an important inspiration. Allen's and Rogers's friendship demonstrates the creative exchange between these two communities in Canada.

Minor Transnationalism

Despite the watershed of comparative scholarship in literary studies, Christine Kim and Sophie McCall question why Indigenous and diasporic literatures are rarely studied together. Although they recognize that this stems from the emphasis on cultural difference and local histories in both diaspora and Aboriginal studies, they suggest that in the era of globalization "the broader project of decolonization requires multiple kinds of tools and strategies." Since indigeneity and diaspora reveal the limits of national categories, albeit from different perspectives, examining the dialogue between them forces us to transform our conceptual frameworks.[7] Resolving the critical gap between Canadian diasporic and First Nations literature is particularly pressing for performance poetry because, as the example of Allen and Rogers illustrates, these poetry communities are already in conversation with one another. Their practitioners often attend the same spoken-word events, slam competitions, open-mic nights, writing workshops, and political rallies. However, scholars have been unsure how to build on this existing dialogue between practitioners while still being respectful of cultural difference. Part of the difficulty stems from the fact that often our comparative frameworks still uphold a nationalistic approach, even though they are designed to expand upon national categories.

This final chapter represents the culmination of my comparative approach. Rather than focus on a single poet, ethnic group, or nation, I bring together Afro-Jamaican dub poets and First Nations performance poets who were influenced by Johnson, Bennett, and Hughes. By building on their predecessors' reinvention of recitation, these poets develop new strategies to liberate personal and collective memory from external forms of control. The minor transnational approach used here examines shifting constellations and alliances, rather than positing rigid categories and firm boundaries. I borrow the term *minor transnationalism* from Françoise Lionnet and Shu-mei Shih, who define it as "the creative interventions that networks of minoritized cultures produce within and across national boundaries."[8] In addition to focusing on creative exchanges in the present, such as the friendship between Allen and Rogers, this chapter excavates networks of reinvention that are embedded in texts, performance practices, and poetry movements. Rather than use the post-colonial model of margin-centre, I trace a network of overlapping counter-publics that do not fit neatly into national traditions to study "the relationships among different margins."[9]

For instance, we know that Hughes inspired many African American poets, yet we know little about the scope of his influence beyond US borders.[10] Although he is now recognized as a poet of the African diaspora, there has been surprisingly little discussion of his relationship with the anglophone Caribbean.[11] This is one of the minor transnational circuits that this chapter examines by looking at how dub poets build on Hughes's blues poetics. Well over twenty years ago, Hughes's biographer Arnold Rampersad suggested in his article "Future Scholarly Projects on Hughes" (1987), that Hughes's preoccupation later in his career with the anglophone Caribbean was in need of examination. Yet far more has been written about his engagements with the francophone and hispanophone Caribbean than the anglophone Caribbean.[12]

Ifeoma Kiddoe Nwankwo attributes this blind spot to the ideologies of cultural nationalism, which have prevented scholars from examining relations between African Americans and West Indians. I focus on dub and Indigenous poets working outside of the United States to overcome US-centric ideas about performance poetry and this nationalistic bias.[13]

In his recent book *Trans-Indigenous: Methodologies for Global Native Literary Studies* (2012), Chadwick Allen argues that indigeneity needs to be at the heart of comparative frameworks "to displace settler interests from the center of intellectual activity and to produce new knowledge."[14] Although he focuses on "Indigenous-to-Indigenous" comparison, his ideas have value for cross-ethnic studies. He critiques traditional comparison in the academy as "a practice of reading that culminates in a statement of similarities and differences, a balanced list of *same* and its mirrored other, *not same*, the familiar 'compare and contrast' ending in 'like' and 'unlike.'"[15] He notes that these types of reductive comparisons create the illusion of objectivity and are often used to justify settler perspectives that deny the cultural uniqueness of tribal identities. He calls for "a together (yet) *distinct*" model, similar to Lionnet and Shih's minor transnationalism, that pursues "purposeful juxtapositions."[16]

While Susan Gingell also cautions against reductive comparisons that overgeneralize oral traditions, she suggests that juxtaposing Caribbean and Indigenous poetries will lead to a more comprehensive understanding of the interplay between oral and textual modes in the Americas.[17] Her essay in Neal McLeod's 2014 collection, *Indigenous Poetics in Canada*, which also includes the Lillian Allen text I cite in the epigraph, lays the groundwork for comparative studies of dub and Indigenous poetics. Gingell notes:

> Despite the two groups' different histories, orality is central to the social lives and verbal arts of each. They both share a belief in the dynamism and potency of the sounded word, and experiences of the silencing of their languages by (neo)colonizers. Moreover, Indigenous and dub poets frequently describe their work as extending ancestral oral traditions even as they thematize the muting of their mother tongues.[18]

Gingell outlines how poets from both groups reinvent the oppressor's language and stress "audible difference" in their performances.[19] She uses the term *sound identity* to characterize how Indigenous and dub poets draw on music and the phonology of language to cultivate self-empowerment and social belonging. For example, dub poets incorporate reggae rhythms and dread talk into their performances, while Cree poets bring Cree syntax and phrases into their poetry to destabilize the dominance of English. By asserting their sound identities, both groups resist the silencing of their voices by the dominant society – a silencing that takes shape through formal education in Canada and Jamaica. Gingell and Lillian Allen both recognize that sound plays an integral role in these freedom discourses. Allen explains this in the following terms: "We must liberate words and forms to more closely reflect our rhythms and tempo."[20] In addition to rhythm as a template for identities in the present, it also connects these poets to the past.

The fragility of memory due to forced relocation is a common theme in dub and Indigenous poetry. Many poets employ different techniques to retrieve silenced or lost memories from the colonial past. For example, in "dis poem," Mutabaruka opens by calling on the Middle Passage:

dis poem
shall speak of the wretched sea
that washed ships to these shores
of mothers cryin for their young
swallowed up by the sea[21]

The Cree scholar Neal McLeod addresses how being removed from one's land causes one to become "alienated from the collective memory of one's people" and the "echoes of the ancestors."[22] Displacement has impelled Indigenous and Afro-Caribbean artists to develop alternative ways to hold on to the past and transmit their cultural narratives through their bodies and through sound.

As the Jamaican critic Michael A. Bucknor establishes, "the cultural survival of the African in the New World demanded recourse to body-memory," which "is mapped out throughout the entire body via a kind of vibrational current." In Allen's work he describes this as "the material configurations of Caribbean linguistic and expressive codes that pulse through her writing."[23] In performance, this "pulse," which comes across through her rhythmic Creole speech, compels her audience to call on their own body-memories. Similarly, Phanuel Antwi characterizes dub as "a living sound archive" of the black Atlantic that travels rhythmically through the body.[24]

Caribbean and Indigenous scholars, such as Bucknor, Antwi, and McLeod, focus primarily on the recovery, storage, and transmission of memory through oral dynamics and performance. However, the history of schoolroom recitation highlights another part of the struggle to decolonize memory: How do individuals overcome the colonial scripts that they were forced to internalize and that distort personal and collective memory? As a classroom ritual, poetry recitation's effectiveness stems from its ability to shape (and even manipulate) body-memory. In the Introduction, I discussed Jamaica Kincaid's protagonist Lucy, who has nightmares of daffodils after being forced to recite Wordsworth's "I Wandered Lonely as a Cloud."[25] Lucy's strong visceral response when she witnesses a field of them for the first time as an adult attests to how the experience has infiltrated her body-memory. Despite her desperation to exorcize this poem from her psyche, it remains a part of her. Although we often equate a powerful memory with a strong intellect, Lucy's memory weakens her mind. This demonstrates how poetry recitation rituals often damage one's memory by making it more docile, receptive, and ultimately trainable.

The poets whom I discuss in this chapter – Lillian Allen, Mutabaruka, LKJ, Jean "Binta" Breeze, Janet Marie Rogers, and Annharte – strengthen counter-forms of body-memory through performance. Their resistant memory politics build on Johnson's, Hughes's, and Bennett's strategies to deflect the negative forces of poetry recitation. To deflect such forces, Johnson, Hughes, and Bennett demonstrated that the daffodils could not simply be extracted. Instead, they refashioned schoolroom poetry practices to challenge their damaging hold on the imagination. Elaborating on their example, contemporary dub and Indigenous poets contend with traumatic memories and reckon with the new forms of language that they unconsciously internalize from their environments. Rather than a classroom assignment, these new forms of internalized language often come from new media technologies.

Recording technologies and digital media have transformed the terrain of performance practices and created an emerging sonic archive for scholars to study. By drawing on a multimedia archive, this chapter moves beyond the excessive focus "on literary and historical documents, and look[s] through the lens of performed, embodied behaviors."[26] John Miles Foley asks why "we are in the habit of understanding poetry as a species of written poetry, not the other way round." As he metaphorically puts it, this leads to scholars "peering through the wrong end of a telescope."[27] Although a recording captures only a trace of "the embodied and contextualized reciprocal relationship between performer(s) and audience," it offers more insight than a printed text and at least allows us to peer through the right end of the telescope.[28] Furthermore, recording technologies have been integral to the development of dub and Indigenous poetries. I will now turn to a discussion of the dub poetry movement's engagements with memory and technology; in the second half of the chapter, I will investigate related methodologies in Indigenous poetry.

Dubbing Over Memories

Bennett's and Hughes's interest in radio anticipates the dub poets' embrace of technology to create a new sound-based poetics that draws on African traditions. In addition to creating new channels of distribution and new opportunities for community building, recording opened up a new terrain of artistic experimentation for neo-oralities. As I discussed in the previous chapter, Bennett expanded on her labrish poetics as a form of subversive mimicry in her topical radio program *Miss Lou's Views*. Hughes also worked as a radio journalist during the Spanish Civil War and the Second World War, and this inspired him to experiment with the metaphor of radio connectivity in his poetry as a way to translate the immediacy of call-and-response across vast geographic distances.[29] This is most evident in his poem "Broadcast to the West Indies" (1943), in which Harlem becomes a poetic persona who calls on the West Indian islands for solidarity:

> I, Harlem, say:
> HELLO, WEST INDIES!
> You are dark like me,
> Colored with many bloods like me,
> Verging from the sunrise to the
> dusk like me,[30]

Hughes evokes his sense of blackness as fluid and hybrid, as "colored with many bloods." This poem reflects his desire to build alliances with West Indian artists and intellectuals, during the 1940s, based on his recognition that they share similar (yet distinct) experiences of racism and racial identity. He travelled to Jamaica in November 1947 to solicit submissions for his and Arna Bontemps's international anthology of black poetry, *The Poetry of the Negro: 1746–1949* (1949). However, many Jamaican poets who were invested in colonial aesthetics were resistant to his efforts to create a transnational black poetics. The discrepancy in how blackness is defined in the United States and the Caribbean created conflict for Hughes in his request for work from certain West Indian contributors who did not consider themselves "black" and did not want to be included in an anthology of black poets.[31] However, a few decades later, the dub poets' technologically infused experiments with black orality and music replied to Hughes's call to the West Indies in the 1940s for a creative dialogue. As I mentioned in the previous chapter, Bennett also held Hughes in high esteem and avidly read his work, and so dub poets make contact with his ideas through her poetics as well.

Similar to Hughes, dub poets situate their work in an Afro-diasporic genealogy of creative innovation. As Lillian Allen maps out:

> Dub poetry is just another chapter in a long succession of dynamic innovative forms which includes the *griots* of Africa, slave narratives, the dialect poetry of Paul Lawrence [*sic*] Dunbar, the Baptist church preacher, There's the blues poets – Langston Hughes, Sterling Brown, and others of the Harlem renaissance – Louise Bennett, Edward Brathwaite, black American jazz and blues with their poets of the sixties, Jamaican DJs and then dub poets and black American rap.[32]

Although the form originates in Africa, Allen stresses that it takes shape only through the synergy of cultures in the Americas.

If for Afro-diasporic people the body has been the primary place to store memory, broadcasting and recording technologies have encouraged performance memory to take new forms. The term *dub* comes from the reggae subgenre that emerged in the late 1960s and literally "refers to the activity of adding and/or removing sounds."[33] In the 1960s, new sound-mixing technologies amplified the possibilities for rearranging a track. In particular, multitrack recording meant that one could remove vocals, which inspired the convention of popular reggae singles including an instrumental version on the B-side of 45-rpm recordings. Without lyrics, these B-sides emphasized the drum and bass pattern – the rhythm. These instrumental tracks became popular in sound-system culture because they provided an ideal template for a DJ to toast his rhymes on, which led to the DJ talk-over style.[34]

Dub poets were inspired by sound-system culture and DJ talk-over stars such as Big Youth, U-Roy, and I-Roy. LKJ first referred to "dub lyricists" in 1976 to characterize DJs as poets; however, his version of dub differs from the role of the DJ.[35] Rather than merely mimic the talk-over DJ, LKJ experiments with using the voice to carry the bass line. As Peter Hitchcock explains, "if dub reggae mixes out the vocals, dub poetry lays down the voice as an instrument within the reggae beat; indeed, the voice is so closely allied with this beat that if you remove the reggae instrumentation you can still hear its sound in the voice of the poem."[36] Dub poets perform both with and without musical accompaniment. When a poet recites without a band, she enacts the inverse of the DJ talk-over. LKJ's poem "Reggae Sounds" demonstrates how the voice becomes an instrument:

> Shock-black bubble-doun-beat bouncing
> rock-wise tumble-doun sound music;
> foot-drop find drum, blood story,
> bass history is a moving
>   is a hurting black story.[37]

LKJ explores language as sound through neologisms like "bubble-doun-beat." As Eric Falci aptly notes about this particular verse, "Like Hughes's blues poems, Johnson's dub poems toggle between describing dub music and trying to become it."[38] In his classic "The Weary Blues," Hughes's opening lines reflect this tactic:

> Droning a drowsy syncopated tune,
> Rocking back and forth to a mellow croon,
>   I heard a Negro play.[39]

The words describe what a blues rhythm sounds like, while the syllables enact it. Hughes delays letting us know that the speaker is a listener in a bar until the indented third line to immerse the reader in the rhythm of the music. LKJ's approach is even more immersive because he never breaks the trance of the rhythm with the intrusion of an "I" statement or a contextual narrative. When LKJ performs this poem, he places emphasis on the second and fourth word in each line to create the one-drop reggae beat.

According to Brathwaite, when poets emphasize the "rhythm and timbre" of words, this accentuates the African aspect of Caribbean Creoles.[40] LKJ stresses that this "reggae sound" becomes a rhythmic structure to convey black collective memory across locations. While LKJ was developing his own poetic response to dub in England, poets in Canada and Jamaica also began to experiment with reggae rhythms. Oku Onuora was the first person to actually define dub poetry as a genre, developing his ideas while he was incarcerated in Jamaica from 1970 to 1977.[41] Initially, he described it as a poem composed with a reggae rhythm. Later, Onuora would widen this definition to include any kind of poetry that has any style of musical rhythms dubbed in.[42] In a talk in 1986, Onuora aimed to clarify the definition by emphasizing dub as a form of substitution:

> Dub poetry simply mean to take out and to put in ... It's dubbing out the little penta-metre and the little highfalutin business and dubbing in the rootsical, yard, basic rhythm that I-an-I know. Using the language, using the body. It also mean to dub out the isms and schisms and to dub consciousness into the people-dem head. That's dub poetry.[43]

Onuora emphasizes *dubbing* as a verb to highlight how it overshadows oppressive, internalized scripts and replaces them with an empowering "dub consciousness." To achieve this, he stresses that poets must perform an embodied language and drum a new rhythmic structure into people's minds that overrides the pentameter. The dub poets avoid trying to erase intractable colonial scripts, which for Kincaid's Lucy proves futile; instead, they override them with their own meanings and rhythms.

Dubbing functions as a form of substitution not through extraction but rather by covering over or drowning out what already exists by accentuating the bass line. The frequent use of onomatopoeia in dub poems exemplifies this point. Lines such as LKJ's "shock-black bubble-doun-beat bouncing" emphasize vocalized words as kinetic forms of rhythm and divorce them from their denotative meanings. Onuora suggests that consciousness is structured by rhythm. As compared to recitation in colonial schools, where internalized English values and language structures encourage a passive engagement with language, dub rhythms invite audiences to activate their embodied relationship to language and their extra-linguistic memories.

Onuora's dub theories relate to Catherine Robson's point that "the compulsorily memorized poem inserted itself into individuals and established its beat in sympathy with, or in counterpoint to, their bodily rhythms."[44] Most of the poets in this study felt that "the little highfalutin business" of schoolroom recitation was a counterpoint rather than a beat in sympathy with their bodily rhythms. Dub poets respond to Bennett's invitation to confront this counterpoint by exploring the clash between their embodied rhythms and the alienating rhythms of pentameter. Hughes's response to the alienating counterpoint of schoolroom recitation was somewhat different. He encouraged young readers to get in touch with their own bodily rhythms and use them to establish the tempo. By drawing on blues and jazz rhythms, he aimed to create poems that "beat in sympathy with" his black audience.

Hughes's advice to black poets to draw on "the meanings and rhythms of jazz," in his 1926 essay "The Negro Artist and the Racial Mountain," forms a key ingredient in the development of dub poetics.[45] According to Morris, "living in Jamaica in the late 1960s, Oku was also influenced by black American trends, including a proliferation of poet-performers who were steeped in the rhythms of black music ... He discovered the poetry of Langston Hughes, which he often adduced as a model."[46] In Britain, LKJ was exposed to Hughes's writings when he joined the Black Panthers and was inspired by the musicality of his poetry.[47] As Michael Smith describes, "We identify the same thing we find run through Langston Hughes poems. Langston Hughes have a blues mood go through it, and we just feel seh, well, we have something, and we seh boy it was the beat."[48] Smith obviously never attended Hughes's poetry workshop at the Chicago Laboratory School, but he picks up on the rhythmic literacy encoded in his poems. Hughes teaches Smith to write through rhythm – to find his own beat.

Although Hughes made significant contributions to dub poets' adaptation of reggae rhythms to create new poetic forms, Bennett's influence on dub poetry is the most pervasive. Allen goes so far as to characterize Bennett as "the mother of dub poetry":

> Dub poetry is something I had evolved into quite naturally, but I didn't call it dub poetry at the time. I loved poetry and recitation/elocution from when I was a little girl. We recited poetry in church, in school and at community happenings. I grew up in Spanish Town, Jamaica in the fifties and sixties. Poetry and storytelling were always very vibrant. Strictly speaking, I would say Louise Bennett would be my first encounter but what she did was not called dub poetry ... I would say Louise Bennett is in fact the mother of dub poetry.[49]

Allen loved "recitation/elocution" when she was a child, a testament to Bennett's reinvention of this practice. Allen also praises Bennett in the introduction to her poetry collection *Women Do This Every Day*. She argues that without Bennett and Bob Marley, who himself "looked to Miss Lou for inspiration," dub poetry would not have developed.[50] Dub poets such as Allen, Mutabaruka, and amuna baraka-clarke acknowledge the importance of Miss Lou in their poems.[51] Allen describes how Bennett provided poets like herself "with room to grow" in her aptly titled "Tribute to Miss Lou":

The voice
strug ug ugg uggling
to be heard

hear dis;
dem sey we sey she sey he sey hear sey
raw rim of soul
her mirror a poem
with room to grow[52]

The elongated struggling enacts the difficulty of finding her voice, as if words are stuck in her throat. Suggesting an intergenerational call and response, Allen emphasizes the reciprocal relationship between saying and listening to emphasize how Bennett's poems provided a generative example for younger poets to build on. She proved to dub poets that the Jamaican language and culture are worthy of poetic expression.[53] Critics and practitioners have firmly established how Bennett's experiments with Jamaican Creole strongly influenced the dub poets.[54] Yet this forms only one part of the story. Bennett, along with Hughes, not only helped dub poets to reclaim black Englishes, but she also laid the foundations for taking back one's memory through her interventions in schoolroom recitation.

Recycling Nursery Rhymes

Although dub poets' reggae-infused style seems to have abandoned the colonial classroom, they respond to their formal schooling in their poems that satirize nursery rhymes. For example, in her dramatic monologue "The arrival of Brighteye," Breeze explores a young girl's psychological experience of migration through a nursery rhyme and a folk song. The BBC commissioned this video poem as part of its fiftieth anniversary Windrush programs to celebrate the arrival of Caribbean people in 1948.[55] The speaker is a seven-year-old girl, nicknamed Brighteye, who migrates to England to meet her mother, who left her at age two to work as a domestic. As I discussed in the previous chapter, Breeze acknowledges that reciting Bennett's female-centred poetics provided a formative model for her to develop her own feminist version of dub, and her exploration of the mother–child relationship in this poem particularly demonstrates this.[56] Breeze may not seek out an audience of children like Hughes and Bennett did, but her portrayal of a child's voice illustrates that she shares their concerns about decolonizing children's minds.[57]

Breeze turns to nursery rhymes and folk songs, oral discourses that often act as intimate currencies between mother and child, to describe her experience of migration from Jamaica to England. These scraps of found language are interspersed with prose sections where Brighteye narrates her journey. In performance, Breeze opens by singing the first stanza a cappella. By portraying a child's voice, Breeze stresses the disparity between what Brighteye feels and what she is able to say based on her subject position and the language available to her. She points to how a young girl must turn to language from her environment to articulate her dislocation. The recycled language acts as a supplement for what cannot be expressed. Through it she exposes the effects of internalized language on the psyche. In the first stanza, Breeze reinvents the Scottish folk song "My Bonnie Lies over the Ocean" to refer to Brighteye's mother:

> My mommy gone over de ocean
> My mommy gone over de sea
> She gawn dere to work for some money
> An den she gawn sen back for me[58]

The lilting tune combined with the romantic theme of the folk song evokes Brighteye's longing for her mother; however, her reinvention of the lines to refer to her mother's financial situation disrupts a purely romanticized interpretation of her predicament. Brighteye sings this lullaby to herself to collapse the distance between her and her mother. Breeze reveals how migration severs family relationships between women. The title is misleading, because the poem depicts how Brighteye never fully arrives in herself because of her alienating experience of migration. She grows up in England, and by the end of the monologue her eyes become red and tired and she must go out and work as a domestic like her mother.

Later in the poem, just before she departs from Jamaica, Brighteye repeats the lines to "Row, Row, Row Your Boat" that she overheard other children reciting while "playing ring game an clapping."[59] By describing how Brighteye learned this rhyme by observing children playing ring games, Breeze illustrates how an archive of oral memory that has roots in the colonizing culture has been reinvented in Jamaica.[60] As Glasceta Honeyghan describes, the nursery rhymes learned in school were "replayed on the playground to jump rope, on the road home from school, and after evening chores."[61] Like Bennett does in "Sammy Intres," dub poets question what happens when the language of the classroom permeates the yard. However, unlike Sammy's mother, who tries to prevent the language from coming into her home, dub poets feel less anxiety about its influence and demonstrate how Jamaican oral cultures appropriate and transform classroom languages.[62]

By sending these reinvented scripts back to England through the voice of Brighteye, Breeze depicts what Bennett characterizes as "colonization in reverse."[63] The doubleness of nursery rhymes, which have a happy tone but often describe dark events, becomes an opportunity to explore the experience of migration. The refrain "merrily, merrily, merrily, merrily / life is but a dream" sounds discordant because Brighteye's reunion with her mother is difficult and alienating.[64] She cannot remember what she looks like after five years of separation and initially mistakes a white woman for her mother. When she realizes that "is nat mi madda at tall," she is so distraught that she urinates on herself.[65] The nursery rhyme inadequately represents the young girl's complex experience of travelling to meet her mother in England. While "rowing" suggests that the speaker has some degree of agency in her journey down the stream, Breeze reveals how Brighteye has little control over what is happening to her. "Row, Row, Row Your Boat" is often interpreted as a lesson to children to meet life's difficulties with a positive outlook. Breeze illustrates how this idealized middle-class tenacity is inadequate for working-class Jamaican children. More pressingly, she demonstrates how external scripts often mediate our innermost feelings and relationships. Yet in spite of its inadequacy, the nursery rhyme allows Brighteye to voice her alienation. Rather than exacerbate the diasporic fragmentation of memory, it helps to connect her to her home in Jamaica.

Other dub poets use phrases from nursery rhymes as part of their social critique, similar to how talk-over DJs like I-Roy use them.[66] For example, in "Me Cyaan Believe It," Michael Smith expresses shock and disbelief over the gross poverty and inequity in 1970s Jamaica by turning to English nursery rhymes as well as ring games and folk sayings. By drawing on these childhood scripts, like Breeze, he demonstrates how Jamaican oral traditions have absorbed British forms. The speaker compares himself to "humpty dumpty," who also had to "face me reality."[67] The phrases from nursery rhymes Smith selects demonstrate how inadequate these lessons are for young children living in poor neighbourhoods in Kingston. Mutabaruka also makes a similar point in his piece "Nursery Rhyme Lament." Like Smith, he underscores the disjunction between the idealized tone of nursery rhymes and the realities of Jamaican poverty. For example, the first stanza rewrites "Jack and Jill":

first time
jack & jill
used to run up de hill every day
now dem get pipe ... an
water rate increase[68]

Mutabaruka omits the last two lines, in which Jack and Jill fall down the hill, to suggest that they may have been better off fetching their own water. He implies that modernization does not always result in a positive benefit for the rural poor in Jamaica.

Mutabaruka characterizes "Nursery Rhyme Lament" as a "social commentary based on what we learn in school."[69] He, Smith, and Breeze were all born in the 1950s, so their early education occurred in pre-Independence Jamaica. Almost all mid-century students in the anglophone Caribbean would learn nursery rhymes at all-age primary schools, even if they never had the opportunity to attend the elite secondary schools. Nursery rhymes were often the first poems that children were taught to memorize and recite before learning the work of authors like Longfellow and Wordsworth. By returning to nursery rhymes, dub poets highlight the more populist aspects of the colonial curriculum. Mutabaruka questions the nonsensical irrelevance of nursery rhymes, pointing out that children frequently learn them without being taught what they mean.

The calypso artist Mighty Sparrow makes a similar critique of nursery rhymes as a dumbed-down curriculum in his 1963 hit "Dan Is the Man (in the Van)." In the song, he attacks Captain James Oliver Cutteridge, the director of education in Trinidad and Tobago, who compiled and implemented Thomas Nelson's *West Indian Readers* in almost every elementary school.[70] The early readers in this series consisted of nursery rhymes, reading instruction, grammar lessons, and simplified versions of British literature and history. Mighty Sparrow argues that these foreign British textbooks sent from England were designed to make West Indian students ignorant. He intersperses his song with lines from nursery rhymes while recalling how being forced to memorize nursery rhymes in school made him feel less intelligent.[71] Mighty Sparrow and Mutabaruka critique the often-meaningless nursery rhymes that students were forced to parrot back in the classroom.[72] However, the nonsensical, catchy rhymes of texts like "Jack and Jill" invite children to relate to words purely as rhythmic entities.

In his study *West Indians and Their Language*, Peter Roberts suggests that the nonsensical quality of nursery rhymes encouraged children to adapt them for playground games:

> In many West Indian children's songs and rhymes, words have evolved to become nonsense words ... A consequence of this which has to be considered is that as a result of the crucial place that the songs and rhymes of childhood have in the linguistic evolution of the individual, freedom to treat language as sounds without meaning may have a spill-over effect on the communicative language of the individual.[73]

Nursery rhymes highlight the hybridity created by the borderless curriculum of recitation. Dub poets relate to these rhymes as both alienating and familiar, rife with meaning and full of nonsense. They become part of a malleable oral archive that also includes Jamaican proverbs, folk tales, and song lyrics. Rather than focus on popular literary recitation classics like Wordsworth's "I Wandered Lonely as a Cloud," dub poets select nursery rhymes because of their fusion with Jamaican oral forms. Children often learn nursery rhymes in the earliest stages of literacy acquisition. Their memorization is typically mediated more through orality than through reading. Even if they encounter them first on the pages of a *West Indian Reader* textbook, their catchy melodies and rhymes are often what capture children's imaginations.

Dub poets' satirical approach to nursery rhymes becomes a way to contend with their unsuitable (yet catchy) rhythms and themes that children absorb. Mighty Sparrow argues that the hidden curriculum of nursery rhymes aims to keep West Indian children ignorant. While he makes a valid point, nursery rhymes also help young students cultivate what Brathwaite characterizes as "syllabic intelligence" and an ability to tune in to the "sonority contrasts" in their environments.[74] Such lessons feed into Bennett's exploration of the sonority contrasts between Jamaican Creole and pentameter and Hughes's instructions to young children to cultivate their own sense of rhythm in *The First Book of Rhythms*. As Breeze's performance of "The arrival of Brighteye" demonstrates, Brighteye manages to express her alienation by accentuating the sonority contrasts between her experience and the melody of "Row, Row, Row Your Boat."

Negotiating Cultural Inheritance

In addition to nursery rhymes, Breeze explores other kinds of language that people unconsciously internalize from their environments. In one of her best-known dramatic monologues, "riddym ravings (the mad woman's poem)," from the album *Riding On De Riddym*, she examines internalized dancehall lyrics. Like "The arrival of Brighteye," this five-minute track explores the impact of globalization on Caribbean working-class women, revealing how their lives have become more difficult than during colonialism. This poem is written in the voice of a homeless pregnant woman who wanders the streets of Kingston searching in vain for someone to talk to. The mad woman believes that she has a radio stuck inside her head because she keeps hearing the chorus of a dancehall song:

mi haffi sleep outa door wid de Channel One riddym box
an de D.J. fly up eena mi head
mi hear im a play seh

Eh, Eh,
no feel no way
town is a place dat ah really kean stay[75]

At first the lyrics bother her; however, as she continually recites them throughout the poem, she begins to cling to them as a reminder of her rural upbringing before she had to leave for the city to find work. Breeze's mad woman wandering the streets of Kingston evokes Louise Bennett's working-class women characters who demand recognition in public space; however, Breeze's mad woman is less optimistic than Bennett's 1940s market women. Critic Jenny Sharpe points out that the mad woman's experience of urban displacement evokes how the International Monetary Fund (IMF) policies and an integrated economy have destroyed the livelihood of many Jamaican farmers.[76]

The authorities repeatedly pick up and take the mad woman to Bellevue, an institution for the mentally ill and poor in Kingston. While she's there, the landlord and doctor try unsuccessfully to remove the radio from her head before eventually administering electric-shock treatment. In the conclusion of the poem, the doctor and the landlord remove the radio from her head, but the woman retrieves it. Instead of returning it to her head, she places it in her belly:

> mi tek de radio
> an mi push i up eena mi belly
> fi keep de baby company
> fah even if mi nuh mek i
> me waan my baby know dis yah riddym yah
> fram before she bawn
> hear de D.J. a play, seh
>
> *Eh, Eh,*
> *no feel no way*
> *town is a place dat ah really kean stay*
> *dem kudda – ribbit mi han*
> *eh – ribbit mi toe*
> *mi waan go a country go look mango*
>
> an same time
> de dactar an de lanlord
> trigger de electric shack
> an me hear de D.J. vice bawl out, seh
>
> *Murther*
> *Pull up Missa Operator!*[77]

Breeze sings the dancehall chorus a cappella, making it distinctively feminine, rather than reciting it in the bravado style of the male dancehall DJ.[78] This poem exemplifies Breeze's performance style, particularly how she uses the modulations of her voice and Creole speech rhythms to inflect the poem with meaning. Her introspective, soft, and wavering voice differs from the declamatory style of much spoken-word and dub poetry. Rather than assume an audience through a direct and forceful address, her unsure voice, especially in the recorded version, makes the listener feel as though she were eavesdropping on this woman's private thoughts. These distinct modulations, absent in the printed version of this poem, convey the unease of the mad woman's state of mind.

In the last two defiant lines, "*Murther / Pull up Missa Operator,*" Breeze raises her voice for the first time in the poem to indicate that the mad woman refuses to be subdued. Sharpe makes a compelling analysis of this conclusion, noting that "these words, also from dancehall culture, allude to a particularly good or 'murderous' track that an audience wants to hear again."[79] The poem ends by assuring us that the recitation of the chorus will continue. Through the rhythms of Creole speech, Breeze combines murder with mother to transfer power from the DJ to the mad woman, who becomes the operator of the radio. *Missa Operator* conflates the roles of the doctor and the DJ, suggesting that the mad woman has scrambled the power of order and dissent in Jamaican culture through her radio receiver. The mad woman takes agency over the technology to communicate with her unborn child. As Sharpe argues, "No matter how many times the forces of law and order try to 'cure' the woman by killing the song in her head, they cannot destroy the memory of her home or prevent her from passing on that memory to the next generation."[80]

While the evocative, futuristic style of "riddym ravings" differs from the use of nursery rhymes in "The arrival of Brighteye," they both emphasize oral memory, identity, the mother–daughter bond, and the psychological effects of internalized lyrics. The fact that a dancehall song replaces a British poem in this context signals some progress. At least the mad woman internalizes a local Jamaican form; however, Breeze's reference to a dancehall DJ still potentially holds problems for women, since dancehall culture often demeans women.[81] Although the lines that the mad woman internalizes sound innocuous, Breeze suggests that even though women no longer have to contend with colonial scripts at the same scale, the ones being produced in Jamaica still may not reflect their interests. She also demonstrates that the experience of linguistic memorization and recitation is often an unconscious one triggered by technological forms.

"The arrival of Brighteye" and "riddym ravings" illustrate how the rhythmic language internalized in social environments can structure one's personal memories and emotional bonds; the mad woman is determined to pass on the rhythm (perhaps more so than the words themselves) to her child before she is born. Breeze enacts Onuora's definition of dubbing as the use of rhythm to overcome the decolonization of the mind. Her urgency to pass on this rhythm underscores the mother's fear that Kingston will not provide her child with rhythms that will connect her to personal history. Similar to the mother character in Bennett's "Sammy Intres," analysed in the previous chapter, the mad woman must fight for her interests to be passed on to her child. The electric cord of the radio, which the mother reclaims as her umbilical cord in the poem, demonstrates how even the most intimate of bonds are mediated (and potentially severed) by external forces. However, the mad woman's literal incorporation of the external transmitter (the radio) into her body and her a cappella rendition of the dancehall chorus underscore how a subject can find physical agency through embodied performance to resist being taken over by these forces. Breeze dramatizes the corporeal dynamic of ingesting or taking in language to expunge or expel the parts of discourse that distort one's experience.

More broadly, "riddym ravings" registers concern about African cultural inheritance in the post-colonial era. It should not be as difficult as it was for Sammy's mother to pass on her Afro-Caribbean interests to her son; however, Breeze's poetry illustrates that globalization creates new forms of memory interference that make this challenging, particularly for mothers and daughters. On the other hand, dub poetry should ease such anxieties, since it clearly displays a strong connection (unshaken by diaspora) to Bennett's and Hughes's legacies and to African musical traditions. As Allen stresses in her "Tribute to Miss Lou," Bennett's "riddim fire" has been passed on to the next generation of Jamaican poets.[82]

Similarly, Janet Marie Rogers and Annharte both write poems that highlight what E. Pauline Johnson has passed on to them as Indigenous women poets. Dub and Indigenous tribute poems demonstrate Lois Parkinson Zamora's point that writers in the Americas often actively construct their own literary genealogies. To evoke Harold Bloom's terminology, these poets feel no "anxiety" about aligning themselves with their chosen influences (what creates anxiety is the influence of the dominant society). Through tribute poems and other writings, they "create [their] precursors rather than cancel them."[83] Remembering their literary ancestors directly activates their resistant politics. By claiming Johnson as their own, Rogers and Annharte challenge how her poetry was used for Indigenization in Canadian curricula.

Creating a Sonic Archive

Rogers establishes how Johnson "engaged in a type of spoken-word delivery well before the genre came into being."[84] In addition to feeling part of Johnson's spoken-word legacy, in her poem "(T)here Is a Time," Rogers expresses kinship with Johnson as "a transplanted import / West Coast Mohawk / on Coast Salish Territory."[85] Rogers was born in Vancouver, grew up in southern Ontario near the Six Nations Reserve, and then eventually settled in Victoria in 1994. When she moved to Victoria she felt welcomed by the Coast Salish people and experienced an instant connection to the land, which inspired her to begin her writing career. As she describes it, on the West Coast "words found me / and took root."[86] Victoria City Council honoured her relationship to the city when they selected her as their poet laureate for 2012–14. In her statement at the beginning of her latest book, *Peace in Duress*, she writes, "I am grateful for the Salish People on whose territory I am allowed to be a visitor. Without the efforts and energies of these brave people, I would not know the great pleasure, enjoy the freedom, and have the ability to fulfill my purpose as a writer and performance poet."[87] Johnson had a similar experience of "homecoming" when she moved to Vancouver towards the end of her life.[88] The Delaware Six Nations poet Daniel David Moses goes so far as to declare, "Rogers is a spiritual descendant of the Mohawk poet Pauline Johnson."[89] In her essay "Pauline Passed Here," Rogers celebrates Johnson's life of travel and her love of adventure: "The roads and roads less travelled informed Pauline's poems as they do mine ... As I travel, especially through the interior of this colonized province [British Columbia], I can't help but think 'Pauline passed here too.'"[90] Although forced relocation through the reserve system, foster care, and residential schooling had devastating effects on First Nations cultures, Rogers draws attention to how self-determined movements can enhance one's critique of colonization and facilitate the growth of pan-Indigenous solidarities. She connects Johnson's life of travel to her celebration of ceaseless movement in her performance poetics. Echoing "the rapids roar" from "The Song My Paddle Sings," she characterizes this as "E. Pauline our rip roar'n ride."[91] Through Johnson, Rogers identifies with what McCall characterizes as "sovereignties-in-motion," which involve a relationship to the land that does not depend on a direct link to one's tribal territory.[92] She stresses a landscape in motion to imagine a diasporic approach to Indigenous citizenship.

In *Peace in Duress*, Rogers celebrates the resiliency of Indigenous oral memory despite (and sometimes even through) geographic displacement. As she puts it, "Our greatest asset / is memory" (6). Her book revolves around the collective memory of the Guswenta Two

Row Wampum Treaty of 1613, the first agreement made between Native people and white settlers in North America, which prioritized peace and friendship. From an Indigenous perspective, this agreement laid the foundations for all subsequent treaties. As Jon Parmenter explains, "*kaswentha* [alternate spelling of Guswenta] emphasizes the distinct identity of the two peoples and a mutual engagement to coexist in peace without interference in the affairs of the other."[93] Rogers's book title *Peace in Duress* evokes how white settlers have repeatedly violated this treaty agreement. The two rows of purple beads on the belt represent a European ship and a Haudenosaunee canoe sailing in peaceful coexistence. The three white rows in the middle symbolize peace, friendship, and forever. Indigenous activists recall this message as a model for contemporary truth and reconciliation.[94] Although controversy exists regarding the authenticity of the paper treaty document and the original wampum no longer exists, the Haudenosaunee maintain that their oral memory holds the more reliable record of the encounter.[95] Rogers's publication of *Peace in Duress* in 2014 builds on the four-hundred-year anniversary celebrations that took place in 2013. She asserts the authority of oral memory over print documents and rejects charges that the treaty is a fake. Rogers begins "Forever" by reciting her own version of lines from the treaty:

> *Forever*
> *as long as the sun shines upon the earth*
> *as long as the water still flows*
> *as long as the grass grows a certain time each year*
> *Forever*
> *as long as Mother Earth is still in motion*
> *still in motion, still in motion*
> (33; italics in the original)

Rogers repeats "still in motion" three times to emphasize movement. Rather than associate forever with stillness, solidity, and paper, she associates it with the shared mobility of land and people.

In the Haudenosaunee memory of the treaty, they stress that both parties must maintain environmental stewardship of the land for friendship to exist. For the land to stay in motion it must be treated with respect. Evoking the wampum belt's image of two lines that should not intersect, Rogers invites her audience to remember white-settler governments violently crossing this line in territorial disputes:

remember Kanonhstaton Caledonia
remember Gustafsen Lake
remember Ipperwash
remember Oka
remember Alcatraz and Eagle Bay
remember Wounded Knee
every day is remembrance day
every day
(35)

Rogers makes Indigenous acts of resistance become part of the Two Row Wampum story as it is passed from one generation to the next. As Rogers describes in "Giving a Shit," a poem about the Idle No More movement, "We are revisiting wampum / We are witnessing commitment" (111). Evoking Remembrance Day, Canada's day to honour war veterans, she questions why these battles get eclipsed in Canadian collective memory. Responding to allegations that a wampum belt cannot record history, she proposes that "anyone who thinks beads are insignificant / should try getting them back from a museum" (34). Building on the metaphor of the canoe in the treaty, she insists, "we paddle a canoe packing values," to underscore how this history of resistance moves with Haudenosaunee people (33). Similar to Johnson, she uses the canoe as a symbol in her poetry; however, she often stresses paddling as a collective action, rather than as a solitary pursuit, to emphasize migratory solidarity.[96]

Rogers released a video recording of "Forever" on the publisher's website as a trailer for *Peace in Duress*. The video uses the text of the poem as a voiceover and features Rogers precariously walking barefoot on a path of white stones. To elongate the path she must return to the beginning, pick up a stone, carry it to the end of the path, and place it carefully down on the ground. She then repeats the process, slowly creating a long trail of stones. The smooth white stones evoke the white whelk-shell beads used to make wampum. Rogers enacts the creation of the middle rows of the Guswenta belt that represent truth. Her performance-art video elaborates on Johnson's embodiment of continuous motion and recalls her use of props, such as a hunting knife and a canoe paddle, to make the characters in her poems more realistic. Rather than embody a specific poetic persona, Rogers embodies the weaving of the wampum belt. By concretizing the belt as embodied action, she reveals that maintaining the wampum treaty requires concerted effort to construct the path with every step that one takes. The lines of peace can be created only through continuous and careful motion. As she lightly steps from stone to stone and struggles to remain balanced, she demonstrates the need to minimize one's footprint on the earth. Most importantly, her circular pattern represents the necessity of returning to the past to build a path forward. Rather than remember the treaty through words or images, Rogers remembers through the movement of her whole body.

Lillian Allen proposes that Rogers's work helps listeners understand "different ways of knowing" through her emphasis on sound and memory.[97] In her essay "Poetics of Renewal: Indigenous Poetics – Message or Medium?" (cited in this chapter's epigraph), Allen describes Rogers's visit to her creative writing class at OCAD University. Imagining these two like-minded poets meeting in a learning environment underscores the intimate relationship between performance poetry and pedagogy. Allen highlights Rogers's disruption of metanarratives and her formal experiments with things like "textures, sounds, silences, [and the] layering of voices."[98] She emphasizes the sonic elements of Rogers's poetics that come through on the page, elements that Rogers has cultivated through her extensive multimedia work. This vein of her poetics – inspired by broadcast technologies and the sound-mixing board – represents her strongest link to the dub poets.

Although Rogers publishes her work in book form, she prioritizes performance and characterizes herself primarily as a spoken-word artist. Her publications – *Peace in Duress* (2014), *Unearthed* (2011), *Red Erotic* (2010), and *Splitting the Heart* (2007) – supplement her live performances and her audio and video recordings. She has also released three albums, *6 Directions* (2013), *Got Your Back* (2012), and *Firewater* (2009). She characterizes her books as "well produced, radio-ready music," positioning them in a sound economy rather than a print one.[99] This reflects her work as a radio broadcaster. She produced the radio documentary *Bring Your Own Drum: 50 Years of Indigenous Protest Music*, and hosts two radio programs – the weekly *Native Waves Radio* on the local Victoria community station and *Tribal Clefs* on CBC Radio One's *All Points West* in British Columbia. Her programs promote new Indigenous music and often feature artists who combine older traditional forms with new electronic and DJ styles such as the hip hop collective Mob Bounce. Such hybrid innovations reflect the influence of black Atlantic protest forms (that emerged out of Jamaican sound-system culture) on First Nations youth. As Glenn Alteen, the curator of *Beat Nation: Hip Hop as Indigenous Culture*, notes, "Hip hop is giving youth new tools to rediscover First Nations culture. What is most striking about this work is how much of it embraces the traditional within its development."[100] Just as the dub poets turn to reggae forms to reinvigorate African griot traditions, Rogers turns to new Indigenous music and emerging media to reinvigorate Mohawk oral traditions. Her experimental spoken word, which plays with sound mixing, reverb, musical accompaniment, and sampling, reflects a complex cultural fusion.

One can silently read Rogers's books and appreciate the musicality of her language, but the experience does not have to stop there. One can easily move off the page and listen to multiple versions of the same poem online. In *Peace in Duress*, she takes advantage of digital forms to loosen the boundaries between a printed poem and the spoken word. The Facebook page for the book provides updates about live events, recordings of live performances, and studio-produced video poems such as the "Forever" book trailer. Rogers also shares audio versions of poems from the book on her SoundCloud page. To borrow terms from Kenneth Sherwood, digital forms facilitate oral poetry's emphasis on "elaboration" and "versioning," to disrupt the stability of the printed poem as the authoritative masterwork. He defines "versioning" as "creating a radically new arrangement of a poem during performance," and "elaboration" as the "improvisational moves" that are often not captured in the page version of a poem.[101] As compared to her first book, *Splitting the Heart*, which contained an accompanying CD, *Peace in Duress* more fully breaks from a page-centric economy through its digital life, which keeps the poems alive and unfinished. Unlike a CD glued into a book, which often encourages a one-to-one relationship between the audio recording and the print version of the poem, digital versioning more fully disrupts the idea of a book as a self-contained object.

On Rogers's SoundCloud page, in addition to the recitations of poems from *Peace in Duress*, she includes performance pieces (with no print version) that extend the dialogue of some of her poems in the book. This approach can be seen in her work about Johnson's possessions in museum collections – "The Celebrity of Famous (includes list of E. Pauline Johnson museum objects)" in *Peace in Duress* and "Wampum Contracts E. Pauline" (2013) and "The Pauline Project" (2012) on

SoundCloud. The former examines Johnson's personal belongings that include "red velvet shoes," a "hair comb," and a "bark rattle," housed in various museums (44–7).[102] The latter two pieces were inspired by her research fellowship at the Smithsonian's National Museum of the American Indian. Although Johnson's material objects are scattered across museum collections throughout North America, Rogers gathers them together and returns them to Mohawk cultural memory through her poetry.

During Johnson's lifetime, she sold her artefacts to different white curators, and she willed many of her possessions, including her buckskin dress and hunting knife, to the Vancouver Museum – even though many felt that her Mohawk items should be returned to the Six Nations community.[103] Traditionally items such as wampum belts are supposed to be collectively owned.[104] Although Rogers is a self-described "Pauline enthusiast," she refrains from idealizing Johnson's legacy by looking at how she facilitated cultural appropriation.[105] Ultimately, Rogers questions who possesses the memory of Johnson through the ownership of these objects.

Rogers produced "Wampum Contracts E. Pauline" for the imagineNATIVE Film + Media Arts Festival in Toronto. It echoes her piece made a year earlier, "The Pauline Project," in that they both use found text from a letter exchange between Johnson and the white collector George Gustav Heye (who founded the National Museum of the American Indian) concerning the sale of one of her wampum belts. They feature two voices – Rogers reads Pauline's letters and Michael Ireton reads Heye's letters. Both pieces demonstrate Patricia Killelea's point that Rogers's sound poems often "creat[e] haunting and, at times, chaotic and dreamlike, sonic atmospheres ... where the listener is made to dwell on a single word in all of its sonic permutations."[106] While the two versions are similar, "Wampum Contracts" is more experimental in its layering of voices and disruption of the narrative exchange between Johnson and Heye. Its dissonant sound more radically refutes the coercion involved in the sale, yet one almost needs to hear "The Pauline Project" first to grasp this. The two pieces reflect the importance of versioning in an oral tradition. Listening to "The Pauline Project," one can discern how she insisted that Heye agree that she could repurchase the wampum belt within two years if she could afford to do so:

> Briefly I find myself in a much better financial position than I had hoped, and my offers from England are most encouraging, so in thinking it all

> over I have concluded to place this proposition before you: will you purchase the belt out and out, giving me $500 for it, and the open possibility of repurchasing it for myself at any time within two years at an advanced figure, you to name the advance, so I will know just where I stand on the matter? You will quite appreciate the fact I know that I do not want to let the belt go completely from my possession at a figure I do not think its full historical value, and I want the opportunity of regaining it again after I get well established in England ... With my most kindly remembrance of our pleasant talk and meeting, I am yours faithfully, E. Pauline Johnson.[107]

Heye agrees to this stipulation as long as Johnson agrees "to give Mr. Heye the first option of repurchasing this belt if she wishes to dispose of it again." Rogers dwells on this phrase by echoing, "if she wishes, if she wishes, if she wishes to dispose of it again." Johnson's frequent overtures of friendship towards Heye underscore her efforts to maintain peace as she sacrifices her own agency. As Hamilton notes, like many public statements about material culture made by Indigenous people in the late nineteenth century, Johnson's letters are "couched in romantic Victorian language," which makes it difficult to discern how she actually felt about the sale.[108] Such language becomes representative of her assimilation. However, her comment about her financial situation reveals her reluctance to lose the belt. She also makes clear that she believes that Heye's price fails to reflect "its full historical value."

"Wampum Contracts" and "The Pauline Project" mourn the cultural loss of Johnson's belt without condemning her for selling it. The audience's background noises amplify this collective mourning. Clapping and laughter turn into jeering, booing, crying, and wailing as Johnson agrees to sell the belt. In "Wampum Contracts," other background noises include buzzing, party sounds, and a synthesizer beat, which create further sound interference. By making this private letter exchange into a performance, Rogers creates a sense of community accountability absent in their original exchange, and draws attention to the performativity of the encounter.

In the "Wampum Contracts" version, Heye's and Johnson's voices often cancel each other out and only traces of their exchange can be heard. Rogers repeats certain phrases, such as "Yours faithfully, E. Pauline Johnson" and "the wampum, the wampum, the wampum." As Johnson's polite words reverb, we hear ambivalence in her colonial mimicry. Did she really remember fondly her "pleasant talk and meeting" with Heye? Rogers implies that Johnson plays the role of the well-mannered Anglo-Canadian lady (much like she did in her poetry performances) because the dominant society expects this from her, but Rogers questions how accurately this persona represents her true feelings. To borrow from another of Rogers's poems, her sound pieces "mak[e] rooms ache / with memory echoes" (109). Such echoes destabilize the origins of the sound and by extension the pain of the memory. In a sense, "Wampum Contracts" laments the inability to know the extent of Johnson's duress when she made this sale. Ultimately, Rogers mourns the impenetrability of Johnson's mimicry. According to the Holocaust scholar Marianne Hirsch, the value of material objects comes from their ability to "carry memory traces from one generation to the next."[109] Yet Rogers underscores the indecipherability of those traces as part of the cultural loss.

Through the letters, Rogers also draws our attention to the less public parts of an archive. While a wampum belt might be featured in museum exhibits, the letters (which explain how it ended up in the museum) often remain out of public view. To think of this in the terms of the Two Row Wampum Treaty, we see evidence of the violation of the peaceful line between the two cultures being crossed in museum exhibits; however, the manner in which the line was violated (and the duress that this causes for Indigenous people) often remains invisible. Rogers reveals how, despite the apparent friendliness between Heye and Johnson, Heye maintains the upper hand due to Johnson's financial need.

Rogers's focus on Johnson's objects (as compared to other aspects of Johnson's legacy) reflects what Hal Foster has characterized as "the archival impulse" in contemporary art practices. He describes how "archival artists seek to make historical information, often lost or displaced, physically present."[110] Their art creates a counter-archive that complicates the institutional record and responds to the "failure of cultural memory."[111] Just as the pedagogy of schoolroom recitation often exerts institutional control over personal and community memory, so do the acquisition and curation of material objects in museums. Given the history of paper records being used to discredit oral ways of knowing, Rogers's sonic recreation of Johnson's written words becomes a political gesture. Drawing on sound-mixing technologies, she creates an Indigenous counter-archive based on sound rather than print. Rather than take a cynical approach (which would be easy to do when writing about museum appropriation of Aboriginal material culture), Foster suggests that archival artists aim "to probe a misplaced past, to collate its different signs (sometimes pragmatically, sometimes parodistically), to ascertain what might remain for the present."[112] Rogers recalls Johnson's sale of the wampum belt to collectively mourn both the cultural loss and Johnson's assimilation. She also brings Johnson's negotiation into the here and now as a lesson for reconciliation. Her book and her sound pieces demonstrate that peace premised on duress will continue to haunt subsequent generations.

Challenging Language Interference

Taking control of cultural memory also figures as a prominent theme in Annharte's performance poetry. Like all of the poets discussed in this book, she works in a variety of genres: as a poet, playwright, community activist, social worker, teacher, storyteller, and mixed-media artist. The author of four trade books of poetry, the Winnipeg-based author has been actively engaged in First Nations arts communities for the past thirty years. She is an outspoken critic of both Canadian-settler literature and also certain First Nations texts that she feels pander to settler concerns.[113]

Despite the centrality of performance to her multi-genre artistic project, Annharte has not released any sound recordings and there are only a few recordings of her work available online. Due to the lack of available recordings, my analysis of Annharte's performance poetics is limited to my memory of seeing her perform at various readings in Vancouver, as well as PennSound's recording of her performance at the Convergence on Poetics conference at the University of Washington, Bothell, in 2012. I also consider her third collection, *Exercises in Lip Pointing*, as a statement of her "lip pointing" performance poetics. Annharte's title refers to the gesture of lip pointing, used as an alternative to finger pointing, which can be considered accusatory, in many Indigenous cultures in North America. The cover image features four sets of lips open to varying degrees to make them appear as if they were in the process of making sounds. The cover image reminds the reader that these poems originate from a mouth rather than from a page. Throughout the book, Annharte underscores remembering as a physical and strenuous gesture that must combat external forces. The poems explore fond childhood recollections, traumatic memories of racial oppression, and the tragic loss of both personal and collective memory evoked by such lines as "a hole in her memory when her mother left."[114] The titles for the three sections of the book dramatize different dimensions involved in the act of remembering. In the first section, "Memory Fishes," the poems explore childhood memories, and Annharte expresses the difficulty of catching and holding on to memories. The middle section, "Red Noise," emphasizes the need to perform memories and to make noise with them in the present to prevent Native voices from being drowned out. The final section, "Coyotrix Recollects," invokes a feminine trickster figure as the agent of memory to fight against the erasure of Indigenous women's collective past.

Similar to Breeze's depiction of the dispossession of working-class Jamaican women, Annharte uses her poetry to address the problems facing many impoverished First Nations women in urban environments. In particular, many of her poems in *Exercises in Lip Pointing* critique the mistreatment of prostitutes in Vancouver's Downtown Eastside as well the disturbing epidemic of murdered and disappeared First Nations women in Canada, of which her own mother was one. Annharte composes poems "with a suppressed scream as subtext."[115] Through her poetry, she rejects the erasure of these women's lives from Canadian collective memory. In her poem "Woman Bath," she describes a "non-white hooker found dead in a ditch this morning." The speaker of the poem acknowledges a direct connection to the prostitute: "I found the dead girl in me   she wasn't killed by my words."[116] Here she underscores the role of language in obscuring First Nations women's existence and her struggle to reinvent a language that can make their lives intelligible. Lally Grauer describes Annharte's compositional process: "She scavenges the scraps littered around, recombines and recycles language so it does not boss *her* around."[117] Annharte recombines "the languages of social control – of government, social work, therapy, [and] self help."[118] For example, in the poem "JJ Bang Bang," which critiques the police shooting of J.J. Harper, a young Native leader who was mistaken for a car thief in the late 1980s in Manitoba, she mimics the authoritative voice of law enforcement telling the Native subject, "get a job go to school / you need a counseling referral" to make apparent the hypocrisy of these words.[119]

Despite the emphasis on oppression in Annharte's work, her poetry is exceedingly funny, and this quality becomes fully realized when she performs it.[120] In her performance at the Convergence conference, her deadpan delivery frequently caused her audience to laugh. Her social critique emerges through the comedy, by drawing attention to the absurdity of colonization and the tired stereotypes of Native identity. Annharte's sardonic tribute to Johnson in *Exercises in Lip Pointing*, "Geriatric Canoe Princess," which features prostitutes on the Downtown Eastside of Vancouver discussing an abusive john, exemplifies her use of humour as a form of social critique. Annharte addresses how First Nations women's self-representation continues to be governed by disempowering social scripts. Her title draws attention to the longevity of what Johnson called the "regulation Indian maiden" stereotype.[121] As the women discuss the abusive john, Johnson hovers like a ghost in the poem. While Annharte never directly names Johnson, she makes frequent references to her life and her iconic depiction of paddling in "The Song My Paddle Sings." She counts on her audience to make the connection because of the power of Johnson's legacy in Canadian collective memory. Similar to Rogers's focus on her museum objects, Annharte also explores who gets to claim Johnson's legacy. They both explore what Hirsch describes as the tension between "the 'guardianship' of a traumatic personal and generational past with which some of us have a 'living connection,' and that past's passing into history or myth."[122] The lives of the prostitutes are juxtaposed with Johnson's to draw attention to how the systemic discrimination against First Nations women has not significantly decreased since Johnson's time. To counter the mythologizing of Johnson, Annharte pairs the word "legend" with descriptions of Johnson's physicality: "legend pukes," "legend had breast cancer," "legend had sex," "legend had fun."[123] Annharte refers to Johnson's breast cancer, which caused her death. She draws attention to how despite her successful performance career she died poor in Vancouver, aligning Johnson's fate with that of the sex workers.

"Geriatric Canoe Princess" does not have a single identifiable speaker. In fact, each stanza in the five-page conversational poem sounds like an interjection. The short lines often leave out prepositions and verbs, or turn nouns into verbs to represent First Nations vernacular English. The first line contradicts the sense of decay evoked by the word *geriatric* in the title: "she poet alive."[124] Annharte turns poet into a verb to emphasize how it brings things to life. Because the title invokes Johnson's canoe legacy, the "she" becomes associated with her.

As part of an Indigenous writers' panel at Calgary's Glenbow Museum, Annharte described her educational experience with Johnson:

> I was forced to read her [Johnson] as a kid … that was my first real knowledge of someone who was trying to write about the environment and who

> was trying to write about settlers and that kind of thing. And actually why I even think highly of her, even though a lot of people don't like her work, is because she did come through Winnipeg and I think she was really inspired by what she saw of Western Indigenous women, so I always feel like she kinda knew something about us and wrote about us.[125]

Like Rogers, Annharte acknowledged Johnson as a groundbreaking figure because she challenged the stereotypical stories writers such as Longfellow told about Indigenous women. Yet she also drew attention to how Johnson herself reinforced the stereotypes that she hoped to challenge and was ultimately unable to tell her own story of being a mixed-race woman.

In "Geriatric Canoe Princess," Annharte uses a conversation between two women to underscore how disenfranchised subjects must directly take control of their own fragmented stories:

> then someone said
> if I had a paddle
> I would have pounded him
> Who's talking to you anyway
> let the speaker interrupt
> her own story[126]

These lines humorously evoke Johnson's representation of the canoe paddle as a symbol of First Nations women's agency to point to its current ineffectiveness. Annharte dispenses with quotation marks to make it ambiguous how many different women are speaking. The short lines and stanzas illustrate how each woman is trying to insert her voice into a very small space, which forces the women to compete against each other. This small poetic space becomes a metaphor for the limited space given to First Nations women in contemporary society. To have one's voice heard, one must say something dramatic to grab the audience's attention. Rather than suggest that the speaker tell "her own story," Annharte stresses that she should be able to "interrupt / her own story" to emphasize the power of the interruptive to reimagine social scripts. The line break underscores the disruption. Similar to Rogers's sonic permutations in "Wampum Contracts," Annharte accentuates the fragmentation to recover traces of Johnson's legacy.

To conclude the poem, Annharte links canoeing with remembering:

jump in my canoe
never mind the sea bus
you don't have time
trouble times we are all legend
if we know it or not
when we go by canoe
we remember to remember
we are remembered[127]

Annharte underscores the importance of First Nations women remembering their own history and being in control of their own movement. She suggests going by canoe rather than the sea bus, which is the public transportation that goes across the Burrard Inlet. This recalls Johnson's exchanges on the North Shore with the Squamish chief Joe Capilano, with whom she used to go canoeing in the Burrard Inlet before she became ill. Throughout her life, Johnson felt disconnected from her Six Nations tribe, and when she met him she finally had a First Nations mentor to teach her directly about Native history, rather than having to learn about it from white writers like Longfellow. The speaker warns that all First Nations women risk losing their humanity because of the persistence of Indigenous stereotypes.

Annharte connects such stereotypes to the damaging effects of English in her essay "Borrowing Enemy Language: A First Nations Woman's Use of Language." She describes how (like so many other writers from colonized sites) she must struggle with her paradoxical relationship to English as a writer: "When I speak of English as the enemy's language, I see the enemy as being *within* the individual person – within one's own language use and how one is programmed to look at things."[128] Rogers also mourns the fact that she learned English as her first language in her poem "Conflicted Loyalties" when she writes, "I miss the language I never had" (28). Annharte stresses that "if a writer does not question imposed language, then, to me, this writer is only passing on oppression to the reader or listener – we are hearing the 'colonized Native' voice."[129] Such "imposed language" interferes with one's ability to remember one's past.

To overcome this, Annharte stresses the role of performing language in the four-page title poem from *Exercises in Lip Pointing*. She describes poems as being crafted through "lips pointed full forward tilt" to make clear that texts such as "Geriatric Canoe Princess" are meant to be spoken aloud – to be made by a mouth emanating sounds – rather than remain static on the page:

Okay today
let's have the lips speak for themselves
shall we let them say what they must
say if asked
if ever asked
as if anyone ever asks
just the lips to speak
                    because the totality
                    of a person counts more
dominates
          what the lips want
                    koochy koo lips
                    lips pursed
          lips pointed full forward tilt
          top lip extended[130]

She invites lips to "speak for themselves," giving agency to the body to make meaning by both taking in and expelling language. She celebrates the right to exercise imaginative freedom and to speak without censorship – something that Johnson struggled to do throughout her life. To point at something is to call someone or something out – her poems do this by calling attention to the damages inflicted from the tyranny of hundreds of years of settler presence in the Americas. However, to suggest that poems are exercises is also reminiscent of the institutional legacy of recitation, when poems were used for rote learning. *Exercises in Lip Pointing* almost sounds like a form of elocutionary training where one might practise how to move one's mouth correctly to produce certain sounds. Yet the image of lips puckering can also be interpreted as the image of a mouth resisting acculturation and refusing to repeat the English that it is being forced to internalize. Annharte teaches her audience how to engage their bodies to reject assimilation by using the lips as the boundary point between the body and its environment. By describing her poems as a form of lip pointing, Annharte underscores the role of bodily gesture in reclaiming signification from dominant forces.

Like the other poets discussed in this chapter, Annharte uses performance to draw attention to how her people are adversely affected by globalization, colonial legacies, and discriminatory government policies. While dub and Indigenous performance poetries emerge through culturally specific forces, they often overlap and mutually inform each other as they resist containment within national borders. These poetries demonstrate that Canada is no longer "a one poem town" beholden to a legacy of Anglocentric values that deny the stage as a site of personal and communal self-creation. The phrase "one poem town" comes from Lillian Allen's infamous conflict with the League of Canadian Poets in 1984.

Allen's story is worth recalling at the end of this book because it highlights how performance poetry untangles the knots of colonial inheritance. When Allen and the dub poets Clifton Joseph and Devon Haughton applied for membership to the League of Canadian Poets in 1984, they were initially rejected because the board members deemed them to be "performers" and "not poets."[131] Many members of the League dismissed their work on the grounds that poetry should not be political and insisted that the dub poets were not writers because the majority of their work had been released as sound recordings. Allen's frosty reception in the Canadian literary world in the 1980s contrasts with her acclaim in the music world, where she won two Juno Awards, for her sound recordings *Revolutionary Tea Party* and *Conditions Critical* in the reggae-calypso category, in 1986 and 1988 respectively. In the spirit of Louise Bennett's newspaper poems, such as "Bans a Killin," which she used to challenge her detractors, Allen published "One Poem Town" as a retort to the League of Canadian Poets in *This Magazine*. Evoking the phrase "one-horse town," Allen accuses the gatekeepers of Canadian culture of provincialism:

> and run you down, down, down
> and out of town
> cause, this is a one poem town
> and hey! What are you doing here anyway?
> So don't come with no pling, ying, jing
> ding something
> calling it poetry[132]

As Diana Brydon argues, the title phrase "becomes a powerful metaphor for the insecure exclusivity of the invader-settler colony, which has displaced the land's original inhabitants and now wishes to exclude further arrivals."[133] Alluding to her conflict with the League in vernacular terms, as if it were a Wild West street fight, Allen rejects poetry as a page-bound art form. The dub poets' conflict with the League proves John Miles Foley's observation that oral poetic forms are often "denied admission by the gatekeepers of the literary arts."[134] Being refused membership also has material consequences, since the League supports poets through funding, advertising, and organizing reading tours.[135]

Allen makes an explicit connection between her situation and Louise Bennett's treatment by the literary establishment in Jamaica in the 1940s, attributing it to how "Jamaica, with its colonial legacy and British influences, is more similar to Canada than one would imagine."[136] Allen's circumstances are also reminiscent of Langston Hughes's struggle to overcome the "racial mountain" in US literature and to have his black folk poetics be recognized as legitimate. More alarmingly, her experiences echo E. Pauline Johnson's desire to gain acceptance as a female poet of colour in Canada almost one hundred years earlier. Like Johnson, she was criticized for her focus on the stage and her insistence that performance poetry should be recognized as literature. Yet these poets' performances of cultural difference were often what really threatened white-settler audiences.

Performance poets' contentious relationships with literary institutions often make us forget the historical link between the classroom and the contemporary poetry stage. To avoid building "a one poem town," this book has examined the distorted echo chamber of recitation in the development of modern performance poetry. In the late nineteenth century, verse recitation provided a way for an everyday person to enter the world of poetry. Holding the stage for a brief moment, the underclasses were permitted to breathe the words of the so-called great literary works. However, the act of embodied recitation engendered unexpected opportunities to challenge the dominant voices designed to interrupt a person's voice. While recitation pedagogies unfurled in the nineteenth century to colonize the voice and homogenize the English language, performance poets have reinvented recitation practices to promote reader agency; hybridize English; champion the disempowered voices of women, children, and colonized subjects; and create a more inclusive public sphere.

Notes

Introduction

1 Lovelace, *A Brief Conversation*, 123–4.
2 Fusco, *English Is Broken Here*, 37–40.
3 Taylor, *The Archive and the Repertoire*, 22.
4 Thomas Sheridan's *A Course of Lectures on Elocution* and John Walker's *Elements of Elocution* were two of the first texts to promote elocution and the idea of a proper and "natural" way of speaking in England.
5 Morrisson, "Performing the Pure Voice," 28.
6 Robson, *Heart Beats*, 51–2.
7 Beran, "In Defense of Memorization." For other defences of memorization in contemporary culture, see Hollander, ed., *Committed to Memory*; Robson, "Why Memorize a Poem?"; Leithauser, "Why We Should Memorize"; and Beachy-Quick, "Inscribe the Poem on Yourself." A common theme in these various pieces is the idea that memorizing poetry is good for improving language skills and for instilling the pleasures of poetry.
8 Beachy-Quick, "Inscribe the Poem on Yourself."
9 McLaren, *Life in Schools*, 212.
10 For a discussion of poetry recitation classes at settlement houses in New York in the 1920s, see Rubin, *Songs of Ourselves*, 186–92.
11 Robson, *Heart Beats*, 137. According to Robson, F.T. Palgrave's series of Golden Treasury anthologies were the most popular classroom readers in the UK until the Second World War. Brathwaite also attests that Palgrave's anthologies were frequently assigned in the anglophone Caribbean when he comments that "we all had to 'do' [them] at school." Brathwaite, *History of the Voice*, 9.

12 I put the term "Standard English" in quotation marks to underscore how the idea of a single grammar and usage for English is a fiction perpetuated by those in power.

13 Coverley is Louise Bennett's married name. Although her legal name was hyphenated after she married Eric Coverley in 1954, she published under the name Louise Bennett throughout her life; therefore, I refer to her as Louise Bennett throughout this study. The issue of names is more complicated with Johnson, who adopted her grandfather's Mohawk name, Tekahionwake, during her performance career when she first went to London. Gerson and Strong-Boag point out that "no evidence survives as to whether she followed proper Mohawk custom to obtain legitimate use of the name." For a discussion on the politics of Johnson's various names and nicknames, see Gerson and Strong-Boag, *Paddling Her Own Canoe*, 116–17; and Willmott, "Paddled by Pauline."

14 The conference, Noh Lickle Twang: Louise Bennett-Coverley: The Legend and the Legacy, was held at the University of the West Indies, Mona, in January 2008.

15 Barack Obama referred to Hughes's description of a dream deferred in his 2008 presidential campaign speeches, and John Kerry invoked Hughes's poem "Let America Be America Again" in his speeches leading up to the 2004 election. Kerry wrote the preface for a coffee table edition of Hughes's *Let America Be America Again and Other Poems* that was released in August 2004 during his campaign. While Hughes's call for America to be America again underscores the opposite – how America has never been America for African Americans – Kerry, perhaps not surprisingly, appropriated this poem in his campaign rhetoric as a straightforward patriotic call to an American past.

16 Critical studies of ethnic women writers tend to group them together. While this is useful to consider the growth and development of female-centred traditions in different geopolitical locations, it also keeps the knowledge produced by women's texts out of wider transnational dialogues. I place Bennett and Johnson in dialogue with Langston Hughes, one of the most famous poets of African American modernism, to pursue alternate lines of affiliation and to bring a wider attention to their work.

17 Additional scholarship on poetry recitation and elocutionary traditions includes Conquergood, "Rethinking Elocution," 325–41; Kirkpatrick, "Hunting the Wild Reciter," 59–71; N. Johnson, "The Popularization of Nineteenth Century Rhetoric," 139–57; and Tiffin, "Cold Hearts and (Foreign) Tongues," 909–21. For a discussion of how recitation

flourished in literary cultures in modern China, see Crespi, *Voices in Revolution*. Crespi notes that Chinese recitation, although quite distinct from anglophone recitation cultures, was also motivated by nationalism, underscoring the link between vocalized performance and national identity.

18 Rubin, *Songs of Ourselves*, 8–9.

19 Ibid., 5.

20 Robson, *Heart Beats*, 22. Throughout this book, I use Robson's term *recitation canon* to characterize the small range of texts that frequently appeared in schoolroom readers for recitation. She notes how the recitation canon differs from the literary canon established by the academy. I bring attention to the transnational reach of the recitation canon, studying how, as it moved across borders, this small range of texts gained some additions and was slightly reconfigured to suit national aims.

21 Sorby, *Schoolroom Poets*, xxvi.

22 *The Mimic Men* is the title of V.S. Naipaul's well-known novel about a colonial subject living in London in the post-colonial era.

23 Walcott, "The Caribbean: Culture or Mimicry?" 9.

24 Ibid., 10.

25 Bhabha, *The Location of Culture*, 122.

26 Ibid.; italics in the original.

27 Ibid., 126; italics in the original.

28 McClintock, *Imperial Leather*, 64.

29 Glissant, *Caribbean Discourse*, 26.

30 Freire describes the banking concept of education in the following passage: "The educator's role is to regulate the way the world 'enters into' the students. His task is to organize a process which already occurs spontaneously, to 'fill' the students by making deposits of information which he considers to constitute true knowledge. And since men 'receive' the world as passive entities, education should make them more passive still, and adapt them to the world … Translated into practice, this concept is well suited to the purposes of the oppressors, whose tranquility rests on how well men fit the world the oppressors have created, and how little they question it." Freire, *Pedagogy of the Oppressed*, 62–3.

31 McLaren, *Schooling as Ritual Performance*, lv.

32 Ibid., 3; italics in the original.

33 Kincaid, *Lucy*, 30. Further reference will be indicated in the text by page number.

34 In her analysis of Kincaid's *Lucy*, Tiffin also notes that it is important to analyze not only the content of the colonial curriculum but also the

teaching methods that were used to disseminate it. She argues that recitation was used "to enforce a separation between mind and body in the colonized subject" and that it inflicted particular damage on Caribbean female bodies. Tiffin, "Cold Hearts and (Foreign) Tongues," 910.

35 Brown-Hinds, "'Can't Leave Home without It,'" 140.

36 Donnell, "Dreaming of Daffodils," 50.

37 Moira Ferguson characterizes Kincaid's representation of the colour yellow in *Lucy* as "the jaundiced marker of white cultural identity." Ferguson, *Jamaica Kincaid*, 112.

38 Braithwaite, *History of the Voice*, 42.

39 Robson, "Standing," 148.

40 Johnson, "A Cry from an Indian Wife," *Collected Poems*, 15; Bennett, "Bans a Killin," *Selected Poems*, 4; and Hughes, "I, Too," *The Collected Poems*, 46.

41 Taylor, *The Archive and the Repertoire*, 274.

42 For a discussion of Bennett as a transnational poet, see Ramazani, *A Transnational Poetics*.

43 Thomas, *Modern Blackness*, 56.

44 I characterize Hughes's contributions to social change as part of the project of decolonization. As I have argued elsewhere, he himself positioned the African American struggle for liberation as part of the wider struggle against imperialism. While Hughes is not technically a colonized subject according to strict definitions of colonialism, many scholars have examined how the African American situation in the United States can be considered in colonial terms. For example, historian Martha Hodes calls the US treatment of African Americans during slavery and segregation a form of "domestic colonialism," which helped to support US "imperial expansion" abroad. See Neigh, "The Transnational Frequency," 265–85; and Hodes, "Fractions and Frictions," 242–3.

45 Kates, *Activist Rhetorics*, 20.

46 Robson, *Heart Beats*, 4. Recitation and rote learning were also widely used in French- and Spanish-speaking countries in the Americas. Although these contexts are beyond the scope of this book, we need more scholarship on how these practices were implemented there and on how writers responded to them. For example in the francophone Caribbean, authors representing the colonial classroom often emphasize the trauma of physical dictation rather than oral recitation of poetry in front of an audience (see Pineau, *Exile*). For a discussion of representations of French education in Caribbean literature, see Léticeé, *Education, Assimilation and*

Identity. For an examination of poetry recitation in public life in Latin America, see Gruesz, *Ambassadors of Culture*; and Kuhnheim, *Beyond the Page*.

47 Buurma and Heffernan, "The Common Reader and the Archival Classroom," 116.

48 In his book *American Poetry in Performance*, Hoffman posits Walt Whitman as the father of performance poetry in the United States. While I draw attention to Longfellow's unacknowledged influence on many poets through his association with recitation, the genealogy mapped out in this project resists positing a single point of origin.

49 Gray, "Preparing for Popularity," 35.

50 Gruesz, *Ambassadors of Culture*, 86. Edgar Allan Poe went so far as to accuse Longfellow of plagiarism because he was so skilful in imitating and adapting other people's ideas (see Poe, "Mr. Longfellow and Other Plagiarists," 292–334). For an analysis of Longfellow's poetry in curricula in the Philippines in the early twentieth century and its relationship to US imperialism, see Wesling, *Empire's Proxy*. For an analysis of how Hebrew translations of *The Song of Hiawatha* influenced Jewish American writers in the late nineteenth and early twentieth centuries, see Katz, *Red, Black, and Jew*; and Rubinstein, *Members of the Tribe*.

51 Ibid., 84.

52 Canada banned potlatch ceremonies as well as "dances associated with religious, supernatural Tamanawas rituals" in 1884. Bans on Thirst dances and Ghost dances followed in 1895. Dickason and Newbigging, *A Concise History of Canada's First Nations*, 199. In Trinidad, after emancipation in 1838, the British government limited carnival celebrations to two days a year, tied to a Christian holiday. Later in the nineteenth century, they also tried (unsuccessfully) to ban stick fighting, which involved chanting and drumming processions in the streets. Dudley, *Carnival Music in Trinidad*, 11–13.

53 For a discussion about the complex relationships among performance, orality, and literacy in colonized sites, see Finnegan, *Oral Traditions*; and Foley, *How to Read*.

54 Arguments about the centrality of orality in Indigenous and black Atlantic poetics often sound quite similar. For example, Zolbrod argues that Native American oral poetry "remains fundamentally a creation of the speaking or singing voice." Zolbrod, *Reading the Voice*, 1. Brathwaite, stresses that Caribbean vernacular poetries "exist not in a dictionary but in the tradition of the spoken word." Brathwaite, *History of the Voice*, 17. In the development of African American literature, Henry Louis Gates

Jr argues for the centrality of the "tension between the spoken and the written word" in the development of African American literature. Gates, *The Signifying Monkey*, 131.

55 Paul Gilroy, "' … to be real,'" 16.

56 Foley, *How to Read*, 68.

57 Street, "The New Literacy Studies," 430. See also Street, *Literacy in Theory*.

58 Foley, *How to Read*, 69.

59 Mignolo, *Local Histories*, 221.

60 For scholarship on the poetry reading in twentieth-century poetics, see Bernstein, *Close Listening*; MacArthur, "Monotony"; and Wheeler, *Voicing American Poetry*. MacArthur notes how "the term *performance poetry* distinguishes more expressivist (read: ethnic and/or nonacademic) poetry-reading styles from the dominant neutral style of academic poetry reading, which is treated as the norm." MacArthur, "Monotony," 59; italics in the original.

61 Sherwood, "Elaborate Versionings," 120.

62 Questions about oral translation into print predominate across different forms of performance poetry. Studies examine how poets animate oral aesthetics in their work and encode the oral dimensions of a poem onto the page for their own performances and for their readers to engage with their poems. Gingell notes that poets are often motivated to publish because doing so earns them cultural capital in the dominant society and helps them to expand their audiences. For scholarship on Caribbean performance poetry in print, see Gingell, "'Always a Poem,'" 220–59; Casas, "Whose Rhythm?" 167–87; Bucknor, "Body-vibes," 301–22; and Morris, *'Is English We Speaking.'* For scholarship on Indigenous poetry in print, see Blaeser, "Writing Voices Speaking," 53–68; and Brill de Ramírez, *Contemporary American Indian Literatures*.

63 The ubiquity of the term *performance*, and its theoretical counterpart *performativity*, in academic discourse has taken away some of the term's critical acuity, yet its mutability reveals the wide-ranging power of performance practices in everyday life. Aside from being the name of an interdisciplinary field, *performance* refers to aesthetic categories, accomplishments, actions, technical practices, and theories of ontology. J.L. Austin originally defined performativity as the ability of performed language to produce identities and social realities. Building on Austin, Judith Butler has established that the repetition of our everyday bodily habits and actions is a performance that constitutes our gendered identities. Deborah Kapchan stresses that *to perform* is a transitive verb to emphasize how the action animates and transforms the object being

performed. Peggy Phelan suggests that what makes performance unique is its "liveness." Yet as Taylor underscores, what performance often brings alive in the present is memory. I explore how these multiple meanings relate to poetry performance. While leaving the definition open, I stress that with poetry, performance becomes an embodied relational practice that animates the intersection between linguistic and extra-linguistic communication. See Austin, *How to Do Things with Words*; Butler, *Bodies That Matter*; Kapchan, "Performance," 121–45; Phelan, *Unmarked*; and Taylor, *The Archive and the Repertoire*.

64 Cowan, "Editorial," 8. The African American poet Tracie Morris is more critical of the pop-culture appropriation of *spoken word* than Cowan, arguing that it has become "a sales term" and that "'poetry' gets lost in the breadth of the definition of 'spoken word.'" (It should be noted that Morris makes this statement in an edited collection with the subtitle *35 Women Leaders in the Spoken Word Revolution*, suggesting that she also accepts Cowan's more radical definition of the term). Similarly, Maria Damon describes spoken word as "a marketing term coined to dispel anxieties about 'poetry.'" Furthermore, I would suggest that the branding of performance poetry as spoken word runs the risk of detaching it from the colonial histories that have shaped it as a mode of social critique. See Morris, "Ad-Libbing," 260; and Damon, "Was That," 332. Foley prefers to use the term *oral poetry* to emphasize how it exists outside of print-centric frameworks; see Foley, *How to Read*, 27–9. For a discussion about the value of the term *verbal arts*, particularly for connecting poetry to traditional forms like folktales and proverbs, see Finnegan, *Oral Traditions*, 10–11; and Bauman, *Verbal Art as Performance*.

65 Cooper, *Noises in the Blood*, 81.

66 For more on the popularity of spoken word in the classroom, see Low, *Slam School*.

67 Recent scholarship on US performance poetry includes Somers-Willett, *The Cultural Politics of Slam Poetry*; Hoffman, *American Poetry in Performance*; and Jones, *The Muse Is Music*. For a multidisciplinary discussion of performance that focuses primarily on Canada, see Gingell and Roy, *Listening Up, Writing Down*.

68 In "Our America [Nuestra América]" (1891), the Cuban writer and activist José Martí makes a call for an inclusive and multi-layered approach to cultures of the Americas in order to resist American imperialism. The historian Edmundo O'Gorman's *The Invention of America: An Inquiry into the Historical Nature of the New World and the Meaning of Its History* (1961) was also an important early work in hemispheric studies that

established the idea of the New World as an invented category central to a Western world view. There are far too many inter-American works to mention them all individually; however, prominent ones include Belnap and Fernández, *José Martí's "Our America"*; Chevigny and Laguardia, *Reinventing the Americas*; Cowan and Humphries, *Poetics of the Americas*; Dash, *The Other America*; Firmat, ed., *Do the Americas Have a Common Literature?*; Fitz, *Rediscovering the New World*; Mignolo, *Local Histories*; and Zamora, *The Usable Past*. The University of Virginia Press's New World Studies series, edited by Michael J. Dash, also includes a number of significant works that have brought more attention to Canadian and Caribbean literatures in hemispheric studies. For example, see Casteel, *Second Arrivals*. Border studies have also played a prominent role in the emergence of inter-American studies (see Anzaldúa, *Borderlands / La Frontera*; and Sadowski-Smith, *Globalization on the Line*). To disrupt notions of linguistic purity in New World identities, recent scholars advocate a multilingual approach to hemispheric studies. Caribbean studies, where older colonial models have obscured the examination of the dialogues between francophone, anglophone, and hispanophone literatures in the region, particularly require this. While *Recalling Recitation in the Americas* focuses on anglophone-derived literatures in the Americas, I hope to contribute to cross-linguistic dialogue by unmooring the disciplinary boundaries of English studies from within. Rather than erase linguistic difference, I draw attention to the multifaceted ways in which English has been pluralized and destabilized throughout the Americas. For multilingual approaches to Caribbean studies, see: Martínez-San Miguel, *Coloniality of Diasporas*; Orlando and Cypress, *Reimagining the Caribbean*; and Van Haesendonck and D'haen, *Caribbeing*.

69 As Jeff Karem stresses, "US Americans have drastically overlooked the contributions of the Caribbean islands to the literary culture of both the Western Hemisphere and the United States itself … [the Caribbean] has rarely been recognized by the United States as a collaborator or interlocutor in the development of New World history." Karem, *The Purloined Islands*, 2. While the United States recognizes Canada more widely than the Caribbean, it is still considered peripheral and the United States has dominated definitions of New World history. As a Canadian scholar who completed her graduate work and now teaches in the United States, I am continually reminded of the virtual invisibility of Canadian literature in English departments in the United States and yet I frequently notice parallels, connections, and dialogues between writers from these two countries.

70 See Wylie, "Hemispheric Studies or Scholarly NAFTA?" 48–61.

71 Philip, "Interview with Empire," 200. J. Edward Chamberlin also notes that Caribbean poets often explore how "the ravaging of aboriginal societies of the new world by the representatives of European civilization is closely related to the story of slavery and to the brutal dispossession and despair that are its legacy." Chamberlin, *Come Back to Me*, 7.

72 Baker, "Borrowing Enemy Language," 60. Annharte has published under the name Marie Annharte Baker, Marie Annharte, and Annharte. I refer to her as Annharte throughout this book because this is currently her preference.

73 Philip, "Interview with Empire," 198, 199.

74 Ibid., 200. Philip writes, "The Caribbean is synonymous with rupture and break and hiatus and held breath. And death. And rebirth."

75 McCall, "Diaspora and Nation," 22–3. For a discussion of Indigenous nationalism in literary studies, see Acoose, "A Vanishing Indian?"; Weaver, Womack, and Warrior, *American Indian Literary Nationalism;* and Womack, *Red on Red*. For a discussion of black diasporic mobility, see Gilroy, *The Black Atlantic*.

76 Kim and McCall, introduction, 1.

77 McCall, "Diaspora and Nation," 37.

78 See Jackson, *Creole Indigeneity*; and Newton, "Return to a Native Land," 108–22.

79 For a critique of post-colonial theory in Indigenous literary studies, see King, "Godzilla vs. the Post-Colonial," 10–16.

80 McCall, "Diaspora and Nation," 22.

81 McLeod, "Coming Home through Stories," 22.

82 McCall, "Diaspora and Nation," 22.

83 Brill de Ramírez, *Contemporary American Indian Literatures*, 10.

84 Literary scholarship has used approaches based in cultural studies to examine popular literature and fiction more often than poetry. This project builds on the work of scholars who have bridged sociological and formal analyses of poetic texts, such as Maria Damon, who coined the term *micropoetries* to refer to informal verse found in diaries, blogs, greeting cards, and bathroom stalls; Rachel Blau DuPlessis's method of "social philology," which interprets the exchange between "the historical terrain and the intimate poetic textures of a work"; Peter Middleton's strategy of "distant reading," which focuses on the performative dimension of reading, tracing how and where texts travel, to explore "a text's intersubjective embeddedness in mutually negotiated histories of cultural and social exchange"; and Michael Davidson's attention to

"form" as part of "a work's institutional and pedagogical functions." See Damon, *Postliterary America*, 5; DuPlessis, *Genders, Races and Religious Cultures*, 1; Middleton, *Distant Reading*, 11; and Davidson, *On the Outskirts of Form*, 6.

85 Chartier, *The Order of Books*, 3.

86 Foley, *How to Read*, 81–2.

87 Lorde, *Sister Outsider*, 43–4.

88 Minh-ha, *Woman, Native, Other*, 101. For uses of "speaking nearby," see Andrews, *In the Belly of the Laughing God*, 35; Gerson and Strong-Boag, *Paddling Her Own Canoe*, 6; and Hoy, *How Should I Read These?* 34.

1. E. Pauline Johnson (Tekahionwake) and Her "Dear Dead Longfellow"

1 Another strong contender for the most recited poem in Canada is John McRae's "In Flanders Fields" (1915).

2 Gray, *Flint and Feather*, 155.

3 Johnson, *Collected Poems*, 81. Unless otherwise noted further references to Johnson are from her *Collected Poems* and will be indicated in the text by page number.

4 Dean, *Inheriting a Canoe Paddle*, 63.

5 See Goldie, *Fear and Temptation*, 13–17; and Deloria, *Playing Indian*. Both Deloria and Goldie study the cultural appropriation of Indigenous cultures, although Deloria examines the United States and Goldie examines Canada, Australia, and New Zealand. While Goldie concentrates on a broad range of cultural production, Deloria focuses primarily on performance, studying how impersonating Native identities has conformed to different needs throughout US history.

6 Gerson, "Pauline Johnson," 228.

7 The following example from a review of the University of Arizona's 1987 edition of Johnson's *The Moccasin Maker*, by the poet Charles Lillard, illustrates how her recitation legacy weakened her literary reputation. He takes a condescending tone when discussing Johnson's unintellectual audience: "The majority of readers (buyers is possibly more accurate) are tourists, grandmothers buying their childhood favourites for their grandchildren, and the curious. None of these buyers/readers constitute an audience willing to plow through Introductions, Bibliographies, and notes; most will not recognize their value." See Lillard, "Choice of Lens," 155. For a discussion about how Johnson's reputation has vacillated between extremes, see Lyon, "Pauline Johnson."

8 For a discussion of how professional elocutionists paved the way for the emergence of author readings, see Byerly, "From Schoolroom to Stage," 125–41.
9 Review of performance at the Toronto Junction, *Daily Tribune*, 23 March 1892, clipping, box 4, file 1, Pauline Johnson Collection.
10 Wheeler, *Voicing American Poetry*, 12–13.
11 Atwood, *Strange Things*, 91–2.
12 Carlson, *Performance*, 5.
13 Rogers, "Blood Moves Us," 257.
14 Gentile, *Cast of One*, 63.
15 As Gerson and Strong-Boag explain, it was difficult for a woman performer "especially if unmarried … to maintain social propriety." Johnson's performances were also much more gregarious than the usual recitation, as she mimicked loud war yells and engaged her whole body in performance. Gerson and Strong-Boag suggest that this might also help to explain why *elocutionist* "slipped from her promoters' vocabulary after she adopted her Native costume" in 1892, and was typically replaced with some variation of "the Indian Poet-Reciter" or "the Mohawk author-entertainer." See Gerson and Strong-Boag, *Paddling Her Own Canoe*, 104–5.
16 Nurhussein, *Rhetorics of Literacy*, 24.
17 For a discussion of the different types of recitation manuals and how the elocution movement appealed to the self-taught learner in the context of the United States, see N. Johnson, "The Popularization of Nineteenth Century Rhetoric," 139–57.
18 Gray, *Flint and Feather*, 53, 60.
19 Pauline's sister, Evelyn Johnson, describes their mother's British approach to childrearing in her unpublished memoir: "We were strictly instructed in etiquette, and many English habits were manifest in our training. Many and varied were the admonitions in behavior given to us, and our table manners were checked with the utmost rigidity." E. Johnson, "Chiefswood," 37.
20 Willmott, "Paddled by Pauline."
21 Gerson, "Pauline Johnson," 220.
22 "Canadian Born" is the title of one of Johnson's poems and her second book-length collection of poetry, published in 1903.
23 Johnson to Kains, 20 April 1890, Archibald Kains Fonds.
24 Sorby, *Schoolroom Poets*, xiii. Archival evidence indicates that Johnson knew some Mohawk but was not fluent in the language. See Gerson and Strong-Boag, *Paddling Her Own Canoe*, 175.
25 Quoted in Johnston, *Buckskin and Broadcloth*, 76.

26 Box 6, file 6, Pauline Johnson Collection.
27 Johnson to Kains, 18 May 1891, Archibald Kains Fonds.
28 Gray, *Flint and Feather*, 124–5.
29 Lyon, "Pauline Johnson."
30 Foley, *How to Read*, 20.
31 A reviewer at the second "Evening of Canadian Authors," held a couple of months later, noted of Johnson that "the gifted authoress is almost as successful an elocutionist as she is a writer." *The Empire*, 15 March 1892, box 4, file 1, Pauline Johnson Collection.
32 Gray, *Flint and Feather*, 142.
33 Gerson and Strong-Boag, *Paddling Her Own Canoe*, 110.
34 After Johnson's death, promoters began calling her "the Mohawk Princess," although they did not use this term during her lifetime. This name became popular after the publication of the first full-length study of her work, *The Mohawk Princess: Being Some Account of the Life of TEKAHION-WAKE (E. Pauline Johnson)* (1931). For a discussion of how this problematic designation developed during her transition into a national icon, see Gerson and Strong-Boag, *Paddling Her Own Canoe*, 124–5.
35 Phillips, "Performing the Native Woman," 124; LaRocque, *When the Other Is Me*, 124.
36 Johnson's performance tours were incredibly demanding. Gray estimates that from October 1892 to May 1893, Johnson performed 125 shows in fifty different towns and cities in Ontario, noting that she would travel and perform anywhere the railway would take her. Gray, *Flint and Feather*, 162.
37 Francis, *The Imaginary Indian*, 114.
38 *Hamilton Spectator*, 31 January 1903, box 4, file 8, Pauline Johnson Collection.
39 Leighton, "Performing Pauline," 159.
40 Bhabha, *Location of Culture*, 128; italics in the original.
41 Leighton, "Performing Pauline," 148.
42 Gray, *Flint and Feather*, 253.
43 *Pale as Real Ladies* is the title of Joan Crate's poetry collection about Pauline Johnson.
44 Brill de Ramírez, *Contemporary American Indian Literatures*, 1–6.
45 P. Gray, "Preparing for Popularity," 34–8.
46 British and American reviewers, rather than Canadian ones, noted the influence of Longfellow. This perhaps reflects Canadian reviewers' desire to de-emphasize foreign influence in order to uphold Johnson's work as uniquely Canadian.

47 Review of *The White Wampum, The Weekly Scotsman*, 8 March 1895, box 4, file 14, Pauline Johnson Collection.

48 Review of *The White Wampum, The Scotsman*, 8 July 1895, box 4, file 14, Pauline Johnson Collection. This Scottish reviewer assumes that Johnson is a male author, indicating that he is unaware of her performances.

49 For a discussion of the canonization of Johnson after her death and the role of John W. Garvin in promoting her as a great Canadian poet, see Shrive, "What Happened to Pauline?" 25–38.

50 The final chapter of this book will examine Johnson's legacy from the perspective of contemporary First Nations women writers. The contemporary Mohawk writer Beth Brant argues, "Pauline Johnson began a movement that has proved unstoppable in its momentum – the movement of First Nations women to write down our stories." Brant, *Writing as Witness*, 5.

51 Gerson, "Rereading Pauline Johnson," 49.

52 LaRocque, *When the Other Is Me*, 122.

53 Lyon, "Pauline Johnson."

54 The dynamic between Aboriginal peoples in the Americas and white settlers is often more all-encompassing than in other colonial settings. The high social standing of Johnson's family in the Six Nations community and her mixed-race parentage also made her very acculturated in white society.

55 Zamora, *The Usable Past*, 7.

56 Gray, *Flint and Feather*, 124.

57 E. Johnson, "Chiefswood," 1.

58 According to Trachtenberg, Longfellow may have been aware that he used the wrong name but selected Hiawatha, rather than the correct Manabozho, because it sounded more poetic. See Trachtenberg, *Shades of Hiawatha*, 52.

59 For Johnson's view of Hiawatha, see also "The Iroquois Women of Canada," in *Collected Poems*, 203.

60 McRaye, *Pauline Johnson*, 1, 40.

61 See Trachtenberg, *Shades of Hiawatha*, 54; and Carr, *Inventing the American Primitive*.

62 Viehmann, "Speaking Chinook," 261.

63 Scott, *Domination*, xii, 4.

64 Jackson, "Longfellow's Tradition," 475.

65 The reception of *The Song of Hiawatha* in the United States will be explored more thoroughly in chapter 2. Although the poem was immensely popular in Canada as well, few scholars have studied the poem's Canadian reception. Fenn Elan Stewart analyses the

performances of *The Song of Hiawatha* by members of the Ojibway tribe in northern Ontario, which were organized by the Canadian Pacific Railway to promote tourism in the area in the early 1900s. Frank Yeigh (Johnson's manager early in her career) writes a glowing but condescending review of one of these performances in 1901. He concludes his review by implying that the Ojibway people are a passive part of the wilderness scenery: "And here we drop the curtain, as the Canadian Ojibways did over the thrilling scenes enacted by these dusky children of nature, amid the blessed islands that adorn the silver sea of Huron." His review suggests that performances of *The Song of Hiawatha* also contributed to nationalist myth making in Canada as well as the United States (albeit in different ways) by reinforcing the idea of the vanishing Native. See Yeigh, "The Drama of Hiawatha," 217; and Stewart, "Hiawatha/Hereafter," 159–80.

66 Review of *The White Wampum, The Sketch*, 24 July 1895, box 4, file 14, Pauline Johnson Collection.

67 Leighton, "Performing Pauline Johnson," 157.

68 Lyon, "Pauline Johnson."

69 Siemerling and Casteel, introduction, 10.

70 For an account of Johnson's performance of this poem, see Gray, *Flint and Feather*, 151–55.

71 Canoeing became a popular hobby among Anglo-Canadians in the late nineteenth century as part of the recreation-in-nature movement, which emerged as a response to industrialization. Along with canoeing, outdoor activities like camping and hiking become widespread as part of this movement. In the popular imagination, nature became domesticated as a leisure space rather than as dangerous wilderness to be feared. For a discussion of how Johnson's writing capitalized on this trend, see the chapter "The Canoeing Craze" in Gray, *Flint and Feather*.

72 Willmott, "Paddled by Pauline."

73 See Gerson and Strong-Boag, *Paddling Her Own Canoe*, 140–54. Gerson and Strong-Boag interpret the canoe as a symbol of independence and freedom akin to American and British women writing about the bicycle as a symbol of the New Woman's mobility and a non-threatening arena to negotiate women's agency in the public sphere.

74 Many of Johnson's reviewers did not pick up on her encrypted challenge to the ideology of the vanishing Native and instead associated her with it. For example, the following reviewer identifies her as the voice of the disappeared: "It was like the voice of the nations who once possessed

this country, who have wasted away before our civilization, speaking through this cultured, gifted, soft-voiced descendant." "Brantford Abroad," 1892, box 4, file 1, Pauline Johnson Collection.

75 Longfellow, *The Song of Hiawatha*, 45. Further reference will be indicated in the text by page number.

76 Dean, *Inheriting a Canoe Paddle*, 25.

77 Ibid., 28–9.

78 Robson, *Heart Beats*, 13.

79 McRaye, *Pauline Johnson*, 64.

80 Francis, *The Imaginary Indian*, 22.

81 Gray quotes the women's rights activist Nellie McClung, who relates her impressions of Johnson's performance in 1899 in her memoirs: "[Her] advertising had shown only the Indian girl in her beaded chamois costume and feather headdress, so when a beautiful young woman in white satin evening dress came out of the vestry door and walked to the platform, there was a gasp of surprise from the audience." McClung goes on to remark that Pauline performed "The Song My Paddle Sings" in the first half of her show before she changed into her Native outfit. Her comments indicate that sometimes Johnson performed "The Song My Paddle Sings" in the first half of her show. McClung's description of the audience's "gasp of surprise" also illustrates how Johnson played with audience expectations to reveal the performativity of race. See Gray, *Flint and Feather*, 253.

82 Lynes, "Claiming Culture, Claiming Voice," 129–30; Moses, "Getting (Back) to Poetry," 127; and Deerchild, "My Poem Is an Indian Woman," 240–1.

83 Zolbrod, *Reading the Voice*, 1.

84 For a discussion of Whittier's abolitionism, see Sorby, *Schoolroom Poets*, 43–56. She characterizes Whittier's racial politics as more radical than those of any of the other schoolroom poets, describing how he fought to end the Massachusetts law that prohibited marriage between blacks and whites in the 1830s.

85 The Metis are a mixed-race people whose existence resulted from the encounter between European and French-Canadian men with Native women during the fur trade.

86 Gerson and Strong-Boag, *Paddling Her Own Canoe*, 169.

87 For a discussion of Johnson's relationship to residential schooling, see, ibid., 197. They point out that in in her fiction from this period, she examines the effects of institutionalized education on Native children and challenges discrimination in Canada's classrooms. While Johnson

did not attend a residential school because the government only began establishing the system in the 1880s, her younger brothers disliked their experiences at the Mohawk Institute, the residential school run by the Church of England in Brantford. On her tours, she also had the opportunity to visit residential schools on the Prairies, and she became an outspoken critic of them once she witnessed their appalling conditions.

88 Gray, *Flint and Feather*, 363–4.

89 Despite widespread discrimination toward mixed-race subjects in late nineteenth-century North America, mixed-race identity afforded power and status to move between cultures. Johnson's character Larocque seems representative of this group, who often used their status to promote the value of Native culture. Gerson and Strong-Boag discuss how in the late nineteenth century there was "something of a mixed-race aristocracy that emerged in North America." Gerson and Strong-Boag, *Paddling Her Own Canoe*, 31.

90 Smith, "Speaking in Tongues."

91 For a discussion of Johnson's loyalty to the British Empire, see Gerson and Strong-Boag, *Paddling Her Own Canoe*, 178–84. They suggest that her efforts to acknowledge Indigenous people as part of the national community were limited by the "racial thinking of her age"; however, at times she also challenged colonial authority even when she appeared on the surface to be upholding it.

92 Ibid., 198–99.

93 Braz, "Outer America," 127.

94 For Fanon's analysis of the alienating psychological effects of the colonizer's gaze on black subjects, which causes one to develop a depersonalized self, see Fanon, *Black Skin, White Masks*.

95 Goldie, *Fear and Temptation*, 12.

96 Fusco, *English Is Broken Here*, 47.

97 Gross, "Coureurs-de-bois," 82.

98 Scott, *Domination*, 4.

99 Whittier, *The Complete*, 69.

100 Ibid., 69.

101 Gray, *Flint and Feather*, 208–12.

2. Langston Hughes's Rhythmic Literacy

1 Quoted in Waggoner, "Teacher Curbed."

2 Nichols, *Arna Bontemps-Langston Hughes Letters*, 266.

3 Waggoner, "Teacher Curbed."
4 Ibid.
5 For a discussion of how the focus on racial identity in Hughes scholarship causes "racial coding" and "over-simplification" in the close readings of his frequently anthologized poems, see Jones, "Listening to What the Ear Demands," 1146.
6 Hughes, *The Collected Poems*, 46.
7 Rampersad, *The Life of Langston Hughes*, 1:94–5.
8 Bernard, *Remember Me to Harlem*, 36.
9 McHenry, *Forgotten Readers*, 4–5.
10 Ibid.
11 Frye, *The Bush Garden*, 191.
12 Nurhussein, *Rhetorics of Literacy*, 213.
13 Another reason why Hughes's children's literature has remained understudied is because he openly stated that he sought an audience of children in order to make money. However, regardless of his monetary intentions, his letters with Bontemps reveal that his children's projects were politically motivated, and that it is through performance that he envisioned their power. See Smith, *Children's Literature of the Harlem Renaissance*, 237.
14 I echo Mervyn Morris's well-known essay, "On Reading Louise Bennett Seriously." As I will discuss in the next chapter, critics often cite Bennett's use of vernacular language as the reason why her work is not taken seriously; however, her focus on children also made it difficult for her to gain credibility as a serious artist.
15 Rampersad, *The Life of Langston Hughes*, 1:140–5.
16 Hughes published numerous works for children, particularly toward the end of his career. See Hughes, *The Collected Works of Langston Hughes*, vol. 11: *Works for Children and Young Adults*.
17 Mickenberg, *Learning from the Left*; and Scott, *Socialist Joy*. See also Anatol, "Langston Hughes and the Children's Literary Tradition," 237–58; Smith, *Children's Literature of the Harlem Renaissance*; and Tracy, "The Dream Keeper," 78–94.
18 Anatol, "Langston Hughes and the Children's Literary Tradition," 243.
19 Hughes's representation of empowered children in his poems can be connected to racial uplift campaigns from the early twentieth century, which often used the black child as a symbol of social progress. See Smith, *Children's Literature of the Harlem Renaissance*, iii.
20 As Freire explains, "the role of the student among students would be to undermine the power of oppression and serve the cause of liberation." Freire, *Pedagogy of the Oppressed*, 62.

21 Hughes, *The Dream Keeper*, 77.
22 Street, *Cross-Cultural Approaches to Literacy*, 2.
23 Hughes, "Cowards from the Colleges," 227.
24 Ibid., 228.
25 Hughes, *The Big Sea*, 335, italics in the original. Further reference will be indicated in the text by page number.
26 See Rampersad, *The Life of Langston Hughes*, 1:54–6.
27 Hughes's representation of himself as a young man sailing back to Africa anticipates later works by Caribbean poets like Kamau Brathwaite, M. NourbeSe Philip, and Mutabaruka, who explore the Atlantic Ocean and the Middle Passage as symbols of black cultural memory. This is particularly true in projects like Philip's *Zong!* which examines the atrocity of enslaved African peoples who were thrown overboard during their journey to the Americas. Hughes counteracts this disempowering history by depicting himself as a young black man with the freedom of mobility to journey back to Africa on his own accord.
28 Mencken, *The American Language*, 71. For a discussion of the African American response to *The American Language*, see Miller, *Accented America*, 196–8.
29 Jones, "Listening to What the Ear Demands," 1158.
30 Street and Street, "The Schooling of Literacy," 148.
31 Ibid., 146–7.
32 McHenry, *Forgotten Readers*, 10.
33 Kates, *Activist Rhetorics*, 54. Hughes follows in the footsteps of black education activists like the elocution professor Hallie Quinn Brown (1845–1949), whom Kates discusses in her book. Like Hughes, she was overwhelmed by illiteracy in the South after her first teaching post at a plantation school, and she devoted her life to black education. She believed that elocution was the ideal vehicle for her mission because of its emphasis on performance. Kates analyses her work "transforming mainstream elocution theory" to address learners who spoke in the black vernacular (54). Brown's recitation manual *Bits and Odds: A Choice Selection of Recitations* (1880), designed for a black audience, figures as a precursor to Hughes's *The Negro Mother and Other Dramatic Recitations*. She included poems in the black vernacular along with recitation classics, and in her elocution instructions, she emphasizes the embodied aspects of the practice. Kates also notes that Brown believed that elocution could contribute to community building and political action, rather than the cultivation of individual taste.
34 McHenry, *Forgotten Readers*, 54.

35 Ibid., 13.
36 hooks, "Performance Practice," 211.
37 Rampersad, *The Life of Langston Hughes*, 1:7.
38 See Robson, "Standing," 148–62. Robson draws a parallel between the use of physical punishment to enforce memorization and recitation and the practice itself as a vehicle for "bodily correction" of a child's speech, demeanour, and carriage.
39 Ibid., 157.
40 Hughes, *The Collected Works of Langston Hughes*, 9:321.
41 Hughes identified Whitman as a primary influence in his own writing, praising him for inspiring his lyric voice. In his introduction to a collection of Whitman's poems, he writes, "One of the greatest 'I' poets of all time, Whitman's 'I' is not the 'I' of the introspective versifiers who write always and only about themselves. Rather it is the cosmic 'I' of all peoples who seek freedom, decency and dignity, friendship and equality between individuals and races all over the world." See Hughes, "The Ceaseless Rings of Walt Whitman," in *The Collected Works of Langston Hughes*, 9:484. For a discussion of Hughes's relationship to Dunbar, see Nurhussein, *Rhetorics of Literacy*, 99, 171–5. Longfellow's recitation model also influenced Dunbar. In fact, he shares many similarities with the poets in this study – he uses recitation to gain social recognition for his poetry, and his work is often remembered through recitation.
42 While Johnson had to contend with Longfellow's cultural prestige in the late nineteenth century, by the time Hughes started writing, Longfellow's cultural capital had diminished considerably. To put it another way, Johnson had to reckon with Longfellow (especially since she wrote about Native themes), while Hughes would have not felt this pressure. This might explain why Hughes only casually mentions him as a part of his literary genealogy.
43 E. Johnson, "Chiefswood," 1. See chapter 1 for a discussion of Johnson's critique of Longfellow's *The Song of Hiawatha*.
44 Lott, *Love and Theft*, 9.
45 See Nyong'o, "Hiawatha's Black Atlantic Itineraries," 85–7.
46 See Sorby, *Schoolroom Poets*, 4; and Jackson, "Longfellow's Tradition."
47 Sorby, *Schoolroom Poets*, 3.
48 Ong, *Orality and Literacy*, 115.
49 See Stewart, "Hiawatha/Hereafter." Stewart illustrates how Anishinaabe performances of *The Song of Hiawatha* in northern Ontario helped to sustain their oral traditions in the early twentieth century during a period when many of their tribal practices were banned.

50 Gaul, "Discordant Notes," 409. Gaul notes the enduring popularity of *Song of Hiawatha* performances, offering the annual Hiawatha Pageant conducted by a white community in Pipestone, Minnesota, as an example. Despite protests by the American Indian Movement going as far back as the 1970s, the pageant ran for sixty years, from 1948 to 2008.

51 Katz, *Red, Black, and Jew*, 9. See also Rubinstein, *Members of the Tribe*.

52 Hughes, "Ten Ways to Use Poetry in Teaching," in *The Collected Works of Langston Hughes*, 9:321.

53 Gaul discusses how there was a rise in *Song of Hiawatha* performances during the Cold War to cultivate a sense of US patriotism. Gaul, "Discordant Notes," 410. See also Deloria, *Playing Indian*, 128–53.

54 Hughes, *The Collected Poems*, 190.

55 For an examination of how racial hierarchies in the United States affected the relationship between African Americans and Native Americans, see Coleman, *That the Blood Stay Pure*. She points out that the categories of African American and Native American in US history are very difficult to unravel because the US census did not use Indian as a separate category until 1870. Prior to this, free black men and Native men would have both been counted as free men of colour.

56 For more on *The Brownies' Book*, see Harris, "Race Consciousness," 192–6; and Phillips, "The Children of Double Consciousness," 590–607. Harris explains how editing *The Crisis*, the official magazine for the National Association for the Advancement of Colored People (NAACP), made Du Bois aware of black children as a neglected reading audience. He received many inquiries from children about the magazine. In response, he published a "Children's Number" annually, which Du Bois claimed was the most popular issue of the publication each year, leading him to start *The Brownies' Book*.

57 Tracy, "The Dream Keeper," 79.

58 Hughes, *I Wonder as I Wander*, 41.

59 For a discussion of Hughes's treatment by his publisher Knopf, see Thomas, *Extraordinary Measures*, 4. Thomas argues that Hughes "was held in low esteem by his own editors at Knopf" because of racist assumptions about the quality of African American poetry.

60 Davey, "Building a Black Audience," 224.

61 Nurhussein, *Rhetorics of Literacy*, 193–94.

62 Hughes, *I Wonder as I Wander*, 3–42.

63 Ibid., 53.

64 Rampersad, *The Life of Langston Hughes*, 1:226. According to Davey, Hughes sold approximately 2,750 copies of *The Negro Mother* for 25 cents each;

1,000 broadsides of five different poems, which he would occasionally give away; and an unknown number of copies of *The Weary Blues*. Davey quotes Hughes in a letter to Taylor requesting that he send more broadsides, which were priced at 10 cents each. Hughes writes, "I shall probably give most of them away, as I read to so many little youngsters who have no money, and who ask me for poems." While he embarked on his tour as a money-making venture, his willingness to give away his poems indicates that his primary goal was getting his poetry into the hands of young black children. Davey, "Building a Black Audience," 238, 237.

65 Davey, "Building a Black Audience," 228.

66 Smethurst, *The Black Arts Movement*, 69.

67 For a discussion of the role of black university students in the Black Arts Movement, see ibid. Offering the example of the Southern Negro Youth Congress, an important black left political group that formed in 1937 in Louisiana, Smethurst argues that it was primarily black students who mobilized the grassroots civil rights movement in the South. He notes that they often used literature and performance to achieve their political goals.

68 C. Johnson, *Growing Up in the Black Belt*, xxii.

69 Burns, *The Letters of Gertrude Stein and Carl Van Vechten*, 1:246.

70 Most notably, Hughes avoided including any of his recitations from *The Negro Mother* in his first collection of poetry for children, *The Dream Keeper and Other Poems* (1932). This book, published by Knopf a year after his tour, was aimed at an integrated audience of black and white children and featured many of his previously published poems from his Harlem Renaissance publications.

71 Davey, "Building a Black Audience," 231.

72 Hughes, *The Collected Poems*, 152.

73 Conquergood, "Rethinking Elocution," 149.

74 For a discussion about the popularity of dialect recitation in the late nineteenth century, see Nurhussein, *Rhetorics of Literacy*.

75 See Davey, "Building a Black Audience," 229–31.

76 Nurhussein, *Rhetorics of Literacy*, 187.

77 Davey, "Building a Black Audience," 233–34.

78 Hughes, *The Collected Poems*, 151.

79 Ibid., 521.

80 Nurhussein, *Rhetorics of Literacy*, 183.

81 Ibid., 191.

82 Hughes, *The First Book of Rhythms*, 40. Further reference will be indicated in the text by page number.

83 Scott, *The Socialist Joy*, 201.
84 Ibid., 193.
85 O'Meally, afterword, 53.
86 Scott, *The Socialist Joy*, 11.
87 Ibid., 192.
88 Hughes, *The Collected Poems*, 387.
89 Ibid., 410.
90 Marsalis, introduction, vi.
91 Mingus, *Beneath the Underdog*, 350–1. See also Moten, "The New International of Rhythmic Feeling(s)."
92 Robson, "Standing," 157.
93 For Scott, Hughes's use of rhythm as a metaphor to dissolve the distinction between African American working-class labour and intellectual creative activity forms the cornerstone of his socialist strategy. See Scott, *Socialist Joy*, 206–8.
94 Hughes, "Ten Ways to Use Poetry in Teaching," in *The Collected Works of Langston Hughes*, 9:319.
95 Hughes's proposal for group recitation is in line with 1930s recitation pedagogy. Rubin discusses how US educators began to promote choral recitation as a mode to recite poetry in the interwar period as way to teach proper elocution through collective activity while learning from one's peers. Rubin, *Songs of Ourselves*, 136–8.
96 Hughes, "Ten Ways to Use Poetry in Teaching," in *The Collected Works of Langston Hughes*, 9:321.
97 For Freire's approach to literacy, see Freire and Macedo, *Literacy: Reading the Word and the World*.
98 See Sorby, *Schoolroom Poets*, 1. Sorby explains how when one-room schoolhouses began to be replaced by multi-room brick buildings after the Civil War it was common to name these new schools after poets as well as political heroes: "Most commonly – or rivaled in popularity only by Lincoln and Washington schools – there were Longfellow schools."
99 The phrase "sing the nation-state" is taken from the Judith Butler and Gayatri Chakravorty Spivak's book title *Who Sings the Nation-State? Language, Politics, Belonging*.

3. Miss Lou Pedagogy and Mimic Women

1 Donna (Aza) Weir-Soley recalls reciting Bennett's poetry in school and how "that was the only way to speak patois in school – and to get applauded for it, at that!" "Interview with Donna (Aza) Weir-Soley," 29.

2 In addition to Breeze, many other women poets have discussed the formative influence Louise Bennett had on their work and how they first encountered it through recitation. For example, the poet Opal Palmer Adisa describes first hearing Bennett poems at the Jamaica Festival in the late 1960s: "I witnessed hosts of children, all ages and both genders, reciting your poems, trying you on, imitating and celebrating you celebrating us – how we spoke and acted at a time when my high school gave detention if we were caught speaking patois (nation language) – the so-called language of the uneducated." Adisa, "Love Letter to Miss Lou," 2.

3 "Speech."

4 Edmondson, *Caribbean Middlebrow*, 87. Other regional dialect poets whom Edmondson mentions include Guyana's Wordsworth McAndrew and Ken Corsbie, and Trinidad's Paul Keens-Douglas.

5 Miner, "Poetic Contests," 926.

6 Quoted in Hewitt, "A Comparative Study," 77. Hewitt's dissertation on Zora Neale Hurston and Louise Bennett offers one of the most comprehensive overviews of Bennett's career and analyses how she acted as a cultural conservator to preserve Jamaican folk culture.

7 For a discussion of Bennett's creolizing of the pantomime, see Edmondson, *Caribbean Middlebrow*, 103–4. Edmondson discusses the huge success of Bennett's first pantomime, originally named "Bluebeard and Brer Anancy" and then renamed "Busha Bluebeard," which retells the fairy tale of Bluebeard by making him into "an evil white plantation owner" who is thwarted by the Jamaican folk hero Anancy.

8 "Interview with Louise Bennett," Cumber Dance, 26–7. John's radio show was on the African American station WWRL (not WWRM).

9 Ramazani, *The Hybrid Muse*, 116.

10 Street and Street, "The Schooling of Literacy," 147.

11 "Interview with Louise Bennett," Scott, 46.

12 Bennett, *Selected Poems*, 4. According to Hewitt, Bennett wrote "Bans a Killin" in 1943; however, it was not published until 10 April 1948, when it appeared in her column in the liberal paper *Public Opinion*. It is not clear whether the editors of the *Gleaner* refused to publish this poem in her weekly column because it directly addressed a reader or because of the argument the poem makes about dialect. Bennett might have also chosen not to publish it at the time for other reasons. See Hewitt, "A Comparative Study," 137.

13 Bennett, *Selected Poems*, 5.

14 Ramazani, *The Hybrid Muse*, 12.

15 This chapter explores the pedagogy of Bennett's Creole poetry for native speakers of Jamaican Creole. However, my experience as a

non-native speaker of Creole learning how to read Bennett, and in turn teaching students in the United States how to read Bennett's poems, suggests to me that her literacy model does translate cross-culturally to a certain extent. Regardless of a reader's native language, Bennett's transcriptions of Creole words demand a phonetic relationship to text and raise an awareness of the multiplicity of English. For a discussion of the usefulness of Bennett's poetry in high school and university curricula outside of the Caribbean, see Nero and Ahmad, *Vernaculars in the Classroom*; and Neigh, "Dreams of Uncommon Languages," 70–92.

16 Brathwaite, *History of the Voice*, 17.

17 Morris, introduction, xi.

18 Brown, *West Indian Poetry*, 108.

19 Hewitt, "A Comparative Study," 137; and Cooper, *Noises in the Blood*, 40.

20 Mignolo, *Local Histories*, 253.

21 For a discussion of humour in Bennett's poetry, see Tidjani-Alou, "'Back to Africa, Miss Mattie?'" 139–53.

22 For a discussion of Bennett's tramcar poems, see Neigh, "The Lickle Space," 5–19.

23 Bennett, *Selected Poems*, 8.

24 Cooper, *Noises in the Blood*, 2–3.

25 Stoler, *Haunted by Empire*, 4.

26 Seager, *The Penguin Atlas of Women*, 76.

27 Blouet, "Slavery and Freedom," 626, 634.

28 Ibid., 643.

29 Quoted in Gordon, *A Century of West Indian Education*, 58.

30 Naipaul, *The Mimic Men*.

31 Mccourtie, "The Politics of Creole Language," 111.

32 Quoted in Gordon, *A Century of West Indian Education*, 58.

33 King and Morrissey, *Images in Print*, 21.

34 Fraser, "School Readers in the Empire," 91. For a discussion of the influence of schoolroom readers on the development of West Indian literature, see Tiffin, "The Institution of Literature," 46.

35 Robson, "Standing," 153.

36 Kincaid, *Lucy*, 17–18.

37 Brathwaite, *History of the Voice*, 42.

38 Senior, *Talking of Trees*, 26. Caribbean literature is littered with references to recitation. Some other notable examples include Brodber, *Myal*; Clarke, *Growing Up Stupid under the Union Jack*; Naipaul, *A House for Mr. Biswas*; and Selvon, *The Housing Lark*.

39 hooks, "Performance Practice," 211.

40 For scholarship on Caribbean creolization, see Glissant, *Caribbean Discourse*; Brathwaite, *The Development of Creole Society*; and Baluntansky and Sourieau, *Caribbean Creolization*. The concept brings into focus the uneven power relations between African, Indigenous, and colonial cultures that fuel the creation of new linguistic and cultural forms in the Caribbean, which are intensified by island environments and plantation slavery systems.

41 Breeze, *Third World Girl*. Breeze discusses her childhood experiences with recitation in the interview included on the DVD that comes with the book.

42 Honeyghan, "Rhythm of the Caribbean," 410.

43 "Interview with Linton Kwesi Johnson," 253.

44 Some of Robert Louis Stevenson's poems appear in the Jamaica Cultural Development Commission's *Children's Speech Anthology* (2011), which provides recommended selections for the Speech Competition at the annual festival, indicating that children still recite his work in Jamaica. See Brodber and Braimbridge, "An Anthology of Creative Works for the Speech Competition."

45 Although Bennett was predominantly schooled in the British tradition of metrical verse, Brathwaite describes Bennett's revelation when her teacher gave her a copy Claude McKay's *Constab Ballads* (1912), written in Jamaican Creole. See Brathwaite, *History of the Voice*, 28.

46 Hewitt, "Taped," 13.

47 Cooper, *Noises in the Blood*, 2.

48 "Interview with Donna (Aza) Weir-Soley," 27.

49 Honeyghan, "Rhythm of the Caribbean," 411.

50 Helen Tiffin also discusses how the commingling of imperial recitation practices with Caribbean oral traditions created unexpected opportunities to reclaim the local voice through parody and subversion. See Tiffin, "Cold Hearts and (Foreign Tongues)," 914.

51 In a 2008 email query to the Excelsior alumni association that the president distributed to the members, I attempted to confirm that Longfellow's poem "Excelsior" was a frequently taught poem at this school in the 1930s. While no one was able to confirm this (mostly likely because members were too young to have attended the school during the 1930s), many people responded by sharing their memories of poetry memorization and recitation in the curriculum.

52 Reckord, "Miss Lou Gets Her First Fee."

53 Ibid. See also Morris, *Miss Lou*, chap. 1. He discusses how the headmaster, Wesley Powell, played a role in nurturing her talent.

54 Quoted in Reckord, "Miss Lou Gets Her First Fee." It should be noted that, as far as I know, this early "Excelsior" poem does not appear in any of Bennett's published writings. In *The Gleaner*, the line breaks in the second and fourth lines occur before the final end rhyme. I have corrected what I am assuming are newspaper column layout restrictions.

55 In her personal papers at McMaster University, there is another short poem called "Excelsior" in a file of poetry manuscripts, which makes fun of how the school has the name of the Jamaican biscuit company Excelsior. By drawing attention to excelsior as a cookie name, she again mocks the seriousness of the Latin meaning of the word, which Longfellow evokes. See box 7, file 10, Louise Bennett Coverley Fonds.

56 Bennett, *Selected Poems*, 7. Further reference for "Sammy Intres" will be indicated in the text by page number.

57 Figueroa, "Coming to Terms with Boys at Risk," 68. Figueroa argues that the emphasis on rote learning partly explains why male test scores are significantly lower than female test scores in the anglophone Caribbean, because the passivity that it demands goes against male socialization.

58 Nero, "De Facto Language Education Policy," 237–40, 225.

59 According to Jamaican Creole grammar, it is debatable whether the title lacks a possessive. The preposition *fi* (meaning "for") is typically used to convey a possessive when attached to a noun, rather than apostrophe *s* in English grammar; however, sometimes a possessive can also be implied. However, this ambiguity still illuminates my point because in the conflict between the two grammar systems (English and Creole), we are not able to determine whether Sammy possesses his interests or not. See Adams, *Understanding Jamaican Patois*, 14.

60 Thomas, *Modern Blackness*, 49.

61 Pollard and Brathwaite argue that T.S. Eliot influenced the development of anglophone Caribbean poetry, yet the populist circulation of Longfellow in poetry anthologies meant that students (particularly ones who were unable to attend elite schools) were far more likely to encounter his verse than Eliot's. See Brathwaite, *History of the Voice*, 30; and Pollard, *New World Modernisms*, 3.

62 While the majority of Bennett scholarship emphasizes her use of Jamaican proverbs and folklore in her poems, Edmondson points out that Bennett also refers to Victorian poetry and English folk stories. Bennett's parody of "Excelsior" is an excellent example of what Edmondson describes as an "anticolonial narrative strategy of rewriting the European text" to challenge colonial educational values through mockery. See Edmondson, *Caribbean Middlebrow*, 104–5.

63 Sorby, *Schoolroom Poets*, xxix.

64 As Ramazani points out, "'Excelsior' metamorphoses into another ironic signifier of the remoteness of such colonial verse from the Jamaican experience." Ramazani, *The Hybrid Muse*, 117.

65 Cooper, *Noises in the Blood*, 3.

66 The Eurocentrism of "Excelsior" likely made it more suitable for colonial curricula than a poem such as *The Song of Hiawatha*, which was more commonly taught in the United States and Canada because it supported national narratives of Native disappearance.

67 Brathwaite, *History of the Voice*, 30. Brathwaite does acknowledge that "Miss Lou erodes and transforms this [the pentameter] with the sound of her language." For a discussion of the debates about Bennett's use of English metre and to what extent this demonstrates that she was constrained by colonial aesthetics, see Rodis, "Vernacular Literacy," 60–72.

68 Longfellow, "Excelsior," 19.

69 Robson, *Heart Beats*, 116.

70 Rodis, "Vernacular Literacy," 65.

71 Usage of *pickney* or *pickny*, meaning a small child, is widespread in Jamaican Creole, and unlike its related American term *pickaninny* it does not have such a negative, racist connotation. It derives from the Portuguese *Pequenino*, which means "little boy, little one." This word is found in Creoles in Sierra Leone, Cameroon, etc., likely due to Portuguese control of the Slave Coast. The word was likely brought to the Caribbean and North America by enslaved peoples. See Allsopp, *Dictionary of Caribbean English Usage*, 438.

72 *Labrish* is the Jamaican word for gossip. Bennett's first book-length collection of poems was called *Jamaica Labrish* (1966) to reflect her frequent depiction of women's labrish in her poems.

73 Longfellow, "Excelsior," 19.

74 Freire, *Pedagogy of the Oppressed*, 67.

75 Giroux, "Literacy," 3.

76 Sorby, *Schoolroom Poets*, xxix.

77 Street and Street, "The Schooling of Literacy," 146.

78 Ibid.

79 Ibid., 163.

80 Bhabha, *The Location of Culture*, 122; italics in the original.

81 Ibid., 126; italics in the original.

82 Ramazani, *The Hybrid Muse*, 115.

83 Ibid., 114–15.

84 Ibid., 117.
85 Chinua Achebe coined the term "malignant fictions" to characterize the destructive myths that colonizers spread and the colonized internalize. See Achebe, *Hopes and Impediments*, 138–53.
86 Oswald, "Preserving Jamaica's Oldest Dance."
87 For a discussion of why scholars have not taken Bennett "seriously," see Mervyn Morris, "On Reading Louise Bennett Seriously."
88 Collins, *Black Feminist Thought*, 182; italics in the original.
89 For a discussion of Bennett's critique of patriarchy, see Narain, *Contemporary Caribbean Women's Poetry*; and Cooper, *Noises in the Blood*.
90 Bennett, *Aunty Roachy Seh*, 23.
91 Morris, *Miss Lou*, chap. 2.
92 Quoted in Sealey, "Miss Lou – Forever Walking Brave."
93 According to *Dictionary of Caribbean Usage*, ring-ding can mean "any kind of noisy excitement, a rousing dance, an open-air row, etc." This doubleness in the affective meaning of the phrase draws attention to how Bennett, while making her show entertaining, encouraged children to question their Eurocentric education, thus inspiring both celebratory and argumentative "noisy excitement." Allsopp, *Dictionary of Caribbean English Usage*, 473.
94 Sealey, "Miss Lou – Forever Walking Brave."
95 In a 2001 interview with Marcia Davidson, Bennett confirms that tapes of *Ring Ding* were not preserved: "To my understanding when I asked about it, the tapes were scrubbed and recorded over with other programs. None to my knowledge were preserved, so there are none available for sale." See "Exclusive Interview with Miss Lou." While a researcher expects challenges when trying to uncover archives of the experiences of Jamaicans from the colonial period, it is discouraging to find that records of nascent post-colonial cultural histories from the 1970s have already been literally erased and dubbed over. The National Library of Jamaica recently published a short video on YouTube called "Behind the Scenes at Ring Ding with Miss Lou." This rare footage emphasizes the difficulty of doing a weekly children's television show in front of a live studio audience.
96 In her memoir, the Jamaican slam poet Staceyann Chin, who now lives in the United States, recalls watching *Ring Ding* on a colour television for the first time as a young girl: "I sit beside her, mesmerized, as I watch the national storyteller, Miss Lou, in a red-and-white plaid bandanna conducting a game of ring-around-the-rosy on the children's show *Ring Ding*. The children are wearing dresses and shirts of every color. Every

time Miss Lou laughs the children laugh too. I lean in toward the screen to get a better look at the people in color." Chin, *The Other Side of Paradise*, 63.

97 McLaren, "Miss Lou, My Mentor."

98 Campbell, "Icon: Miss Lou."

99 Quoted in Morris, introduction, xiii.

100 I borrow the term "black vernacular intellectual" from Grant Farred. His exclusive focus on black men in his study *What's My Name? Black Vernacular Intellectuals* replicates the stereotype that intellect is a masculine trait and neglects to examine women's contributions to "vernacular thinking."

101 Duncan, "Aunt(y) Jemima in Spiritual Experience," 107. Duncan's essay discusses Spiritual Baptist women's reappropriation of Aunt Jemima, the racist pancake mix symbol. Aunt Jemima's costume with headscarf and long skirts resembles both that of the Spiritual Baptist women who wear a head tie as part of their spiritual dress and Bennett's costume for her public performances. Duncan argues that while Aunt Jemima represents black women's servility in North American popular culture, the Spiritual Baptist Caribbean immigrant women from the Toronto congregation, who put Aunt Jemima's statue on their alter, reclaimed her as mythic symbol of spiritual strength.

102 Bennett, *Aunty Roachy Seh*, 11.

103 Ibid., 11.

104 Adisa, "Culture and Nationalism," 129.

105 Brathwaite, *History of the Voice*, 18.

106 For debates about the role of Creole in Jamaican education, see Low, "*Creare*," 84–101; Bryan, *Between Two Grammars*; Mccourtie, "The Politics of Creole Language," 108–27; and Nero, "De Facto Language Education Policy," 221–42.

107 Meditz and Hanratty, *Islands of the Commonwealth Caribbean*, 63.

108 UNESCO, *Jamaica*, 91.

109 King and Morrissey, *Images in Print*.

110 Mccourtie, "The Politics of Creole Language," 113–14, 122.

111 Jamaican Foundation for Lifelong Learning, "The Development and State."

112 Pollard, *From Jamaican Creole to Standard English*. For scholarship on transitional bilingualism in the anglophone Caribbean, see also Carrington, "Determining Language Education Policy," 27–44; Craig, "Models for Educational Policy," 245–65; Craig, *Teaching Language and Literacy*; Simmons-McDonald, "Language Education Policy (2)," 120–42; and Bryan, *Between Two Grammars*.

113 Nero, "De Facto Language Education Policy, 222–3, 226. Nero uses Rosini Lippi-Green's term *standard language ideology* to characterize how the dominant language – often the one spoken by the upper middle class – becomes idealized in a society. Nero notes how in Jamaica standard language ideology creates contradictory attitudes toward Creole. For example, a person may refer to Creole with affection but also reject its use in public discourse, and feel embarrassment about using it in certain situations. See Lippi-Green, *English with an Accent*.
114 Nero, "De Facto Language Education Policy," 227. See also the Ministry of Education's draft of the *Language Education Policy*.
115 Hewitt, "Taped," 4. In recent years, language attitudes have begun to change. In a 2005 national survey, 78 per cent of the respondents viewed themselves as bilingual in Jamaican Creole and English, and 70 per cent of them approved of bilingual education for children. Devonish and Carpenter, "Towards Full Bilingualism," 300–1.
116 Bryan, "Language and Literacy," 93–4.
117 See Devonish and Carpenter, "Towards Full Bilingualism." The Jamaican Language Unit was started in 2002. Building on Bennett's legacy, a central part of its mission is to eventually add freedom from discrimination on the grounds of language to the Charter of Rights in the Jamaican Constitution.
118 Ibid., 294.
119 "Bilingual Education Project," *The Jamaican Language Unit*.
120 "Interview with Donna (Aza) Weir-Soley," 55.

4. Recitation Legacies in Dub and Indigenous Poetics

1 L. Allen, "Poetics of Renewal," 294.
2 Ibid., 294.
3 In an interview, Rogers explains how Gottfriedson edited her collection *Unearthed*. She notes: "I had always admired him as a writer, now I know he is a great editor and mentor." See "Interview with Mohawk Poet Janet Marie Rogers."
4 A key part of Craig Womack's Native literary separatism entails Indigenous writers developing their own critical frameworks because "Native people have been excluded from discourse concerning their own cultures." By exploring Johnson as her predecessor, Rogers upholds Womack's separatist approach to literary study by aiming to construct a Native history of performance poetry. However, Rogers's approach avoids foreclosing cross-ethnic solidarities. For her, these enrich (rather

than detract from) her efforts "to disrupt the powers of the literary status quo as well as the powers of the state." Womack, *Red on Red*, 4–5.

5 L. Allen, "De Dub," 17. For an overview of the development of dub poetry, see Habekost, *Verbal Riddim*; and Bucknor, "Dub Poetry as a Postmodern Art Form," 255–64.

6 Antwi, "Dub Poetry," 75–6.

7 Kim and McCall, introduction, 6.

8 Lionnet and Shih, *Minor Transnationalism*, 8. Lionnet and Shih distinguish minor transnationalism from major transnationalism, which they identify as the hegemonic and homogenizing force of globalization.

9 Ibid., 2.

10 For scholarship on Hughes's influence on African American poetry, see Jones, *The Muse Is Music*; Schultz, *The Afro-Modernist*; and Smethurst, *The Black Arts*. For scholarship on Hughes's influence on the broader category of US performance poetry, see Hoffman, *American Poetry*; and Wheeler, *Voicing American Poetry*.

11 Brent Hayes Edwards noted in 2007 that "it is now commonplace to describe Langston Hughes as a writer of the 'African diaspora.'" Edwards, "Langston Hughes," 691.

12 Rampersad, "Future," 312. Some examples of scholarship on Hughes's relationship to the francophone and hispanophone Caribbean, include Leary, "Havana Reads"; Patterson, *Race*; and Cobb, *Harlem, Haiti, and Havana*.

13 Nwankwo, "Cosmopolitan," 269. I would add that more work needs to be done to assess the development of dub poetry within US borders (where it has been less prominent) because nationalistic frameworks often downplay its cross-cultural dynamics and categorize it as African American. In turn, the distinctions between post-slavery Jim Crow and British colonial legacies of recitation that play out in contemporary spoken-word communities in the United States deserve more thorough examination.

14 C. Allen, *Trans-Indigenous*, xiii.

15 Ibid.; italics in the original.

16 Ibid., xiii, 143; italics in the original.

17 Gingell, "Coming Home through Sound," 46.

18 Gingell, "The 'Nerve of Cree,' the Pulse of Africa," 272.

19 Ibid., 271.

20 L. Allen, "Poetics of Renewal," 295.

21 Mutabaruka, *The Next*, 10. For an examination of the legacy of slavery in Caribbean poetics, see Chamberlin, *Come Back to Me*.

22 McLeod, "Coming Home through Stories," 19.

23 Bucknor, "Body Vibes," 301–02, 302.
24 Antwi, "Dub Poetry," 65.
25 Kincaid, *Lucy*, 17–18.
26 Taylor, *The Archive and the Repertoire*, xviii.
27 Foley, *How to Read*, 28.
28 Hodges, "Poetry and Overturned Cars," 103.
29 Rampersad, *Life of Langston Hughes*, 2:39.
30 Hughes, *The Collected Poems*, 273. For an in-depth analysis of "Broadcast to the West Indies," see Neigh, "The Transnational Frequency of Radio Connectivity."
31 Rampersad, *Life of Langston Hughes*, 2:155.
32 L. Allen, "De Dub," 18–19; italics in the original.
33 Morris, *"Is English We Speaking*," 36.
34 Dick Hebdige explains in more detail the style of the instrumental B-side: "On the dub the original tune is still recognisably there but it is broken up. The rhythm might be slowed down slightly, a few snatches of song might be thrown in and then distorted with echo. The drums and bass will come right up to the listener and demand to be heard." The DJ talk-over style emerged from these B-sides. DJs such as U-Roy improvised monologues over these instrumental tracks at live sound-system parties, which became so popular that these artists began to release their own toasting LPs. Hebdige, *Cut 'N' Mix*, 83.
35 Johnson, "Jamaican Rebel Music," 398.
36 Hitchcock, "'It Dread Inna Inglan.'"
37 Johnson, *Mi Revalueshanary Fren*, 15.
38 Falci, *The Cambridge*, 160.
39 Hughes, *The Collected Poems*, 50.
40 Brathwaite, *History of the Voice*, 13.
41 Kei Miller describes how prison guards confiscated Onuora's writing notebook after his first performance because they feared that it might incite the other prisoners to rebel. He explains how the distinct sound of dub poetry responded to oppressive situations in the 1970s: "It made the kind of sound that is more than a sound – it is an action. It acted on things that needed to be acted upon. It went around the city of Jericho; it shouted, and walls came down – in Kingston, and in Brixton, and in Bristol. It taught us that there are times to be angry, indeed, to be furious, and that fury can be composed into a thing of eloquence." See Miller, *Writing Down*, 89.
42 Bucknor, "Dub Poetry as a Postmodern Art Form," 256. Bucknor discusses how both practitioners and critics debate the meaning and

usefulness of the term *dub*. Part of the controversy stems from the fact that dub emerged simultaneously in different locations in the 1970s (London, Toronto, and Kingston) and it was only later that poets began to recognize the connections in their work. Certain poets express ambivalence over the term *dub* being used to characterize their work, while others view it as a valuable label that gives their work critical visibility. LKJ has suggested that it might be too limiting to encompass the range of his experimentation with oral modes, music, and poetic expression. For this reason, Carolyn Cooper and Mervyn Morris prefer the more inclusive term *performance poetry* to refer to dub because this places it in a subversive African oral tradition that predates reggae music. However, Lillian Allen embraces the term because she feels it situates Caribbean poetics within a broader Afro-diasporic community. As these artists struggle to be recognized as poets, rather than as musicians, the dub label has both helped and hindered this process. Kei Miller goes so far as to provocatively declare the death of dub poetry, because he views its militant tone as intrinsically linked to 1970s protest politics. Regardless of these debates about dub as an appropriate aesthetic label (and ongoing artistic movement), Jamaican poets' engagements with reggae forms since the 1970s are indisputable. What concerns me is the relationship between dub poets' reggae innovations and recitation legacies. For more on the debates about the term, see Habekost, *Verbal Riddim*, 3–5; Cooper, *Noises in the Blood*, 80–1; Morris, *"Is English We Speaking,"* 36–44; and Miller, *Writing Down*.

43 Quoted in Morris, *"Is English We Speaking,"* 37–8.

44 Robson, "Standing," 157.

45 Hughes, "The Negro Artist," 94.

46 Morris, *"Is English We Speaking,"* 37.

47 Johnson, "Dub Poetry."

48 "Interview with Michael Smith," 281.

49 "Lillian Allen: All the More 'Anxious for Revolution.'"

50 L. Allen, *Women Do This Every Day*, 14. Big Youth also acknowledges Bennett's legacy in his 1976 hit single "Miss Lou Ring Ding." Known by many in Jamaica as "the human *Gleaner*" for his songs that comment on local political issues, he continues Bennett's tradition of topical newspaper poetry in performance form. Hebdige, *Cut 'N' Mix*, 88.

51 Other references to Louise Bennett in dub poems include Mutabaruka, "Miss Lou," in *The First Poems*, 28–29; and baraka-clarke, "mih mudda tongue," in *Utterances and Incantations*, 37–39.

52 L. Allen, *Women Do This Every Day*, 44.

53 Although Bennett was an important influence on the dub poets, they were often not encouraged to view her as a poet. As Mutabaruka points out, when he was growing up he was taught to think of Miss Lou "as a folklorist" and "as a comedian," rather than as a poet. Mutabaruka, "From Page-Poet to Recording Artist," 25.

54 Many critics have explored Bennett's linguistic influence on dub poetry. For example, Brathwaite identifies the marriage between vernacular speech and reggae rhythms in dub poetry as the culmination in the development of nation language poetics, which finally allows poets to fully break from the tyranny of English metrical verse. In turn, Carolyn Cooper views dub as part of an ongoing subversive oral tradition that extends back to slavery and that resists being "appropriated by the official culture." See Brathwaite, *History of the Voice*, 33; and Cooper, *Noises in the Blood*, 136.

55 Breeze's primary mode of distribution has been live performance and recordings, rather than print. In addition to publishing, she has released many sound recordings and video productions of her poems. Breeze's frequent use of recordings emphasizes the limitations of print for her poetics and the value of bodily gesture, sound, and the performer's relationship to her audience in the production of a poem's meaning. She turned to publishing her poetry in the late 1980s with her first collection *Riddym Ravings*, which also has an audiocassette version, *Riding On De Riddym*. She also released the album *Tracks* in 1991 on LKJ's label. Her most recent book of selected poems, *Third World Girl*, also includes a DVD recording of her performing many of the poems in the collection for a live audience.

56 Breeze, "Can a Dub Poet Be a Woman?" 498–502.

57 Certain dub poets do carry on Hughes and Bennett's legacy of performing and writing for children. For example, Lillian Allen published the book *Nothing But a Hero: Poetry for Children and Young People* (1992) because she wanted to provide children with more empowering content than what is available to them in nursery rhymes and fairy tales. The collection, which is also available in a CD version, features poems about Harriet Tubman, Nelson Mandela, and Jamaican folk tales.

58 Breeze, *Third*, 124.

59 Ibid., 125.

60 The origins of "Row, Row, Row Your Boat" are unclear. Some believe that the song actually developed in the United States before becoming popular in England. One possible theory suggests that the song may have originated in minstrel shows. See Studwell, *The Americana Song Reader*, 82.

61 Honeyghan, "Rhythm of the Caribbean," 410.

62 As I discussed in the previous chapter, Bennett also explores how nursery rhymes function as a discourse between mother and child in her poem "Bed-Time Story."

63 Bennett, *Selected Poems*, 106. Bennett's poem "Colonization in Reverse" depicts the influx of West Indian immigrants to the United Kingdom in the post–Second World War era.

64 Breeze, *Third*, 125.

65 Ibid., 126.

66 Hebdige, *Cut 'N' Mix*, 85.

67 Smith, "Me Cyaan Believe It," 284.

68 Mutabaruka, *The First Poems*, 12. For a discussion of Smith and Mutabaruka's play with the idealized tone of nursery rhymes to explore Jamaican poverty, see Habekost, *Verbal Riddim*, 73.

69 Mutabaruka, "From Page-Poet to Recording Artist," 25.

70 The story of the Thomas Nelson and Sons publishing company and their *West Indian Readers* reveals another dimension of the borderless curriculum of schoolroom recitation and how we must track its development (and the dispersal of imperial power) across different peripheral sites. In the late nineteenth century, Thomas Nelson and Sons's *Royal Readers* became the pre-eminent school readers in domestic and imperial schools. As the company established itself, it opened branch offices in colonial outposts, which in turn led to the localization of these readers. This began in the Canadian office in Toronto in 1882 when they produced a Canadian version of the reader that included Indigenous sources, and then they went on to produce readers for individual provinces. Because of a new trade agreement between Canada and the West Indies in the early twentieth century, the Toronto office took responsibility for sales in the Caribbean. The Canadian office recommended that the West Indies develop local readers just as Canada had done. This led to S.B. Watson (the head of the Toronto office) hiring Cutteridge in the 1920s to compile the *West Indian Readers*. While the content was still overwhelmingly British, Cutteridge also included some Anancy stories and information about West Indian geography. His readers were used in West Indian schools until the mid-sixties. See Robert Fraser, "School Readers in the Empire," 89–106.

71 Mighty Sparrow, *Volume 1*.

72 Mutabaruka, "From Page-Poet to Recording Artist," 26.

73 Roberts, *West Indians and Their Language*, 160.

74 Brathwaite, *History of the Voice*, 8, 46.

75 Breeze, *Riddym*, 58; italics in the original.
76 Sharpe, "Cartographies of Globalisation," 452.
77 Breeze, *Riddym*, 60–1; italics in the original.
78 I analyse "the mad woman's poem" track on the 2006 rerelease of the *Riding On De Riddym* album available as an iTunes download and on CD. For a discussion of how Breeze's voice differs from the male DJ, see Joan Dayan, "Caribbean Cannibals," 59–60.
79 Sharpe, "Cartographies of Globalisation," 454.
80 Ibid.
81 Elizabeth Wheeler and Sharpe interpret "the mad woman's poem" as emblematic of Breeze's Caribbean feminist politics in its reclaiming of the male-dominated form of dancehall for black women's subjectivity through the use of technology. See Sharpe, "Cartographies of Globalisation," 454; and Wheeler, "Riddym Ravings," 139–54.
82 L. Allen, *Women Do This Every Day*, 43.
83 Zamora, *The Usable Past*, ix.
84 Rogers, "Blood Moves Us," 257.
85 Rogers, *Unearthed*, 100.
86 Ibid., 101.
87 Rogers, *Peace*; her statement occurs after the copyright page before pagination begins. Further reference will be indicated in the text by page number.
88 Johnson embraced Vancouver as her home, and she chose to be buried there rather than on the Six Nations Reserve, which upset her sister Evelyn. See Gray, *Flint and Feather*, 385.
89 Rogers, *Unearthed*, back cover.
90 Rogers, "Pauline Passed Here," 40.
91 Johnson, *Collected Poems*, 82; and Rogers, *Unearthed*, 100.
92 McCall, "Diaspora and Nation," 22.
93 Parmenter, "The Meaning of *Kaswentha*," 83.
94 The lines in the wampum belt represent "a separate-but-equal relationship ... based on mutual benefit and mutual respect for each party's inherent freedom of movement" (Parmenter, "The Meaning of *Kaswentha*," 84–5).
95 For a discussion of debates about the treaty, see ibid.
96 Rogers feels no pressure to disentangle the symbol of the canoe from white-settler poetry like Longfellow's. For her, it is firmly rooted in Indigenous poetics through the Two Row Wampum Treaty and Johnson's poetry.
97 L. Allen, "Poetics of Renewal," 298.

98 Ibid., 299.
99 Rogers, "Waaseyaa'sin in Conversation."
100 Alteen, *Beat Nation.*
101 Sherwood, "Elaborate Versionings," 130, 127.
102 Rogers also explores the legacy of Johnson in her play *Pauline and Emily: Two Women.* She depicts a fictional encounter between Johnson and the painter Emily Carr. The two women meet while canoeing on the waters of English Bay in Vancouver.
103 Johnson sold many of her Mohawk artefacts that she inherited from her parents to well-known ethnographers such as Ernest Thompson Seton and David Boyle. Johnson's transactions were not the first break with tradition, since many of her father's artefacts were not acquired through proper Mohawk custom. However, Michelle Hamilton points out that "the nineteenth-century sale of an ethnographic object by an Aboriginal person did not necessarily mean, as collectors presumed, that it was considered to be irrelevant to contemporary life. Instead, its sale could mean its preservation in a time made uncertain by missionary coercion to convert to Christianity, by the presence of Indian agents, and by fears that an assimilated youth would no longer be able or willing to participate in their culture." Johnson's letters suggest that her sale of artefacts was motivated primarily by financial need. See Hamilton, *Collections*, 114–15, 10.
104 Ibid., 136.
105 Rogers, "Pauline Passed Here," 39.
106 Killelea, Review of *Peace in Duress.*
107 Quoted in Rogers, "The Pauline Project."
108 Hamilton, *Collections*, 17.
109 Hirsch, *The Generation*, 178.
110 Foster, "An Archival Impulse," 4.
111 Ibid., 21.
112 Ibid.
113 Baker, "'Guerilla Backchat,'" 63.
114 Annharte, *Exercises*, 7.
115 Baker, "'Guerilla Backchat,'" 63.
116 Annharte, *Exercises*, 30, 33; extra space in the original.
117 Baker and Grauer, "'A Weasel Pops,'" 117; italics in the original.
118 Ibid., 122.
119 Annharte, *Exercises*, 45.
120 For an analysis of humour in Annharte's poetry, see Andrews, *In the Belly of a Laughing God.*

121 Johnson, *Collected Poems*, 178.
122 Hirsch, *The Generation*, 2.
123 Annharte, *Exercises*, 22–23.
124 Ibid.
125 Annharte, "I'POYI Panel."
126 Annharte, *Exercises*, 24.
127 Ibid., 25.
128 Baker, "Borrowing," 61; italics in the original.
129 Ibid.
130 Annharte, *Exercises*, 40.
131 L. Allen, "De Dub Renegades," 14.
132 Ibid., 14. Allen also republished "One Poem Town" in *Women Do This Every Day*.
133 Brydon, "One Poem," 211.
134 Foley, *How to Read*, 28.
135 The dub poets' initial rejection caused controversy within the League, and later that year the League reviewed their decision. They voted to accept the dub poets' membership applications, and the following year they also approved new membership criteria at their annual general meeting. A poet's recordings and performances would now be recognized as a part of her resume. See Gingell, "'Always a Poem,'" 228–30.
136 L. Allen, "De Dub," 15–16. The parallels between Bennett and Allen are even more pointed in that the League of Jamaican Poets in the 1940s did not view Bennett as a poet and never invited her to any of their meetings (see "Interview with Louise Bennett," Scott, 46).

Permissions

Epigraph, excerpt from "Postscript," excerpts from "Beyond Sandy Hook," and excerpts from "The Mother of Gracchi" from THE BIG SEA by Langston Hughes. Copyright © 1940 by Langston Hughes. Copyright renewed 1968 by Arna Bontemps and George Houston Bass. Reprinted by permission of Hill and Wang, a division of Farrar, Straus and Giroux, LLC.

Photograph of Langston Hughes from the Beinecke Rare Book and Manuscript Library, Yale University. Reprinted with permission of the Langston Hughes Estate.

Excerpts from "The Black Clown" from THE COLLECTED POEMS OF LANGSTON HUGHES by Langston Hughes, edited by Arnold Rampersad with David Roessel, Associate Editor, copyright © 1994 by the Estate of Langston Hughes. Used by permission of Alfred A. Knopf, an imprint of the Knopf Doubleday Publishing Group, a division of Penguin Random House LLC. All rights reserved. Any third party use of this material, outside of this publication, is prohibited. Interested parties must apply directly to Penguin Random House LLC for permission.

Excerpts from *The First Book of Rhythms* by Langston Hughes. Copyright © 1954 Franklin Watts. Reprinted with permission of the Langston Hughes Estate.

Excerpts from Daryl Cumber Dance's interview with Louise Bennett in *New World Adams: Conversations with West Indian Writers*. Copyright © 1992 Daryl Cumber Dance. Reprinted by permission of Peepal Tree Press.

Excerpts from "Rhythm of the Caribbean: Connecting Oral History and Literacy" by Glasceta Honeyghan, published in *Language Arts*. Copyright © 2000 by the National Council of Teachers of English. Reprinted with permission.

Excerpts from "Miss Lou Gets Her First Fee" by Michael Reckord. Copyright © 2013 The Gleaner Company (Media) Limited. Reprinted with permission.

Excerpts from *Selected Poems* by Louise Bennett and excerpts and photographs from The Louise Bennett Coverley Fonds at the William Ready Division of Archives and Research Collections at McMaster University. Permission to use Materials of Dr, The Honourable Louise Bennett Coverley, has been granted by the Co-Executors of the LBC, Estate, Judge Pamela Appelt, and Fabian Coverley, B.Th, emails appelt@cogeco.ca, and fcoverley@gmail.com.

Excerpts from "Miss Lou, My Mentor" by Audrey McLaren, published in *Jamaica Gleaner*. Copyright © 2006 Audrey McLaren. Reprinted by permission of the author.

Excerpts from "All the More 'Anxious for Revolution,'" an interview with Lillian Allen by Christopher Laursen. Copyright © 2013 *Sound Addictions: Social Consciousness and Well-Being in Global Music*. Reprinted by permission of Christopher Laursen, *Sound Addictions: Social Consciousness and Well-Being in Global Music*, https://soundaddictions.wordpress.com/2013/04/04/lillian-allen-lead-page/.

Excerpts from "De Dub Renegades in a One Poem Town" by Lillian Allen, published in *This Magazine*. Copyright © 1987 Lillian Allen. Reprinted with permission of the author, www.lillianallen.ca.

Excerpts from *The First Poems / The Next Poems* by Mutabaruka. Copyright © 2005 Mutabaruka. Reprinted by permission of Paul Issa Publications.

Excerpts from *Peace in Duress* by Janet Rogers. Quoted by permission of the publisher from *Peace in Duress* © 2014 Janet Rogers, Talonbooks, Vancouver, B.C.

Excerpts from "The Pauline Project" by Janet Rogers. Copyright © 2012 Janet Rogers audio, by Pauline Johnson. Reprinted by permission of the author.

Bibliography

Achebe, Chinua. *Hopes and Impediments: Selected Essays, 1965–1987*. New York: Doubleday, 1988.

Acoose, Janice. "A Vanishing Indian? On Acoose: Women Standing above Ground?" In *(Ad)dressing Our Words: Aboriginal Perspectives on Aboriginal Literatures*, edited by Armand Garnet Ruffo, 37–56. Penticton, BC: Theytus Books, 2001.

Adams, L. Emilie. *Understanding Jamaican Patois: An Introduction to Afro-Jamaican Grammar*. Kingston, Jamaica: LMH Publishing, 1991.

Adisa, Opal Palmer. "Culture and Nationalism on the World Stage: Louise Bennett's Aunty Roachy Seh Stories." *The Global South* 4, no. 2 (2010): 124–35.

– "Love Letter to Miss Lou: Memories Intersect History." In "Critical Approaches to Louise Bennett," edited by Ifeoma Nwankwo. Special issue, *Journal of West Indian Literature* 17, no. 2 (2009): 1–4.

Allen, Chadwick. *Trans-Indigenous: Methodologies for Global Native Literary Studies*. Minneapolis: University of Minnesota Press, 2012.

Allen, Lillian. "De Dub Renegades in a One Poem Town." *This Magazine* 21, no. 7 (1987/1988): 14–21.

– "Lillian Allen: All the More 'Anxious for Revolution.'" Interview by Christopher Laursen, *Sound Addictions: Social Consciousness and Well-being in Global Music*. 4 April 2013. https://soundaddictions.wordpress.com/lillian-allen/.

– *Nothing but a Hero: Poetry for Children and Young People*. Toronto: Well Versed Publications, 1992.

– "Poetics of Renewal: Indigenous Poetics – Message or Medium?" In McLeod, *Indigenous Poetics*, 293–301.

– *Women Do This Every Day: Selected Poems of Lillian Allen*. Toronto: Women's Press, 1993.

Allsopp, Richard, ed. *Dictionary of Caribbean English Usage*. 1996. Kingston, Jamaica: University of the West Indies Press, 2003.

Alteen, Glenn. Curatorial Statement. *Beat Nation: Hip Hop as Indigenous Culture*. http://www.beatnation.org.

Anatol, Giselle Liza. "Langston Hughes and the Children's Literary Tradition." In *Montage of a Dream: The Art and Life of Langston Hughes*, edited by John A. Tidwell and Cheryl R. Ragar, 237–58. Columbia: University of Missouri Press, 2007.

Andrews, Jennifer. *In the Belly of a Laughing God: Humour and Irony in Native Women's Poetry*. Toronto: University of Toronto Press, 2011.

Annharte (see also Baker, Marie Annharte), perf. *Convergence on Poetics*. PennSound. University of Washington Bothell. Filmed 29 September 2012. http://writing.upenn.edu/pennsound/x/Convergence-on-Poetics.php.

– *Exercises in Lip Pointing*. Vancouver: New Star Books, 2003.

– "I'POYI Panel 6." Aboriginal Writer's Gathering. YouTube video, 8.36. Filmed 27–9 March 2008. Posted December 2009. https://www.youtube.com/watch?v=aEE6kzCR0Ww.

Antwi, Phanuel. "Dub Poetry as a Black Atlantic Body-Archive." *Small Axe* 19, no. 3 (2015): 65–83.

Anzaldúa, Gloria. *Borderlands / La Frontera: The New Mestiza*. San Francisco: Aunt Lute Books, 1987.

Archibald Kains Fonds. Library and Archives Canada.

Atwood, Margaret. *Strange Things: The Malevolent North in Canadian Literature*. Oxford: Clarendon Press, 1995.

Austin, J.L. *How to Do Things with Words*. Cambridge, MA: Harvard University Press, 1962.

Baker, Marie Annharte (see also Annharte, Marie). "Borrowing Enemy Language: A First Nations Woman's Use of Language." *West Coast Line* 10, no. 27/1 (1993): 59–66.

– "'Guerilla Backchat' with Marie Annharte Baker." By Reg Johanson. *Capilano Review* 3, no. 10 (2010): 61–70.

Baker, Marie Annharte, and Lally Grauer. "'A Weasel Pops In and Out of Old Tunes': Exchanging Words." *Studies in Canadian Literature / Études en littérature canadienne* 31, no. 6 (2006): 116–27.

Baluntansky, Kathleen, and Marie-Agnes Sourieau, eds. *Caribbean Creolization: Reflections on the Cultural Dynamics of Language, Literature, and Identity*. Miami: University Press of Florida, 1998.

baraka-clarke, amuna. "mih mudda tongue." In *Utterances and incantations: Women, Poetry and Dub*, edited by Afua Cooper, 37–9. Toronto: Sister Vision Press, 1999.

Bauman, Richard. *Verbal Art as Performance*. Prospect Heights, IL: Waveland Press, 1977.

Beachy-Quick, Dan. "Inscribe the Poem on Yourself," *Poetry Off the Shelf: The Poetry Foundation*. Podcast audio. Accessed 23 June 2015. http://www.poetryfoundation.org/features/audioitem/3218.

"Behind the Scenes at Ring Ding with Miss Lou," YouTube video, 4.28. Posted by The National Library of Jamaica, 7 September 2012. https://www.youtube.com/watch?v=pgS1mSWpP9s.

Belnap, Jeffrey, and Raúl Fernández, eds."*José Marti's "Our America": From National to Hemispheric Cultural Studies*. Durham, NC: Duke University Press, 1998.

Bennett, Louise. *Aunty Roachy Seh.* Edited by Mervyn Morris. Kingston, Jamaica: Sangster's Book Stores, 1993.

– "Exclusive Interview with Miss Lou." By Marcia Davidson. *Jamaicans.Com*. http://jamaicans.com/misslouinterview/.

– "Interview with Louise Bennett." In *New World Adams: Conversations with Contemporary West Indian Writers*, by Daryl Cumber Dance, 25–30. Leeds, UK: Peepal Tree Press, 1992.

– "Interview with Louise Bennett." By Dennis Scott. In Markham, *Hinterland*, 45–50.

– *Jamaica Labrish: Jamaica Dialect Poems*. Notes and introduction by Rex Nettleford. Kingston, Jamaica: Sangster's Book Stores, 1966.

– *Selected Poems*. Edited by Mervyn Morris. Kingston, Jamaica: Sangster's Book Stores, 1982.

Beran, Michael Knox. "In Defense of Memorization." *City Journal* (2004). http://www.city-journal.org/html/14_3_defense_memorization.html.

Bernard, Emily, ed. *Remember Me to Harlem: The Letters of Langston Hughes and Carl Van Vechten*. New York: Vintage, 2001.

Bernstein, Charles, ed. *Close Listening: Poetry and the Performed Word*. New York: Oxford University Press, 1998.

– "Poetics of the Americas" *Modernism/modernity* 3, no. 3 (1996): 1–23.

Bhabha, Homi K. *The Location of Culture*. New York: Routledge, 1994.

"Bilingual Education Project." *The Jamaican Language Unit, The University of the West Indies at Mona*. Last modified 2014. Accessed 2 October 2015. http://www.mona.uwi.edu/dllp/jlu/projects/index.htm.

Blaeser, Kimberly. "Writing Voices Speaking: Native Voices and an Oral Aesthetic." In *Talking on the Page: Editing Aboriginal Texts*, edited by Laura A. Murray and Karen D. Rice, 53–68. Toronto: University of Toronto Press, 1999.

Blouet, Olwyn Mary. "Slavery and Freedom in the British West Indies, 1823–33: The Role of Education." In *History of Literacy*. Special issue, *History of Education Quarterly* 30, no. 4 (1990): 625–43.

Brant, Beth. *Writing as Witness: Essay and Talk*. Toronto: Women's Press, 1994.

Brathwaite, Edward Kamau. *The Development of Creole Society in Jamaica, 1770–1820*. Oxford: Oxford University Press, 1971.

– *History of the Voice: Development of Nation Language in Anglophone Caribbean Poetry*. London: New Beacon Books, 1984.

Braz, Albert. "Outer America: Racial Hybridity and Canada's Peripheral Place in Inter-American Discourse." In Siemerling and Casteel, *Canada and Its Americas*, 119–33.

Breeze, Jean "Binta." "Can a Dub Poet Be a Woman?" In *The Routledge Reader of Caribbean Literature*, edited by Alison Donnell and Sarah Lawson Welsh, 498–502. New York: Routledge, 1996.

– *Riddym Ravings and Other Poems*. London: Race Today, 1988.

– *Riding On De Riddym*. 57 Productions, 2005. MP3. Originally released in 1996.

– *Third World Girl: Selected Poems with Live Readings DVD*. Tarset, Northumberland: Bloodaxe Books, 2011.

Brill de Ramírez, Susan Berry. *Contemporary American Indian Literatures and the Oral Tradition*. Tucson: University of Arizona Press, 1999.

Brodber, Andrew, and Sandra Braimbridge, eds. "An Anthology of Creative Works for the Speech Competition. Children's Speech Anthology." *Jamaica Cultural Development Commission*. 2011. http://www.jcdc.gov.jm/uploads/advisories/SPEECH%20ANTHOLOGY%20_2_.pdf.

Brodber, Erna. *Myal*. London: New Beacon Books, 1988.

Brown, Lloyd W. *West Indian Poetry*. 2nd ed. London: Heinemann, 1984.

Brown-Hinds, Paulette. "'Can't Leave Home without It': The Paradox of Memory in Jamaica Kincaid's *Lucy*." In *Post-Colonial Perspectives on Women Writers from Africa, the Caribbean, and the US*, edited by Martin Japtok, 133–49. Trenton: Africa World Press, 2003.

Bryan, Beverley. *Between Two Grammars: Research and Practice for Language Learning and Teaching in a Creole-Speaking Environment*. Kingston, Jamaica: Ian Randle Publishers, 2010.

– "Language and Literacy in a Creole-Speaking Environment: A Study of Primary Schools in Jamaica." *Language, Culture, and Curriculum* 17, no. 2 (2004): 87–96.

Brydon, Diana. "One Poem Town? Contemporary Canadian Cultural Debates." In *Voices of Power: Co-operation and Conflict in English Language and Literatures*, edited by Marc Maufort and Jean-Pierre van Noppen, 211–20. Liège, Belgium: Université de Liège, 1997.

Bucknor, Michael A. "Body Vibes: (S)pacing the Performance in Lillian Allen's Poetry." *Thamyris* 5, no. 2 (1998): 301–22.

– "Dub Poetry as a Postmodern Art Form: Self-Conscious of Critical Reception." In *The Routledge Companion to Anglophone Caribbean Literature*, edited by Michael A. Bucknor and Alison Donnell, 255–64. New York: Routledge, 2011.

Burns, Edward, ed. *The Letters of Gertrude Stein and Carl Van Vechten*, vol. 1: *1913–1935*. New York: Columbia University Press, 1986.

Butler, Judith. *Bodies That Matter: On the Discursive Limits of "Sex."* New York: Routledge, 1993.

Butler, Judith, and Gayatri Chakravorty Spivak. *Who Sings the Nation-State? Language, Politics, Belonging*. New York: Seagull Books, 2011.

Buurma, Rachel Sagner, and Laura Heffernan. "The Common Reader and the Archival Classroom: Disciplinary History for the Twenty-First Century." *New Literary History* 43, no. 1 (2012): 113–35.

Byerly, Alison. "From Schoolroom to Stage: Reading Aloud and the Domestication of Victorian Theater." In *Culture and Education in Victorian England*, edited by Patrick Scott and Pauline Fletcher, 125–41. Lewisburg, PA: Bucknell University Press, 1990.

Campbell, Howard. "Icon: Miss Lou – 'Ring Ding! Concert Time!'" *Jamaica Gleaner*, 1 August 2006. Accessed 5 November 2009. http://jamaica-gleaner.com/gleaner/20060801 (page no longer on site).

Carlson, Marvin A. *Performance: A Critical Introduction*. London and New York: Routledge, 1996.

Carr, Helen. *Inventing the American Primitive: Politics, Gender, and the Representation of Native American Literary Traditions, 1789–1936*. New York: New York University Press, 1996.

Carrington, Lawrence D. "Determining Language Education Policy in Caribbean Sociolinguistic Complexes." *International Journal of the Sociology of Language* 8 (1976): 27–44.

Casas, Maria Caridad. "Whose Rhythm? Textualized Riddim in Lillian Allen's *Women Do This Everyday*." *Essays in Canadian Writing* 83 (2004): 167–87.

Casteel, Sarah Phillips. *Second Arrivals: Landscape and Belonging in Contemporary Writing in the Americas*. Charlottesville: University of Virginia Press, 2007.

Chamberlin, J. Edward. *Come Back to Me My Language: Poetry and the West Indies*. Chicago: University of Illinois Press, 1993.

Chartier, Roger. *The Order of Books: Readers, Authors, and Libraries in Europe between the Fourteenth and Eighteenth Centuries*. Translated by Lydia G. Cochrane. Stanford: Stanford University Press, 1994.

Chevigny, Bell Gale, and Gari Laguardia, eds. *Reinventing the Americas: Comparative Studies of Literature of the United States and Spanish America*. Cambridge: Cambridge University Press, 1986.

Chin, Staceyann. *The Other Side of Paradise: A Memoir*. New York: Scribner, 2009.

Clarke, Austin. *Growing Up Stupid under the Union Jack*. Toronto: McClelland and Stewart, 1980.

Cobb, Martha. *Harlem, Haiti, and Havana: A Comparative Study of Langston Hughes, Jacques Roumain, and Nicolás Guillén*. Washington, DC: Three Continents Press, 1979.

Coleman, Arica L. *That the Blood Stay Pure: African Americans, Native Americans, and the Predicament of Race in Virginia*. Bloomington: Indiana University Press, 2013.

Collins, Patricia Hill. *Black Feminist Thought: Knowledge, Consciousness, and the Politics of Empowerment*. New York: Routledge, 1990.

Conquergood, Dwight. "Rethinking Elocution: The Trope of the Talking Book and Other Figures of Speech." *Text and Performance Quarterly* 20, no. 4 (2000): 325–41.

Cooper, Carolyn. *Noises in the Blood: Orality, Gender, and the Vulgar in Jamaican Popular Culture*. London: Palgrave Macmillan, 1993.

Cowan, Bainard, and Jefferson Humphries, eds. *Poetics of the Americas: Race, Founding, and Textuality*. Baton Rouge: Louisiana State University Press, 1997.

Cowan, T.L. "Editorial: An Emerging Discourse." In "Spoken Word Performance," edited by T. L. Cowan and Rick Knowles. Special issue, *Canadian Theatre Review* 130 (2007): 7–9.

Craig, Dennis R. "Models for Educational Policy in Creole-Speaking Communities." In *Theoretical Orientations in Creole Studies*, edited by Albert Valdman and Arnold Highfield, 245–65. New York: Academic Press, 1980.

– *Teaching Language and Literacy: Policies and Procedures for Vernacular Students*. Georgetown, Guyana: Education and Development Services, 1999.

Crate, Joan. *Pale as Real Ladies: Poems for Pauline Johnson*. London, ON: Brick Books, 1989.

Crespi, John A. *Voices in Revolution: Poetry and the Auditory Imagination in Modern China*. Honolulu: University of Hawai'i Press, 2009.

Damon, Maria. *Postliterary America: From Bagel Shop Jazz to Micropoetries*. Iowa City: University of Iowa Press, 2011.

– "Was That 'Different,' 'Dissident,' or 'Dissonant'? Poetry (n) the Public Spear: Slams, Open Readings, and Dissident Traditions." In Bernstein, *Close Listening: Poetry and the Performed Word*, 324–42.

Dash, Michael J. *The Other America: Caribbean Literature in New World Context*. Charlottesville: University of Virginia Press, 1998.

Davey, Elizabeth A. "Building a Black Audience in the 1930s: Langston Hughes, Poetry Readings, and the Golden Stair Press." In *Print Culture in a Diverse America*, edited by James P. Danky and Wayne A. Wiegand, 223–43. Chicago: University of Illinois Press, 1998.

Davidson, Michael. *On the Outskirts of Form: Practicing Cultural Poetics*. Middletown, CT: Wesleyan University Press, 2011.

Dayan, Joan. "Caribbean Cannibals and Whores." *Raritan* 9, no. 2 (1989): 45–67.

Dean, Misao. *Inheriting a Canoe Paddle: The Canoe in Discourses of English-Canadian Nationalism*. Toronto: University of Toronto Press, 2013.

Deerchild, Rosanna. "My Poem Is an Indian Woman." In McLeod, *Indigenous Poetics*, 237–44.

Deloria, Philip Joseph. *Playing Indian*. New Haven, CT: Yale University Press, 1998.

Devonish, Hubert, and Karen Carpenter. "Towards Full Bilingualism in Education: The Jamaican Bilingual Primary Education Project." *Social and Economic Studies* 56, no. 1/2 (2007): 277–303.

Dickason, Olivia Patricia, and William Newbigging. *A Concise History of Canada's First Nations*. 2nd ed. Don Mills, ON: Oxford University Press, 2010.

Donnell, Alison. "Dreaming of Daffodils: Cultural Resistance in Narratives of Theory." *Kunapipi* 14 (1992): 45–52.

Dudley, Shannon. *Carnival Music in Trinidad: Expressing Music, Expressing Culture*. New York: Oxford University Press, 2004.

Duncan, Carol B. "Aunt(y) Jemima in Spiritual Experience in Toronto: Spiritual Mother or Servile Woman?" *Small Axe: A Caribbean Journal of Criticism* 5, no. 1 (2001): 97–122.

DuPlessis, Rachel Blau. *Genders, Races and Religious Cultures in Modern American Poetry, 1908–1934*. Cambridge: Cambridge University Press, 2001.

Edmondson, Belinda. *Caribbean Middlebrow: Leisure Culture and the Middle Class*. Ithaca, NY: Cornell University Press, 2009.

Edwards, Brent Hayes. "Langston Hughes and the Futures of Diaspora." *American Literary History* 19, no. 3 (2007): 689–711.

Falci, Eric. *The Cambridge Introduction to British Poetry, 1945–2010*. New York: Cambridge University Press, 2015.

Fanon, Frantz. *Black Skin, White Masks*. Translated by Charles Lam Markmann. New York: Grove Press, 1967.

Farred, Grant. *What's My Name? Black Vernacular Intellectuals*. Minneapolis: University of Minnesota Press, 2003.

Ferguson, Moira. *Jamaica Kincaid: Where the Land Meets the Body*. Charlottesville: University of Virginia Press, 1994.

Figueroa, Mark. "Coming to Terms with Boys at Risk in Jamaica and the Rest of the Caribbean." *Commonwealth Education Partnerships* (2010): 66–9. http://www.cedol.org/wp-content/uploads/2012/02/66-69-2010.pdf.

Finnegan, Ruth. *Oral Traditions and the Verbal Arts: A Guide to Research Practices*. New York: Routledge, 1992.

Firmat, Gustavo Pérez, ed. *Do the Americas Have a Common Literature?* Durham, NC: Duke University Press, 1990.

Fitz, Earl E. *Rediscovering the New World: Inter-American Literature in a Comparative Context*. Iowa City: University of Iowa Press, 1991.

Foley, John Miles. *How to Read an Oral Poem*. Chicago: Illinois University Press, 2002.

Foster, Hal. "An Archival Impulse." *October* 110 (2004): 3–22.

Francis, Daniel. *The Imaginary Indian: The Image of the Indian in Canadian Culture*. Vancouver: Arsenal Pulp Press, 1993.

Fraser, Robert. "School Readers in the Empire and the Creation of Post-Colonial Taste." In *Books without Borders*, vol. 1: *The Cross-National Dimension in Print Culture*, edited by Robert Fraser and Mary Hammond, 89–106. New York: Palgrave Macmillan, 2008.

Freire, Paulo. *Pedagogy of the Oppressed*. Translated by Myra Bergman Ramos. New York: Herder and Herder, 1970.

Freire, Paulo, and Donaldo Macedo. *Literacy: Reading the Word and the World*. Westport, CT: Bergin and Garvey Press, 1987.

Frye, Northrop. *The Bush Garden: Essays on the Canadian Imagination*. Concord, ON: House of Anansi, 1995.

Fusco, Coco. *English Is Broken Here: Notes on Cultural Fusion in the Americas*. New York: New Press, 1995.

Gates, Jr, Henry Louis. *The Signifying Monkey: A Theory of African-American Literary Criticism*. New York: Oxford University Press, 1988.

Gaul, Theresa Strouth. "Discordant Notes: Longfellow's *Song of Hiawatha*, Community, Race, and Performance Politics." *Journal of American Culture* 27, no. 4 (2004): 406–14.

Gentile, John Samuel. *Cast of One: One-Person Shows from the Chautauqua Platform to the Broadway Stage*. Chicago: University of Illinois Press, 1989.

Gerson, Carole. "Pauline Johnson and Celebrity in Canada: 'The Most Unique Feature in the Literary World Today.'" In *Women Writers and Celebrity in the Long Nineteenth Century*, edited by Ann R. Hawkins and Maura Ives, 219–32. Surrey, UK: Ashgate, 2012.

– "Rereading Pauline Johnson." *Journal of Canadian Studies / Revue d'études canadiennes* 46, no. 2 (2012): 45–61.

Gerson, Carole, and Veronica Strong-Boag. Introduction to *Collected Poems and Selected Prose*. By E. Pauline Johnson, xiii–xliv.

– *Paddling Her Own Canoe: The Times and Texts of E. Pauline Johnson (Tekahionwake)*. Toronto: University of Toronto Press, 2000.

Gilroy, Paul. *The Black Atlantic: Modernity and Double Consciousness*. Cambridge, MA: Harvard University Press, 1992.
– "'... to be real': The Dissident Forms of Black Expressive Culture." In *Let's Get It On: The Politics of Black Performance*, edited by Catherine Ugwu, 12–33. Seattle: Bay Press, 1995.
Gingell, Susan. "'Always a Poem, Once a Book': Motivations and Strategies for Print Textualizing of Caribbean-Canadian Dub and Performance Poetry." *Journal of West Indian Literature* 14, no. 1/2 (2005): 220–59.
– "Coming Home through Sound: See-Hear Aesthetics in the Poetry of Louise Bennett and Canadian Dub Poets." In "Critical Approaches to Louise Bennett," edited by Ifeoma Nwankwo. Special issue, *Journal of West Indian Literature* 17, no. 2 (2009): 32–48.
– "The 'Nerve of Cree,' the Pulse of Africa: Sound Identities in Cree, Cree-Métis, and Dub Poetries in Canada." In McLeod, *Indigenous Poetics*, 271–91.
Gingell, Susan, and Wendy Roy, eds. *Listening Up, Writing Down, and Looking Beyond: Interfaces of the Oral, Written, and Visual*. Waterloo, ON: Wilfrid Laurier University Press, 2012.
Giroux, Henry A. "Literacy and the Pedagogy of Empowerment." Introduction to *Literacy: Reading the Word and the World*. By Freire and Macedo, 1–28.
Glissant, Édouard. *Caribbean Discourse: Selected Essays*. Translated by Michael J. Dash. Charlottesville: University of Virginia Press, 1989.
Goldie, Terry. *Fear and Temptation: The Image of the Indigene in Canadian, Australian, and New Zealand Literatures*. Montreal and Kingston: McGill-Queen's University Press, 1989.
Gordon, Shirley C. *A Century of West Indian Education: A Source Book*. London: Longman, 1963.
Gray, Charlotte. *Flint and Feather: The Life and Times of E. Pauline Johnson, Tekahionwake*. Toronto: Harper Perennial Canada, 2003.
Gray, Paul H. "Preparing for Popularity: Origins of the Poet-Performer Movement." *Literature in Performance* 6, no.1 (1985): 34–41.
Gross, Konrad. "Coureurs-de-Bois, Voyageurs and Trappers: The Fur Trade and the Emergence of an Ignored Canadian Literary Tradition." *Canadian Literature* 127 (1990): 76–91.
Gruesz, Kirsten Silva. *Ambassadors of Culture: The Transamerican Origins of Latino Writing*. Princeton, NJ: Princeton University Press, 2002.
Habekost, Christian. *Verbal Riddim: The Politics and Aesthetics of African-Caribbean Dub Poetry*. Amsterdam: Rodopi, 1993.
Hamilton, Michelle A. *Collections and Objections: Aboriginal Material Culture in Southern Ontario*. Montreal and Kingston: McGill-Queen's University Press, 2010.

Harris, Violet J. "Race Consciousness, Refinement, and Radicalism: Socialization in *The Brownies' Book*." *Children's Literature Association Quarterly* 14, no. 4 (1989): 192–6.

Hebdige, Dick. *Cut 'N' Mix: Culture, Identity and Caribbean Music*. New York: Routledge, 1990.

Hewitt, Mary Jane. "A Comparative Study of the Careers of Zora Neale Hurston and Louise Bennett as Cultural Conservators." PhD diss., University of the West Indies, 1986.

– "Taped Discussion Session – Louise Bennett and Mary Jane Hewitt – 23 August 1975." *TS*. Louise Bennett Coverley Fonds.

Hirsch, Marianne. *The Generation of Postmemory: Writing and Visual Culture after the Holocaust*. New York: Columbia University Press, 2012.

Hitchcock, Peter. "'It Dread Inna Inglan': Linton Kwesi Johnson, Dread, and Dub Identity." *Postmodern Culture* 4, no. 1 (1993). http://www.pomoculture.org/2013/09/25/it-dread-inna-inglan-linton-kwesi-johnson-dread-and-dub-identity/.

Hodes, Martha. "Fractions and Frictions in the United States Census." In Stoler, *Haunted by Empire*, 240–70. Durham, NC: Duke University Press, 2006.

Hodges, Hugh. "Poetry and Overturned Cars: Why Performance Poetry Can't Be Studied (and Why We Should Study It Anyway)." In Gingell and Roy, *Listening Up*, 97–110.

Hoffman, Tyler. *American Poetry in Performance: From Walt Whitman to Hip Hop*. Ann Arbor: University of Michigan Press, 2011.

Hollander, John, ed. *Committed to Memory: 100 Best Poems to Memorize*. New York: Turtle Point Press, 2000.

Honeyghan, Glasceta. "Rhythm of the Caribbean: Connecting Oral History and Literacy." *Language Arts* 77, no. 5 (2000): 406–13.

hooks, bell. "Performance Practice as a Site of Opposition." In *Let's Get It On: The Politics of Black Performance*, edited by Catherine Ugwu, 210–21. Seattle: Bay Press, 1995.

Howard, Anne Halleck Kelsey. *The Canadian Elocutionist: Designed for the Use of Colleges, Schools and Self Instruction, Together with a Copious Selection, in Prose and Poetry, of Pieces Adapted for Reading, Recitation and Practice*. Toronto: Rose Publishing, 1885.

Hoy, Helen. *How Should I Read These? Native Women Writers in Canada*. Toronto: University of Toronto Press, 2001.

Hughes, Langston. *The Big Sea: An Autobiography*. New York: Hill and Wang, [1940] 1993.

– *The Collected Poems of Langston Hughes*. Edited by Arnold Rampersad and David Roessel. New York: Random House, 1994.

– *The Collected Works of Langston Hughes*, vol. 9: *Essays on Art, Race, Politics, and World Affairs*. Edited by Christopher C. De Santis. Columbia: University of Missouri Press, 2002.

– *The Collected Works of Langston Hughes*, vol. 11: *Works for Children and Young Adults: Poetry, Fiction, and Other Writing*. Edited by Dianne Johnson. Columbia: University of Missouri Press, 2003.

– "Cowards from the Colleges." *Crisis* 41, no. 8 (August 1934): 226–8.

– *The Dream Keeper and Other Poems*. New York: Alfred Knopf, 1932.

– *The First Book of Rhythms*. New York: Franklin Watts, 1954.

– *I Wonder as I Wander: An Autobiographical Journey*. New York: Hill and Wang, 1956.

– "The Negro Artist and the Racial Mountain." In *The Portable Harlem Renaissance Reader*, edited by David Lewis, 91–5. New York: Penguin, 1994.

– *The Negro Mother and Other Dramatic Recitations*. New York: Golden Stair Press, 1931.

Jackson, Shona N. *Creole Indigeneity: Between Myth and Nation*. Minneapolis: University of Minnesota Press, 2012.

Jackson, Virginia. "Longfellow's Tradition: or, Picture-Writing a Nation." *Modern Language Quarterly* 59, no. 4 (1998): 471–96.

Jamaican Foundation for Lifelong Learning. "The Development and State of the Art of Adult Learning and Education." National Report of Jamaica: Ministry of Education, 2008. Accessed 25 July 2015. http://www.unesco.org/fileadmin/MULTIMEDIA/INSTITUTES/UIL/confintea/pdf/National_Reports/Latin%20America%20- %20Caribbean/Jamaica.pdf.

Johnson, Charles S. *Growing Up in the Black Belt: Negro Youth in the Rural South*. Washington, DC: American Council on Education, 1967.

Johnson, E. Pauline (Tekahionwake). *Canadian Born*. Toronto: George N. Morang, 1903.

– *Collected Poems and Selected Prose*. Edited by Carole Gerson and Veronica Strong-Boag. Toronto: University of Toronto Press, 2002.

Johnson, Evelyn H.C. "Chiefswood," Typescript compiled and edited by Dorothy Keen and Martha McKeon, 1936. Fur Trade Collection, F 471-3-0-8, Archives of Ontario.

Johnson, Linton Kwesi. "Dub Poetry." Interview by Marco Werman, *PRI's The World*. 7 March 2013. http://www.publicbroadcasting.net/wnti/.artsmain/article/9/70/747703/WNTI.Highlights/%E2%80%99Dub.Poetry%E2%80%99.Linton.Kwesi.Johnson/.

– "Interview with Linton Kwesi Johnson." By Mervyn Morris. In Markham, *Hinterland*, 250–61.

– "Jamaican Rebel Music." *Race and Class* 17, no. 4 (1976): 397–412.

– *Mi Revalueshanary Fren*. Keene, NY: Ausable Books, 2006.

Johnson, Nan. "The Popularization of Nineteenth Century Rhetoric: Elocution and the Private Learner." In *Oratorical Culture in Nineteenth-Century America: Transformations in the Theory and Practice of Rhetoric*, edited by Gregory Clark and S. Michael Halloran, 139–57. Carbondale: Southern Illinois University Press, 1993.

Johnston, Sheila F. *Buckskin and Broadcloth: A Celebration of E. Pauline Johnson Tekahionwake, 1861–1913*. Toronto: Dundurn Press, 1997.

Jones, Meta DuEwa. "Listening to What the Ear Demands: Langston Hughes and His Critics." *Callaloo* 25, no. 4 (2002): 1144–75.

– *The Muse Is Music: Jazz Poetry from the Harlem Renaissance to Spoken Word*. Chicago: University of Illinois Press, 2011.

Kapchan, Deborah. "Performance." In *Eight Words for the Study of Expressive Culture*, edited by Burt Feintuch, 121–45. Urbana: University of Illinois Press, 2003.

Karem, Jeff. *The Purloined Islands: Caribbean–U.S. Crosscurrents in Literature and Culture, 1880–1959*. Charlottesville: University of Virginia Press, 2011.

Kates, Susan. *Activist Rhetorics and American Higher Education, 1885–1937*. Carbondale: Southern Illinois University Press, 2001.

Katz, Stephen. *Red, Black, and Jew: New Frontiers in Hebrew Literature*. Austin: University of Texas Press, 2009.

Killelea, Patricia. Review of *Peace in Duress*, by Janet Marie Rogers. *Transmotion* 1, no. 1 (2015). https://journals.kent.ac.uk/index.php/transmotion/article/view/150/556.

Kim, Christine, Sophie McCall, and Melina Baum Singer, eds. *Cultural Grammars of Nation, Diaspora, and Indigeneity in Canada*. Waterloo, ON: Wilfrid Laurier University Press, 2012.

Kim, Christine, and Sophie McCall. Introduction to *Cultural Grammars*, 1–18.

Kincaid, Jamaica. *Annie John: A Novel*. New York: Farrar, Straus and Giroux, 1985.

– *Lucy: A Novel*. New York. Farrar, Straus and Giroux, 1990.

King, Ruby, and Mike Morrissey. *Images in Print: Bias and Prejudice in Caribbean Textbooks*. Jamaica: Institute of Social and Economic Research, 1988.

King, Thomas. "Godzilla vs. the Post-Colonial." *World Literature Written in English* 30, no. 2 (1990): 10–16.

Kirkpatrick, Peter. "Hunting the Wild Reciter: Elocution and the Art of Recitation." In *Talking and Listening in the Age of Modernity: Essays on the History of Sound*, edited by Joy Damousi and Delsey Deacon, 59–71. Canberra: Australian National University Press, 2007.

Kuhnheim, Jill S. *Beyond the Page: Poetry and Performance in Spanish America*. Tucson: University of Arizona, 2014.

LaRocque, Emma. *When the Other Is Me: Native Resistance Discourse, 1850–1990*. Winnipeg: University of Manitoba Press, 2010.

Leary, John Patrick. "Havana Reads the Harlem Renaissance: Langston Hughes, Nicolás Guillén, and the Dialectics of Transnational American Literature." *Comparative Literature Studies* 47, no. 2 (2010): 133–58.

Leighton, Mary Elizabeth. "Performing Pauline Johnson: Representations of 'the Indian Poetess' in the Periodical Press, 1892–95." *Essays in Canadian Writing* 65 (1998): 141–64.

Leithauser, Brad. "Why We Should Memorize." *New Yorker*, 25 January 2013. http://www.newyorker.com/books/page-turner/why-we-should-memorize.

Léticeé, Marie. *Education, Assimilation and Identity: The Literary Journey of the French Caribbean*. Coconut Creek, FL: Caribbean Studies Press, 2009.

Lillard, Charles. "Choice of Lens." *Canadian Literature* 118 (1988): 154–5.

Lionnet, Françoise, and Shu-mei Shih, eds. *Minor Transnationalism*. Durham, NC: Duke University Press, 2005.

Lippi-Green, Rosini. *English with an Accent*. New York: Taylor and Francis, 1997.

Longfellow, Henry Wadsworth. "Excelsior" [1841]. In *The Poetical Works of Longfellow: Cambridge Edition*, edited by Horace E. Scudder, 19. New York: Houghton Mifflin, 1975.

– *The Song of Hiawatha*. New York: Dover Publications, [1855] 2006.

Lorde, Audre. *Sister Outsider: Essays and Speeches*. Berkeley, CA: Crossing Press, 1984.

Lott, Eric. *Love and Theft: Blackface Minstrelsy and the American Working Class*. New York: Oxford University Press, 1993.

Louise Bennett Coverley Fonds. William Ready Division of Archives and Research Collections, McMaster University Library, Hamilton, ON.

Lovelace, Earl. *A Brief Conversation and Other Stories*. Portsmouth, NH: Heinemann, 1988.

Low, Bronwen E. "*Creare*: Re-imagining the Poetics and Politics of the Jamaican Creole Language Debates." *Caribbean Journal of Education* 20, no. 1 (2000): 84–101.

– *Slam School: Learning through Conflict in the Hip-Hop and Spoken Word Classroom*. Stanford, CA: Stanford University Press, 2011.

Lynes, Jeanette. "Claiming Culture: Claiming Voice: Rita Joe of Eskasoni." In *Words Out There: Women Poets in Atlantic Canada*, edited by Jeanette Lynes, 129–34. Lockeport, NS: Roseway, 1999.

Lyon, George W. "Pauline Johnson: A Reconsideration." *Studies in Canadian Literature / Études en littérature canadienne* 15, no. 2 (1990). http://journals.hil.unb.ca/index.php/scl/article/view/8124/9181.

MacArthur, Marit J. "Monotony, the Churches of Poetry Reading, and Sound Studies." *PMLA* 131, no. 1 (2016): 38–63.

Markham, E.A., ed. *Hinterland: Caribbean Poetry from the West Indies and Britain.* Newcastle upon Tyne: Bloodaxe Books, 1990.

Marsalis, Wynton. Introduction to *The First Book of Rhythms*, by Langston Hughes, vi–viii. New York: Oxford University Press, 1995.

Martí, José. "Our America." 1891. *José Martí: Selected Writings*. Translated by Esther Allen. New York: Penguin, 2002.

Martínez-San Miguel, Yolanda. *Coloniality of Diasporas: Rethinking Migrations in a Pan-Caribbean Context*. Basingstoke: Palgrave Macmillan, 2014.

McCall, Sophie. "Diaspora and Nation in Métis Writing." In Kim, McCall, and Singer, *Cultural Grammars*, 21–41.

McClintock, Anne. *Imperial Leather: Race, Gender, and Sexuality in the Colonial Contest*. New York: Routledge, 1995.

Mccourtie, Lena. "The Politics of Creole Language Education in Jamaica: 1891–1921 and the 1990s. *Journal of Multilingual and Multicultural Development* 19, no. 2 (2010): 108–27.

McHenry, Elizabeth. *Forgotten Readers: Recovering the Lost History of African American Literary Societies*. Durham, NC: Duke University Press, 2002.

McLaren, Audrey. "Miss Lou, My Mentor." Letter. *Jamaica Gleaner*, 30 July 2006. Accessed 5 November 2009 (page no longer on site)..

McLaren, Peter. *Life in Schools: An Introduction to Critical Pedagogy in the Foundations of Education*. 5th ed. Los Angeles: University of California Press, 2007.

– *Schooling as a Ritual Performance: Towards a Political Economy of Educational Symbols and Gestures*. 3rd ed. Lanham, MD: Rowman and Littlefield, 1999.

McLeod, Neal. "Coming Home through Stories." In *(Ad)dressing Our Words: Aboriginal Perspectives on Aboriginal Literatures*, edited by Armand Garnet Ruffo, 17–36. Penticton, BC: Theytus Books, 2001.

– ed. *Indigenous Poetics in Canada*. Waterloo, ON: Wilfrid Laurier University Press, 2014.

McRaye, Walter. *Pauline Johnson and Her Friends*. Toronto: Ryerson, 1947.

Meditz, Sandra W., and Dennis M. Hanratty, eds. *Islands of the Commonwealth Caribbean: A Regional Study*. Washington, DC: United States Government, 1989.

Mencken, H.L. *The American Language: An Inquiry into the Development of English in the United States*. New York: Alfred A. Knopf, 2000.

Mickenberg, Julia L. *Learning from the Left: Children's Literature, the Cold War, and Radical Politics in the United States*. New York: Oxford University Press, 2006.

Middleton, Peter. *Distant Reading: Performance, Readership, and Consumption in Contemporary Poetry*. Tuscaloosa: University of Alabama Press, 2005.

Mighty Sparrow. *Volume 1: Mighty Sparrow*. Ice Records, 2000, compact disc.

Mignolo, Walter D. *Local Histories / Global Designs: Coloniality, Subaltern Knowledges, and Border Thinking*. Princeton, NJ: Princeton University Press, 1999.

Miller, Joshua L. *Accented America: The Cultural Politics of Multilingual Modernisms*. New York: Oxford University Press, 2011.

Miller, Kei. *Writing Down the Vision: Essays and Prophecies*. Leeds, UK: Peepal Tree Press, 2013.

Miner, Earl. "Poetic Contests." In *The New Princeton Encyclopedia of Poetry and Poetics*, edited by Alex Preminger and T.V.F. Brogan, 925–7. Princeton, NJ: Princeton University Press, 1993.

Minh-ha, Trinh T. *Woman, Native, Other: Writing Post-Coloniality and Feminism*. Bloomington: Indiana University Press, 1989.

Ministry of Education, Youth and Culture. *Language Education Policy* (Jamaica, 2001). http://dlpalmer.weebly.com/uploads/3/5/8/7/3587856/language_educationpolicy.pdf. (Page no longer online.)

Mingus, Charles. *Beneath the Underdog: His World as Composed by Mingus*. Edited by Nel King. New York: Vintage, 1991.

Morris, Mervyn. Introduction to *Selected Poems*. By Louise Bennett, iii–xx.

– *'Is English We Speaking': And Other Essays*. Kingston, Jamaica: Ian Randle Press, 1999.

– *Miss Lou: Louise Bennett and Jamaican Culture*. Oxford: Signal Books, 2014. Kindle Edition.

– "On Reading Louise Bennett Seriously." *Jamaica Journal* 1, no. 1 (1967): 60–74.

Morris, Tracie. "Ad-Libbing." *Word Warriors: 35 Women Leaders in the Spoken Word Revolution*, edited by Alix Olson, 256–64. Berkeley: Seal Press, 2007.

Morrisson, Mark. "Performing the Pure Voice: Elocution, Verse Recitation, and Modernist Poetry in Prewar London." *Modernism/modernity* 3, no. 3 (1996): 25–50.

Moses, Daniel David. "Getting (Back) to Poetry: A Memoir." In McLeod, *Indigenous Poetics*, 121–35.

Moten, Fred. "The New International of Rhythmic Feeling(s)." In *Sonic Interventions*, edited by Sylvia Mieszkowski, Joy Smith, and Marijke de Valck, 31–56. Amsterdam: Rodopi, 2007.

Mutabaruka. *The First Poems (1970–1979)*. Kingston, Jamaica: Paul Issa Publications, 2005.

– "From Page-Poet to Recording Artist: Mutabaruka Interviewed by Eric Doumerc." *Journal of Commonwealth Literature* 44, no. 23 (2009): 23–31.

– *The Next Poems (1980–2002)*. Kingston, Jamaica: Paul Issa Publications, 2005.

Naipaul, V.S. *A House for Mr. Biswas*. New York: Vintage, 1961.

– *The Mimic Men*. London: Penguin, 1967.

Narain, Denise Decaires. *Making Style: Contemporary Caribbean Women's Poetry*. New York: Routledge, 2002.

Neigh, Janet. "Dreams of Uncommon Languages: Transnational Feminist Pedagogy and Multilingual Poetics." *Feminist Formations* 26, no. 1 (2014): 70–92.

– "The Lickle Space of the Tramcar in Louise Bennett's Feminist Post-Colonial Poetics." In "Critical Approaches to Louise Bennett," edited by Ifeoma Nwankwo. Special issue, *Journal of West Indian Literature* 17, no. 2 (2009): 5–19.

– "The Transnational Frequency of Radio Connectivity in Langston Hughes's 1940s Poetics." *Modernism/modernity* 20, no. 2 (2013). 265–85.

Nero, Shondel. "De Facto Language Education Policy through Teachers' Attitudes and Practices: A Critical Ethnographic Study in Three Jamaican Schools." *Language Policy* 12 (2014): 221–42.

Nero, Shondel, and Dohra Ahmad. *Vernaculars in the Classroom: Paradoxes, Pedagogy, Possibilities*. New York: Routledge, 2014.

Newton, Melanie J. "Return to a Native Land: Indigeneity and Decolonization in the Anglophone Caribbean." *Small Axe* 17, no. 2 (2013): 108–22.

Nichols, Charles H., ed. *Arna Bontemps-Langston Hughes Letters: 1925–1967*. New York: Dodd, Mead and Company, 1980.

Nurhussein, Nadia. *Rhetorics of Literacy: The Cultivation of American Dialect Poetry*. Columbus: Ohio State University Press, 2013.

Nwankwo, Ifeoma Kiddoe, "Cosmopolitan Consciousness: Inter-American Engagements in the Scripting of African-American and Caribbean Identities." PhD diss., Duke University, 1999.

Nyong'o, Tavia. "Hiawatha's Black Atlantic Itineraries." In *The Traffic in Poems: Nineteenth-Century Poetry and Transatlantic Exchange*, edited by Meredith L. McGill, 81–96. New Brunswick, NJ: Rutgers University Press, 2008.

O'Gorman, Edmundo. *The Invention of America: An Inquiry into the Historical Nature of the New World and the Meaning of Its History*. Bloomington: Indiana University Press, 1961.

O'Meally, Robert G. Afterword to *The First Book of Rhythms*. By Langston Hughes. 50–5. New York: Oxford University Press, 1995.

Ong, Walter J. *Orality and Literacy: The Technologizing of the Word*. New York: Methuen, 1982.

Orlando, Valérie K., and Sandra Messinger Cypess, eds. *Reimagining the Caribbean: Conversations among the Creole, English, French, and Spanish Caribbean*. Lanham, MD: Lexington Books, 2014.

Oswald, Janelle. "Preserving Jamaica's Oldest Dance." *The Voice Online*. 17 August 2011. http://www.voice-online.co.uk/article/preserving-jamaicas-oldest-dance.

Parmenter, Jon. "The Meaning of *Kaswentha* and the Two Row Wampum Belt in Haudenosaunee (Iroquois) History: Can Indigenous Oral Tradition be Reconciled with the Documentary Record?" *Journal of Early American History* 3 (2013): 82–109.

Patterson, Anita. *Race, American Literature and Transnational Modernisms*. New York: Cambridge University Press, 2008.

Pauline Johnson Collection. William Ready Division of Archives and Research Collections, McMaster University Library, Hamilton, ON.

Phelan, Peggy. *Unmarked: The Politics of Performance*. New York: Routledge, 1993.

Philip, M. NourbeSe. "Interview with Empire." In *Assembling Alternatives: Reading Postmodern Poetries Transnationally*, edited by Romana Huk, 195–206. Middletown, CT: Wesleyan University Press, 2003.

Phillips, Michelle H. "The Children of Double Consciousness: From *The Souls of Black Folk* to the *Brownies' Book*." *PMLA* 128, no. 3 (2013): 590–607.

Phillips, Ruth B. "Performing the Native Woman: Primitivism and Mimicry in Early Twentieth-Century Visual Culture." In *Antimodernism and Artistic Experience: Policing the Boundaries of Modernity*, edited by Lynda Jessup, 26–49. Toronto: University of Toronto Press, 2001.

Pineau, Gisèle. *Exile: According to Julia*. Translated by Betty Wilson. Charlottesville: University of Virginia Press, 2003.

Poe, Edgar Allan. "Mr. Longfellow and Other Plagiarists." *The Works of the Late Edgar Allan Poe*, vol. 3. Edited by Rufus W. Griswold, 292–334. New York: J.S. Redfield, 1850.

Pollard, Charles W. *New World Modernisms: T.S. Eliot, Derek Walcott, and Kamau Brathwaite*. Charlottesville: University of Virginia Press, 2004.

Pollard, Velma. *From Jamaican Creole to Standard English: A Handbook for Teachers*. Kingston, Jamaica: University of the West Indies Press, 2003.

Ramazani, Jahan. *The Hybrid Muse: Post-Colonial Poetry in English*. Chicago: University of Chicago Press, 2001.

– *A Transnational Poetics*. Chicago: University of Chicago Press, 2009.

Rampersad, Arnold. "Future Scholarly Projects on Langston Hughes." *Black American Literature Forum* 21, no. 3 (Autumn 1987): 305–16.

– *The Life of Langston Hughes*, vol. 1: *I, Too, Sing America: 1902–1941*. New York: Oxford University Press, 1986.

– *The Life of Langston Hughes*, vol. 2: *I Dream a World: 1941–1967*. New York: Oxford University Press, 1988.

Reckord, Michael. "Miss Lou Gets Her First Fee." *The Gleaner*, 6 September 2013. http://jamaica-gleaner.com/gleaner/20130906/ent/ent2.html.

Roberts, Peter A. *West Indians and Their Language*. New York: Cambridge University Press, 1988.

Robson, Catherine. *Heart Beats: Everyday Life and The Memorized Poem*. Princeton, NJ: Princeton University Press, 2012.

– "Standing on the Burning Deck: Poetry, Performance, History." *PMLA* 120, no. 1 (2005): 148–62.

– "Why Memorize a Poem?" *The Chronicle Review: The Chronicle of Higher Education*. 26 November 2012. http://chronicle.com/article/Why-Memorize-a-Poem-/135878/.

Rodis, Katherine Verhagen. "Vernacular Literacy and Formal Analysis: Louise Bennett-Coverley's Jamaican English Verse." In "Critical Approaches to Louise Bennett: Part 2," edited by Ifeoma Nwankwo. Special issue, *Journal of West Indian Literature* 18, no. 1 (2009): 60–72.

Rogers, Janet. "Blood Moves Us – Story Poetry Lives Inside." In McLeod, *Indigenous Poetics in Canada*, 253–7.

– "Interview with the Mohawk Poet Janet Marie Rogers." By Black Coffee Poet. 2011. http://blackcoffeepoet.com/2011/11/09/interview-with-mohawk-poet-janet-marie-rogers-2/.

– *Pauline and Emily: Two Women*. Alexandria, VA: Alexander Street Press, 2006.

– "Pauline Passed Here." In McLeod, *Indigenous Poetics in Canada*, 39–41.

– "The Pauline Project." SoundCloud audio, 3.35. 2012. https://soundcloud.com/janet-marie-rogers/the-pauline-project.

– *Peace in Duress*. Vancouver: Talonbooks, 2014.

– *Peace in Duress* Book Trailer. *Vimeo* video, 3:09. 2014. http://talonbooks.com/books/peace-in-duress.

– *Unearthed*. Lantzville, BC: Leaf Press, 2011.

– "Waaseyaa'sin Christine Sy in Conversation with Janet Marie Rogers." By Waaseyaa'sin Christine Sy. *Lemon Hound*. 2014. http://lemonhound.com/2014/06/16/waaseyaasin-christine-sy-in-conversation-with-janet-marie-rogers/.

– "Wampum Contracts E. Pauline." SoundCloud audio, 2:13. 2013. https://soundcloud.com/janet-marie-rogers/wampum-contracts-e-pauline.

Rubin, Joan Shelley. *Songs of Ourselves: The Uses of Poetry in America*. Boston: Harvard University Press, 2007.

Rubinstein, Rachel. *Members of the Tribe: Native America in the Jewish Imagination*. Detroit: Wayne State University Press, 2010.

Sadowski-Smith, Claudia. *Globalization on the Line: Culture, Capital, and Citizenship at U.S. Borders.* New York: Palgrave Macmillan, 2002.

Schultz, Kathy Lou. *The Afro-Modernist Epic and Literary History: Tolson, Hughes, and Baraka.* New York: Palgrave Macmillan, 2013.

Scott, James C. *Domination and the Arts of Resistance: Hidden Transcripts.* New Haven, CT: Yale University Press, 1990.

Scott, Jonathan. *Socialist Joy in the Writing of Langston Hughes.* Columbia: University of Missouri Press, 2006.

Seager, Joni. *The Penguin Atlas of Women of the World.* 3rd ed. New York: Penguin, 2003.

Sealey, Alicia. "Miss Lou – Forever Walking Brave." *Caribbean Camera.* 26 February 2015. http://thecaribbeancamera.com/?p=4768.

Selvon, Samuel. *The Housing Lark.* Colorado Springs, CO: Three Continents Press, 1965.

Senior, Olive. *Talking of Trees.* Kingston, Jamaica: Calabash, 1985.

Sharpe, Jenny. "Cartographies of Globalisation, Technologies of Gendered Subjectivities: The Dub Poetry of Jean 'Binta' Breeze." *Gender and History* 15, no. 3 (2003): 440–59.

Sheridan, Thomas. *A Course of Lectures on Elocution.* London: W. Strachan, 1762.

Sherwood, Kenneth. "Elaborate Versionings: Characteristics of Emergent Performance in Three Print/Oral/Aural Poets." *Oral Tradition* 21, no. 1 (2006): 119–47.

Shrive, Norman. "What Happened to Pauline?" *Canadian Literature* 13 (1962): 25–38.

Siemerling, Winfried, and Sarah Phillips Casteel, eds. *Canada and Its Americas: Transnational Navigations.* Montreal and Kingston: McGill-Queen's University Press, 2010.

– Introduction to *Canada and Its Americas*, 3–28.

Simmons-McDonald, Hazel. "Language Education Policy (2): The Case for Creole in Formal Education in St. Lucia." In *Caribbean Language Issues: Old and New*, edited by Pauline Christie, 120–42. Kingston, Jamaica: University of the West Indies Press, 1996.

Smethurst, James Edward. *The Black Arts Movement: Literary Nationalism in the 1960s and 1970s.* Chapel Hill: University of North Carolina Press, 2005.

Smith, Katharine Capshaw. *Children's Literature of the Harlem Renaissance.* Bloomington: Indiana University Press, 2004.

Smith, Michael. "Interview with Michael Smith." By Mervyn Morris. In Markham, *Hinterland*, 275–83.

– "Me Cyaan Believe It." In Markham, *Hinterland*, 284–6.

Smith, Zadie. "Speaking in Tongues." *New York Review of Books*. 26 February 2009. http://www.nybooks.com/articles/archives/2009/feb/26/speaking-in-tongues-2/.

Somers-Willett, Susan B.A. *The Cultural Politics of Slam Poetry: Race, Identity, and the Performance of Popular Verse in America*. Ann Arbor: University of Michigan Press, 2009.

Sorby, Angela. *Schoolroom Poets: Childhood, Performance, and the Place of American Poetry, 1865–1917*. Lebanon, NH: University of New Hampshire Press, 2005.

"Speech." *Jamaica Cultural Development Commission*. 26 April 2013. Accessed 27 April 2013. http://www.jcdc.gov.jm/get_content.php?cid=49.

Stewart, Fenn Elan. "Hiawatha / Hereafter: Re-appropriating Longfellow's Epic in Northern Ontario." *Ariel* 44, no. 4 (2014): 159–80.

Stoler, Ann Laura, ed. *Haunted by Empire: Geographies of Intimacy in North American History*. Durham, NC: Duke University Press, 2006.

Street, Brian V., ed. *Cross-Cultural Approaches to Literacy*. New York: Cambridge University Press, 1993.

– *Literacy in Theory and Practice*. New York: Cambridge University Press, 1984.

– "The New Literacy Studies." In *Literacy: A Critical Sourcebook*, edited by Ellen Cushman, Eugene R. Kintgen, Barry M. Kroll, and Mike Rose, 430–42. New York: Bedford/St Martin's, 2001.

Street, Joanna C., and Brian V. Street. "The Schooling of Literacy." In *Writing in the Community*, edited by David Barton and Roz Ivanič, 143–66. Newbury Park, CA: Sage, 1991.

Studwell, William Emmett. *The Americana Song Reader*. New York: Haworth Press, 1997.

Taylor, Diana. *The Archive and the Repertoire: Performing Cultural Memory in the Americas*. Durham, NC: Duke University Press, 2003.

Thomas, Deborah. *Modern Blackness: Nationalism, Globalization, and the Politics of Culture in Jamaica*. Durham, NC: Duke University Press, 2004.

Thomas, Lorenzo. *Extraordinary Measures: Afrocentric Modernism and Twentieth-Century American Poetry*. Tuscaloosa: University of Alabama Press, 2000.

Tidjani-Alou, Antoinette. "'Back to Africa, Miss Mattie?': Autobiographical Notes from Global Africa on Apprehending Texts and Subtexts of Popular Culture." *The Global South* 5, no. 2 (2012): 139–53.

Tiffin, Helen. "Cold Hearts and (Foreign) Tongues: Recitation and the Reclamation of the Female Body in the Works of Erna Brodber and Jamaica Kincaid." *Callaloo* 16, no. 4 (1993): 909–21.

– "The Institution of Literature." In *A History of Literature in the Caribbean*, vol. 2: *English- and Dutch-Speaking Regions*, edited by A. James Arnold, 41–66. Philadelphia: John Benjamins, 1992.

Trachtenberg, Alan. *Shades of Hiawatha: Staging Indians, Making Americans*. New York: Hill and Wang, 2004.

Tracy, Stephen. "The Dream Keeper: Langston Hughes's Poetry, Fiction, and Non-Biographical Books for Children and Young Adults." *Langston Hughes Review* 17 Centennial Edition (2002): 78–94.

UNESCO. *Jamaica: Development of Secondary Education*. Paris: UNESCO, 1983. http://unesdoc.unesco.org/images/0008/000806/080615EB.pdf.

Van Haesendonck, Kristian, and Theo D'haen, eds. *Caribbeing: Comparing Caribbean Literatures and Cultures*. Amsterdam: Rodopi, 2014.

Viehmann, Martha L. "Speaking Chinook: Adaptation, Indigeneity, and Pauline Johnson's British Columbia Stories." *Western American Literature* 47, no. 3 (2012): 258–85.

Waggoner, Walter. "Teacher Curbed on Negro Poems." Special to the *New York Times*, 12 November 1966.

Walcott, Derek. "The Caribbean: Culture or Mimicry?" *Journal of Interamerican Studies and World Affairs* 16, no. 1 (1974): 3–13.

Walker, John. *Elements of Elocution*. London: T. Cadell, 1781.

Weaver, Jace, Craig S. Womack, and Robert Warrior. *American Indian Literary Nationalism*. Albuquerque: University of New Mexico Press, 2006.

Weir-Soley, Donna (Aza). "Interview with Donna (Aza) Weir-Soley." By Ifeoma Nwankwo. In "Critical Approaches to Louise Bennett: Part 2," edited by Ifeoma Nwankwo. Special issue, *Journal of West Indian Literature* 18, no. 1 (2009): 26–59.

Wesling, Meg. *Empire's Proxy: American Literature and U.S. Imperialism in the Philippines*. New York: New York University Press, 2011.

Wheeler, Elizabeth A. "Riddym Ravings: Female and National Identity in Jamaican Creole Poetry." In *Imagination, Emblems and Expressions: Essays on Latin American, Caribbean, and Continental Culture and Identity*, edited by Helen Ryan-Ranson, 139–54. Bowling Green, OH: Bowling Green State University Press, 1993.

Wheeler, Lesley. *Voicing American Poetry: Sound and Performance from the 1920s to the Present*. Ithaca, NY: Cornell University Press, 2008.

Whittier, John Greenleaf. *The Complete Poetical Works of John Greenleaf Whittier*. Boston: Houghton Mifflin Company, 1892.

Willmott, Glenn. "Paddled by Pauline," *Canadian Poetry* 46 (2000). http://canadianpoetry.org/volumes/vol46/willmott.html.

Womack, Craig S. *Red on Red: Native American Literary Separatism*. Minneapolis: University of Minnesota Press, 1999.

Wylie, Herb. "Hemispheric Studies or Scholarly NAFTA? The Case for Canadian Literary Studies." In Siemerling and Casteel, *Canada and Its Americas*, 48–61.

Yeigh, Frank. "The Drama of Hiawatha or Mana-Bozho as Played by a Band of Canadian Ojibway Indians." *Canadian Magazine* 17, no. 3 (1901): 207–17.

Zamora, Lois Parkinson. *The Usable Past: The Imagination in Recent Fiction of the Americas*. New York: Cambridge University Press, 1997.

Zolbrod, Paul G. *Reading the Voice: Native American Oral Poetry on the Page*. Salt Lake City: University of Utah Press, 1995.

Index

Page numbers in italics refer to photographs.

www.ingramcontent.com/pod-product-compliance
Lightning Source LLC
LaVergne TN
LVHW090156080826
844660LV00013B/836/J

* 9 7 8 1 4 8 7 5 0 1 8 3 9 *